AF553207

WIRELESS AD HOC AND SENSOR NETWORKS

WIRELESS AD HOC AND SENSOR NETWORKS

By

Rohtash Ghuriya

2016

SBS Publishers & Distributors Pvt. Ltd.
New Delhi

ISBN 13 : 9789380090733

First Published in 2016

Published by:

SBS PUBLISHERS & DISTRIBUTORS PVT. LTD.

2/9, Ground Floor, Ansari Road, Darya Ganj,

New Delhi - 110002,

INDIA

Tel: 0091.11.23289119 / 41563911

Email: mail@sbspublishers.com

www.sbspublishers.com

Preface

A wireless ad hoc and sensor network consists of a number of sensors spread across a geographical area. Each sensor has wireless communication capability and some level of intelligence for signal processing and networking of the data. A wireless ad hoc network (WANET) is a decentralized type of wireless network. The network is ad hoc because it does not rely on a preexisting infrastructure, such as routers in wired networks or access points in managed wireless networks. Instead, each node participates in routing by forwarding data for other nodes, so the determination of which nodes forward data is made dynamically on the basis of network connectivity. An ad hoc network typically refers to any set of networks where all devices have equal status on a network and are free to associate with any other ad hoc network device in link range. A wireless sensor network (WSN) of spatially distributed autonomous sensors to monitor physical or environmental conditions, such as temperature, sound, pressure, etc. and to cooperatively pass their data through the network to a main location. The more modern networks are bi-directional, also enabling control of sensor activity. The development of wireless sensor networks was motivated by military applications such as battlefield surveillance; today such networks are used in many industrial and consumer applications, such as industrial process monitoring and control, machine health monitoring, and so on.

Editor

Contents

Chapter 1

RELATION-BASED MESSAGE ROUTING IN WIRELESS SENSOR NETWORKS

Jan Nikodem, Maciej Nikodem, Marek Woda and Ryszard KlempousWroclaw University of Technology Poland Zenon Chaczko

University of Technology Sydney Australia

INTRODUCTION

Sensor networks and their related topics represent some of the greatest and challenging possibilities in the research field that have come about in recent years. Emerging technologies like wireless sensor network (WSN), standards enabled legacy sensors, ubiquitous and cloud computing, middleware, communication systems, internet protocols (IP) and next generation networks are leading to a set of new paradigms where wireless sensors can be treated as vital components of common infrastructure and a shared resource with an ability to serve multiple and concurrently executing applications run by various users in distributed environment. This is in strong contrast to traditional concepts where dedicated sensor devices are being physically and logically hard-wired to communication and computing infrastructure serving very specific and dedicated data/information processing applications. Wireless sensor networks consist of a number of small electronic devices (nodes) distributed in an area that by far exceeds the communication range of a single sensor. Message routing is one of the most important issues in such networks. This is mainly due to the large number of nodes, variety of possible communication paths, restricted power source and variability (in time and space) of environmental conditions in which the WSN operates. A shared communication channel and restricted communication ranges require that nodes of the WSN cooperate and/or coordinate their actions while messages are routed from nodes to the base station (BS).

It is a well-known idea Descartes & Lafleur (1960) to solve large and complex problems by dividing them into smaller and possibly simpler tasks. The most crucial element of such an attempt is to decide how to divide the problem in order to get a problem that can be solved efficiently and, what is more important, can be used to find a solution to the original problem. A distributed system, such as a WSN, is traditionally seen as a set of spatially distributed nodes that communicate, coordinate their actions and inform other nodes about their status using special messages sent over the communication channel Dollimore et al. (2005). Such a system is usually assumed to be isolated from the outside word – even if it measures its parameters and/or listens to the status messages from other nodes, it is still not affected by the environmental conditions and its changes. We are going to look at such a system as it consists of independent elements that adjust their actions according to the actual situation in their neighbourhood and WSN in order to achieve globally defined goals. Surroundings of each node is composed of two elements:

- neighbourhood – a set of WSN elements (i.e. nodes) that are in the surroundings of the node,
- environment – a set of elements that are in the surroundings of a node, influence its behaviour, but are not elements of the WSN.

The above approach enables to describe any system as an open system in which communication activity adapts to stimulus that originates both from system elements as well as from environment.

This enables the system to respond to harsh and unpredictable situations that may be beneficial in many applications.

When analysing WSN it is important to capture four related components:

- independence of WSN elements,
- cooperation, and
- communication between WSN elements,
- interaction of elements with the environment.

This chapter focuses on communication in a distributed system such as a WSN. The main purpose of communication in WSNs is to retransmit messages and route them to the base station. Our interest in distributed WSNs is not only due to spatial distribution of nodes of the network, but also due to the fact that decisions on message routing and communication paths are taken in distributed manner as an effect of cooperation between nodes.

THE RELATIONAL MODEL OF COMMUNICATION IN WSN

Investigation of activities in wireless sensor network can be based on relational model of cooperation between nodes of the network Nikodem (2009). Relational model captures dependencies (relations) between nodes of the network and defines actions that nodes may take in different situations. Actions are taken by every node individually, so the relational model can be used to describe independent elements that cooperate within the network in order to achieve globally defined goals. since the relational model reflects the nature of real WSNs, therefore, it includes all previous proposals to efficient network organisation, communication and routing. Moreover, it enables to construct new algorithms that will achieve globally defined goals through local actions taken be each node of the network.

Actions and Relations between Nodes

Communication activity in WSN can be described using three binary relations defined over set of actions - Act. Set of actions contain all activities that can be carried out by every node of the network individually but with respect to other nodes and environment (i.e. situation in the neighbourhood). Ability to execute specific action depends on the state of the node (e.g. network establishment actions, network management, and normal operation) and its execution cause the state of the node to be changed. Therefore, all actions that can be taken by nodes of the WSN are defined over a Cartesian product of set of nodes Nodes and set of all

possible states States:

$$\text{Act} : \text{Nodes} \times \text{States} \rightarrow \text{States}. \quad (1)$$

Measurement of environment parameters, data aggregation, sending messages to a single (or group) node and message receiving are examples of actions that can be taken by nodes. Since nodes are autonomous, therefore each node can execute actions independently from other nodes. Undoubtedly, this is an advantage since this enables nodes in a different part of the WSN to perform various (possible related) actions simultaneously. On the other hand a number of actions become essential only when two or more nodes cooperate. In such situation cooperation requires that nodes execute actions that are related which is formally denoted as:

$$a_i^{(1)} \mathscr{R} a_j^{(2)}, \quad (2)$$

Where $a_i^{(1)}, a_j^{(2)} \in \text{Act}$ and $a_i^{(k)}$ denotes i-th action that is executed by k-th node. Eq. (2) should be read as: action $a_i^{(1)}$ is in relation with $a_j^{(2)}$. Relations are used to determine actions that are related to each other and are either executed together (but not necessarily in the same time instant) or cannot be executed together. Since nodes can execute a vast number of actions that can be part of different relations, therefore relations have their names and symbols. Since this chapter focuses on communication, therefore, we will only consider communication related relations and simplify the notation. From now on sending and receiving a message will be denoted as x where x is an ID of node that is either sending or receiving the packet. Whether node x sends or receives the message will arise from the context or will be explained in the text. To describe a variety of possible dependencies between different elements of real world WSN it is enough to define three elementary relations Jaron (1978); Nikodem (2008):

- subordination - π,
- tolerance - ,
- collision - κ.

When message sending and receiving actions are considered then subordination

$$x_R \pi y_S, \tag{3}$$

means that node y receives data whenever node y send it. Subordination is transitive which means that if x is subordinated to y and z is subordinated to x then z is also subordinated to y:

$$x_R \pi y_S \text{ and } z_R \pi x_S \Rightarrow z_R \pi y_S. \tag{4}$$

Subordination is antisymmetric which means that if x is subordinated to y then y is not subordinated to x:

$$x_R \pi y_S \Rightarrow \neg (y_R \pi x_S). \tag{5}$$

We can define a set Π of pairs of nodes of the WSN that are in subordination relation. This set consist of ordered pairs of nodes such that:

$$\Pi = \{\langle x, y \rangle \mid x_R, y_S \in \text{Act and } x_R \pi y_S\} \tag{6}$$

When dealing with communication tolerance relation between nodes x and y

$$x_R \vartheta y_S \tag{7}$$

means that x may receive messages send by node y. When x tolerates y then it is less likely that node y sends messages to x - y prefers subordinated nodes. Nevertheless, y may send message to x and whenever this happens node x will receive the message and route it towards the base station. In contrast to previous relation tolerance is symmetrical

$$x_R \vartheta y_S \Rightarrow y_R \vartheta x_S, \tag{8}$$

but is not transitive. Subordination and tolerance relation can be composed - if x is subordinated to y and z tolerates x then z also tolerates y:

$$x_R \pi y_S \text{ and } z_R \vartheta x_S \Rightarrow z_R \pi y_S. \tag{9}$$

Set of all nodes that tolerate each other is a set of pairs < x, y > such that

$$\Theta = \{\langle x, y \rangle \mid x_R, y_S \in \text{Act and } x_R \vartheta y_S\}. \tag{10}$$

It follows From the definition of relations п, □ for corresponding sets of subordinated and tolerated nodes (Π and Θ) that

$$\Pi \subseteq \Theta. \tag{11}$$

The final relation that we need to consider is the relation of collision which for data transmission and reception activities in WSN specifies all those sensor nodes that don't exchange messages among themselves. The relation of collision between node x and node y is denoted as:

$$x_R \kappa y_S, \tag{12}$$

The above relation takes place when a node x does not receive any messages transmitted by the node y, including both broadcasted and explicitly addressed messages from the node y to the node x. Additionally, if a node x has a collision relation with node y and the node z is subordinated to the node x, then the node z has also a collision relation with the node y. This can be expressed as:

$$x_R \kappa y_S \wedge z_R \pi x_S \Rightarrow z_R \kappa y_S. \tag{13}$$

The relations of tolerance and collision are mutually exclusive therefore only thoseWSNnodes that are not in a relation of tolerance can remain to stay in a relation of collision. Hence, if we denote a set of nodes that remains in relation of collision as:

$$K = \{< x, y >\mid x_R, y_S \in Act \wedge x_R \kappa y_S\}, \tag{14}$$

then the sets of nodes that remain in relations of tolerance and collision meet the following criterion:

$$\Theta \cap K = \varnothing. \tag{15}$$

Since, $\Pi \subseteq \Theta$ also applies therefore sensor nodes that are both in relation of tolerance and subordination cannot remain in relation of collision

$$\Pi \cap K = \varnothing. \tag{16}$$

NEIGHBOURHOOD, NEIGHBOURING AND ENVIRONMENT

When studying multi-hop communication in sensor networks it is not possible to omit such specific aspects of WSN as sensor node cooperation. Due to limited radio range, the majority of nodes in the WSN are not able to transmit data directly to the base station, therefore the nodes have to rely on the mechanism of retransmission offered by other nodes in their surroundings. Wireless sensor networks are truly distributed systems where sensor nodes characterised by limited communication resources cooperating among each other in order to support the network infrastructure activity as a whole. Events and entities that are in the perception range of a node belong to its surroundings. In the set that we call the surroundings we can identify two distinctive subsets: neighbourhood and environment. Considering that we are interested in communication aspects of WSN, the concept of neighbourhood is particularly significant; hence we dedicate this concept in our further investigation. In WSN related literature the definition of neighbourhood is frequently used, often becoming a basis for the definition of several routing algorithms Braginsky & Estrin (2002); Burmester et al. (2007); Manjeshwar & Agrawal (2001); Younis & Fahmy (2004). Let us begin from explaining the meaning of Map(X, Y) expression that can be defined as a collection of mappings of set X onto set Y (surjection). Let us define Sub(X) as a family of subsets X and the neighbourhood as

N ⊠ Map(Nodes, Sub(Nodes)). (17)

Furthermore, if N(x) belongs to neighborhood of the node x and N(S) is a neighborhood of the set S of nodes then, using the neighborhood relation (here denoted as η) we can define a collection of nodes which are neighbors of the given node x as:

$$N(x) = \{y \mid y \boxtimes Nodes \boxtimes x\eta y\}, \qquad (18)$$

and denote the set of neighbours of all nodes that belong to the set S as:

$$N(S) = \{y \mid y \in Nodes \wedge (\exists x \in S \mid x\eta y)\}. \qquad (19)$$

In this discussion, we assume that the neighbourhood relation is a symmetric:

$$x \, \eta \, y \Rightarrow y \, \eta \, x. \qquad (20)$$

This implies, that if a node x remains in a neighbourhood relation with y (i.e. x is able to communicate with y) then the node y is also in a neighbourhood relation with x.

In WSN literature several various locality models were proposed Nikodem et al. (2009). Various benefits and drawbacks of sensor node clasterization or unique transmission paths in context of the applied definition of neighbourhood are also discussed. However, the most accepted approach for defining the locality is the one based on the concept of the neighbourhood that is derived from the technological limitation of radio communication. In some specific situations the partitioning of network into clusters can be very beneficial, to a degree this can be seen as an oversimplification that makes our computation much easier. However, the trade-off is a reduction of the solution space. In the case of a singular retransmission path the solution space consists only of one element. Let us consider the neighbourhood family of N = {Ni | i ∈ I} for which the following conditions are met:

$$(\forall i \in \mathrm{I} \mid \mathrm{N}_i \neq \varnothing)(\cup_i \mathrm{N}_i = Nodes), \qquad (21)$$

$$(\exists^{\succ} i, y \in \mathrm{I} \mid i \neq j)(\mathrm{N}_i \cap \mathrm{N}_j \neq \varnothing). \qquad (22)$$

This translates onto a local mode (for each node) and takes the form of:

$$|(\forall y \in Nodes)(\exists^{\succ} i \in \mathrm{I} \mid y \in \cap \mathrm{N}_i \neq \varnothing). \qquad (23)$$

The expression ∃ can be translated as: "there are as many instances as the structure of the network allows for". The neighbourhood obtained when taking this approach can be interpreted as the most natural of all possible instances that can also guarantee the maximum retransmission capabilities for all allowable solutions. Referring back to concepts of surroundings (S), neighbourhood (N) and environment we could

observe that:

$$((N \subset WSN) \wedge (E \not\subset WSN)) \wedge ((N \cup E \subset S) \wedge (N \cap E = \emptyset)). \quad (24)$$

Neighbourhood is a collection of all of the neighbouring surrounding that belong to the WSN, while the environment (E) consists of all of the elements of surrounding that do not belong to the wireless sensor network but that do have an effect on its behaviour.

FORMING ACTIONS - CHAINS

Relational dependencies of the chain functions of WSN in most cases describe connections between the neighbouring nodes and adapt general principles of neighbourhood. To deal with it, let us focus on the relation of subordination π. Out of all four relations only this one is transitive, which allows us to model the retransmission paths. The π relation which is both transitive and reflective, forms a preorder in the set of actions Act (1). Further investigation requires a stronger order of the set of actions Act. Introducing a partial order does not appear difficult. In real time applications, nodes are distributed more or less randomly over a given area (i.e. they may be dispersed out of a aeroplane). In the case where two network, nodes are found very close to each other, one of them becomes tacit (mute) and in reserve. In this way, a singular communication node substantially greater robustness and survivability is formed. In mathematical terms, such "binding" of two elements can be expressed as:

$$(\forall x, y \in \mathrm{Act})(x\, \pi\, y \wedge y\, \pi\, x) \Rightarrow (y = x). \quad (25)$$

The above expression shows that subordination happens asymmetrically which in turn may lead to a partial set order (asymmetric preorder). Therefore, the set of actions Act is partially ordered (poset). In the discussed formal apparatus we have a stronger relationship than the one indicated in expression (25). As shown in (5), the subordination relation is of an antisymmetric nature; hence this is equivalent to irreflexivity as every relation that is antisymmetric is both asymmetric and irreflexive. Indeed in WSN, a situation when a sensor node transmits to itself does not belong to a category of logical behaviours. Irreflexivity put together with transitivity provides a strict partial order. The set of actions Act being finite and partially ordered can be represented in many ways as any two argument relation can be represented in a form of a directed graph or a diagram. For such a graphic representation we can use the Hasse diagrams which can help us to show the subordination relation between pairs of elements and the whole structure of partial classification of the set of actions. Although, the Hasse diagrams are simple and very intuitive tools for dealing with finite posets, it turns out to be a difficult task to draw "clear" diagrams for more complex situations when we try to represent all possible communication links in the structure of WSN. In most cases when we apply the Hasse technique by first drawing a graph with the minimal elements of an order and then incrementally adding other missing elements we may end-up producing rather poor and unreadable diagrams where internal structure and symmetries of the order are no longer present due to a large number of connections. Therefore, we need to search for a better solution. Our approach using the relations may in the future lead to more viable solution for the representation of connectivity in WSN. In multi-hop sensor networks, the subordination relation that reflects communication aspects of WSN, is not a relation that is cohesive or finite. This means that

$$(\exists x, y \in \mathrm{Act})(\neg(x\,\pi\,y \vee y\,\pi\,x)), \tag{26}$$

hence, there are elements for which such a relation does not take place, thus the subordination relation can be described as a set of a partial order (poset). It is possible to select subsets of such a set that are linearly ordered so that the partial order will additionally meet the condition of cohesion such as:

$$(\forall x, y \in \mathrm{Act})(x\,\pi\,y \vee y\,\pi\,x). \tag{27}$$

It needs to be noted that this expression contradicts the previous one. In multiplicity and partial order theories, ordered subsets for which the order relation is found to be cohesive are called chains. To form the chain we shall define the subordination relation setting by the following induction:

$$\pi^n = \pi^{n-1} \circ \pi, \ldots \pi^2 = \pi^1 \circ \pi, \pi^1 = \pi. \quad (28)$$

$$\pi^n = \{< x, y >| < x, y > \in \text{Act}^{n-1} \times \text{Act}\}, \quad (29)$$

where x shall be called the direct successor of y, while y will be called direct predecessor of x. Forming the communication activities in multi-hop WSNs is the fundamental problem because there is a question whether messages from the network area can be passed onto the base station. On a global scale (this involves the whole WSN), to build suitable structure that allows us to find the answer for this question we could draw on a concept from the theory of multiplicity - transitive closure of 2-argument relation of subordination π on the set Act. However, in this work, the problem of solving the communication activity is perceived from the local level (node neighbourhood). Therefore, we shall consider a case when a packet is transmitted from the node y and after certain number of retransmissions should reach the base station (BS). Applying the setting of subordination relation π, for each sensor node y we define sets of its ascenders Asc and descenders Des using the following expressions

$$\text{Asc}_\pi(y) = \{z \in \text{Act} \mid (\exists n \in \text{N})(y\pi^n z)\}, \quad (3$$

$$\text{Des}_\pi(y) = \{z \in \text{Act} \mid (\exists n \in \text{N})(z\pi^n y)\}. \quad (3$$

Expressions (30),(31) define sets with full communication space of the node y. One of our main aims, however, is to find an answer to the question "to whom send a packet in open space?" hence we need to pay more attention to the set Desπ. It is worth to notice, that for a packet to arrive from the sensor node y to its destination at the node BS it is necessary for the base station to be one of the elements of the set Desπ. Additionally, we could form many subsets of the Desπ set and some of these subsets may help us to determine communication activity in WSN. Among the subsets of Desπ, we can distinguish two types of subsets:

- four sets that are partially ordered, and
- family of well-ordered chains (linearly ordered sets)

The selected ordered chains can be defined as:

$$\text{Des}_{\pi}^{min}(y) = \{x \in \text{Des}_{\pi}(y) \mid \text{BS}\ \pi\ x)\}. \quad (32)$$

The subset (32) contains the selected nodes that are the direct ascenders of the base station (BS). Hence, only the retransmission that involves these nodes allows the packets sent from the node y reaching the BS. The power of this set determines the maximum number of packets that can be delivered from the node y to the BS. Second subset

$$\text{Des}_{\pi}^{max}(y) = \{x \in \text{Des}_{\pi}(y) \mid x\ \pi\ y)\}, \quad (33)$$

contains the nodes that are direct followers of the y node, in other words, these are the nodes that are required to execute the retransmission of the packet issued from the node y. The power of this set determines the maximum number of packets that could be sent from the node y to the BS. Third subset

$$\text{Des}_{\pi}^{mis}(y) = \{x \in \text{Des}_{\pi}(y) \mid \neg(\exists n \in \text{N})(\text{BS}\pi^{n}x)\}, \quad (34)$$

contains nodes that become the dead end on the paths to the base station. A packet that arrives at such a node does not have even a chance to reach the BS. The last subset

$$\text{Des}_{\pi}^{pfex}(y) = \{x \in \text{Des}_{\pi}(y) \mid \text{Card}(\text{Asc}_{\pi}(x)) > 1\}, \quad (35)$$

is made up of nodes called pontifixes that are located at intersections of the packet routes. These nodes become the bottlenecks on the routing path from node y to the BS. Skilful shaping of the communication activity allows for the best utilisation of these elements. The power of the set of pontifixes defines the capability of packet to escape from one routing path onto another during the retransmission to the base station (BS).

From the perspective of shaping the communication activity in WSN, the second most interesting subset group Desπ(y) represents a family of chains Chnπ(y) that constitutes linearly ordered subsets. For each iteration of the Chni π(y) chain the following condition applies:

$$(\forall \mathrm{Chn}^{i}_{\pi}(y) \subset \mathrm{Des}_{\pi}(y) \mid i \in \mathrm{I})(\mathrm{BS} = \perp \wedge y = \top), \tag{36}$$

where the symbol ⊥ denotes the smallest element BS and the symbol denotes the biggest element (y).

COMMUNICATION TOWARDS BASE STATION

In a wireless sensor network nodes are responsible for the collection of information (individual action) and forwarding them to the base station (collective action). As it was described previously, such action may be described using the three relations - subordination, tolerance and collision. Subordination relation is particularly important, because of its transitivity and asymmetry, and it was used in the developed simulator.

At first, let's consider subordination relation only and suppose that the node x is a source of information. Then, the set Π(x) contains all nodes, to which x can send messages directly. Using the subordination relation, a node that receives the information is able to forward it to its neighbors that are in the subordination relation with it. Therefore, we can define the set of the node descendants that contains all nodes to which the message may be sent to:

$$\mathrm{Des}_{\pi}(x) = \{y \mid (\exists n \in \mathrm{N})(y\pi^{n}x)\}, \tag{37}$$

where yπnx indicates that there are n intermediate nodes y(i) such that one can build a chain of relationships

$$y\pi y_n, y_n\pi y_{n-1}, y_{n-1}\pi y_{n-2}, \ldots, y_2\pi y_1, y_1\pi x. \tag{38}$$

When subordination reflects direction towards the base station then it is ensured that the base station belongs to the set Desπ(x) for each node x. Therefore, each message generated by x will eventually reach the base station. Moreover, it follows from the properties of subordination relation and the fact BS belongs to Desπ(x) that a message sent from the node x and retransmitted to subordinated nodes, always reaches the BS (assuming that all nodes on the communication path have enough energy). This is due to transitivity property of the subordination relation and the fact that in chain of relationships (38) we have yiπx for every i = 1, 2, . . . , n and yiπyj for any i > j. Since the subordination relation is asymmetric, so in the chain of relationships each node occurs only once - otherwise, if

$$y_{i+1} = y_j \tag{39}$$

for some i > j then from the fact that yi+1πyi follows that yjπyi . However, since i > j

therefore yiπyj and so the relation becomes symmetric which contradicts the assumption (5). This means that in sequence (38) each node can occur only once. Therefore, and due to the fact that Desπ(x) is finite and contains the BS follows that for every x there exists a finite subordination relationship chain that leads to the BS, i.e.:

$$\mathrm{BS}\pi y_n, y_n \pi y_{n-1}, y_{n-1} \pi y_{n-2}, \ldots, y_1 \pi x. \tag{40}$$

The above property results directly from the definition of set Desπ(x) that includes only these nodes that are closer to the BS than node x. As a consequence each node yi in relationship chain (40) is closer to the BS then x and yj for any i > j. If x is located in the communication range of the BS then set Desπ(x) is a singleton that consists only of the BS. Set Desπ(x) consists of a number of nodes y that are subordinated to x and, in connected networks (i.e. networks in which each node can communicate directly or using retransmission with BS), constitute one or more relationship chains. These chains may differ in number of elements but always lead to the BS.

Similar properties do not hold for tolerance relation since BS does not necessarily belong to

$$\mathrm{Des}_{\vartheta}(x) = \{y \min(\exists n \in \mathrm{N})(y \vartheta^{n} x)\}. \tag{41}$$

Moreover, there is no guarantee that yi = yj in the tolerance relationship chain

$$y \vartheta y_n, y_n \vartheta y_{n-1}, \ldots, y_2 \vartheta v_1, y_1 \vartheta x \tag{42}$$

for any combination of i = j. This is a direct consequence of symmetry property that may lead to loops in chain where part of the chain begins and ends with the same node, e.g

$$x \vartheta y_n, y_n \vartheta y_{n-1}, \ldots, y_2 \vartheta y_1, y_1 \vartheta x. \tag{43}$$

As a result tolerance relationship chain may be infinite even if Des(x) is always finite (since number of nodes in the network is finite). Above considerations present that tolerance relation itself is not sufficient to guarantee that cooperation within the sensor network will lead to proper routing of messages (i.e. that messages will reach the base station). However, tolerance has features that make it very useful as an auxiliary to the subordination. In real life application of WSN it may be particularly useful to cope with locality effects - this corresponds to situations when divided problems cannot be solved or does not improve the overall result. Similarly in WSN, tolerance will enable routing paths variation in order to prevent message loss (e.g. due to dead ends). In an extreme case tolerance relation (that is symmetric) may force a node to send a packet back to its ascender in order to find an alternative routing path. The combination of subordination and tolerance relations allows drawing on advantages of both relations. Subordination ensures that messages always reach the base station while tolerance increases by far the number of available communication paths.

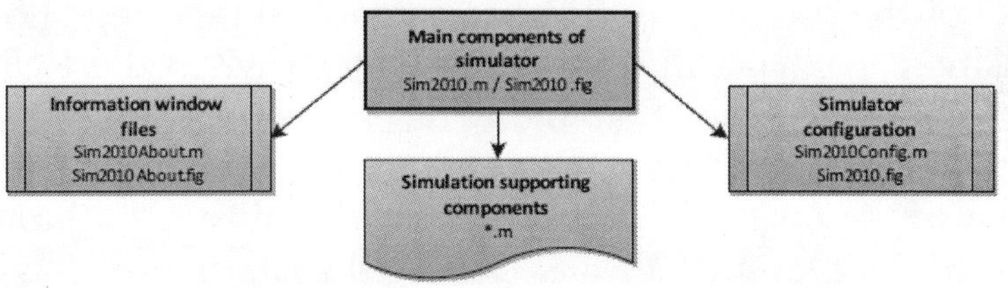

Figure. 1. Simulator architecture - key components

SIMULATION OF WSN COMMUNICATION BEHAVIOUR

In order to present the relational approach that can model behaviour and operation of WSN we have developed a network simulator. Our simulator models behaviour of every single sensor that operates independently in order to meet globally defined criteria and with respect to situation in its environment.

Simulator

The MATLAB environment is required for set up and proper operation of the simulator. The simulator was written and had been tested in MATLAB version R2009b. Only the basic features of the MATLAB environment were used, so no additional tool kits (Toolboxes) are required. The architecture of the simulator is presented in Fig. 1. The entry point of the simulator is Sim2010.fig file which starts the simulator GUI.

Work with the simulator Fig. 2 starts from parameters being setup (Phase I). This includes such parameters as network size, number of sensors, etc. This stage is surmounted by the deployment of sensors in the defined working area, visible in the visualisation area of the main simulator. The first action undertaken in Phase II, is the selection of one of the seven algorithms available in the simulator. Then, depending on the choice made, one can change the default parameters of the algorithm. At this stage, one can also decide how to present the results of simulationand its detail by setting additional parameters in the configuration window. Approval of the configuration changes made in this step allows for the transition to Phase III. Simulation begins when the RUN SIM button is pressed. From that moment, the simulation runs, with time as well as simulation results/parameters being visualised on the screen in the form of graphs and numerical results. Simulation can be also saved to an AVI file. During the simulation, a user can control it (stop and resume it), using the simulation control panel or configuration window to change the appearance of visualisation window. Completion of the simulation process ends PHASE III. Pressing the RESET DATA button, allows the user to jump back to the first stage and resuming simulation from the beginning (possibly with new parameters). Fig. 3 shows the main window of the simulator in which the basic parameters of WSN are defined, the simulation is visualised and information about the current state of the simulation (number of loops, number of messages etc.) and values of network parameters

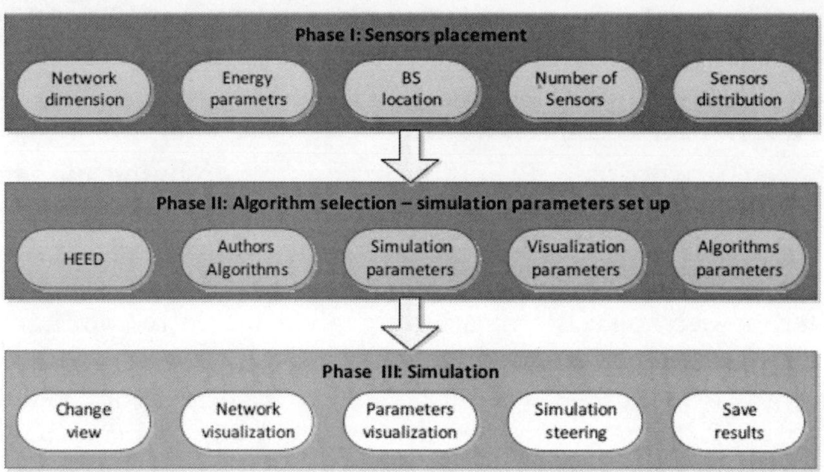

Figure. 2. Main simulation phases

(the average cost of energy, lifespan, etc.) are presented. The basic network parameters that can be entered by the user are:

- size of the network and its area - it is determined by defining a rectangular area in which WSN nodes will be deployed. Because one of the vertices of the area is permanently located at the point (0,0) this area is defined by specifying the length of two sides of the rectangle along the X and Y axis ("Network Size" field). It should be noted that currently the simulator operates for a two-dimensional network, which means that it is not possible to determine the size of the nets along the Z axis.
- position of the base station - we have assumed that there is only one base station in the simulated WSN that can be located at any point of the network area. It is common to place the base station in a corner of the area which is the worst possible position
- number of parameters and sensors - simulator allows to control such network parameters as the number of WSN nodes deployed ("Sensor - Number"), the maximal communication range of a single node ("Sensor - Range") and initial energy of each node ("Sensor- Energy"). In determining the number

of nodes and their maximum range, one has to remember that these parameters are related to the size of the network. Setting too few nodes, or too short communication range can cause the network to be disconnected (some nodes of the network will not be able to communicate with the base station).

Given network area (P) and the maximum communication range of a node (Rt), the number of nodes required to ensure network is connected, can be estimated. Note that if in each circular area of the diameter Rt/2 at least one node is located then any two nodes located in two adjacent areas will be always able to communicate directly. This will be ensured regardless of their position within this area. Since the entire network area is rectangular, we assume that the area of Rt/2 diameter can be approximated by a square of diagonal $R_t/2$, inscribed in the circle.

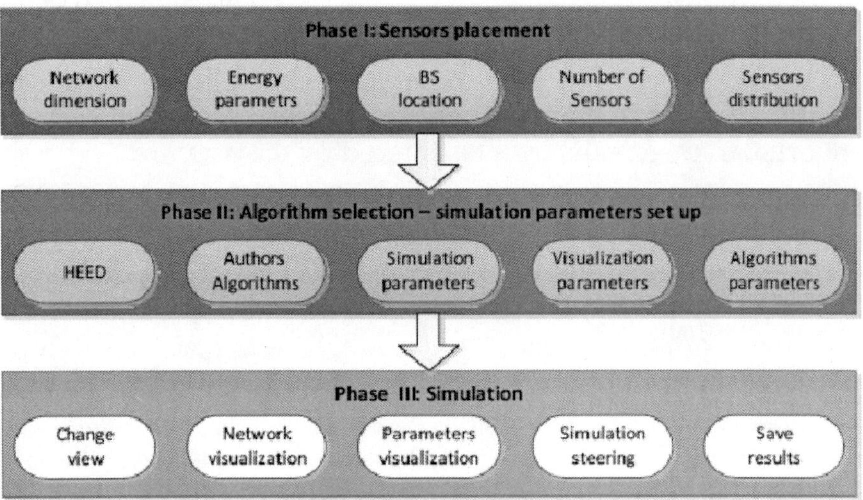

Figure. 3. Main simulator window

If so then the number of areas that will fit on the entire network is equal to

$$N = \frac{R_t^2}{2\sqrt{2}P}. \tag{44}$$

Once the number of areas is known, one can estimate the number of nodes to be scattered in the network that ensures each of N areas is covered with at least one node. This problem is equivalent to the ball-and-bins problem in which balls are thrown randomly to bins, which is the well-known in mathematics. It was presented that when

$$n = 2N \log N = \frac{R_t^2}{\sqrt{2}P} \log\left(\frac{R_t^2}{2\sqrt{2}P}\right), \tag{45}$$

nodes (balls) are used then the probability that there is at least one node (ball) in each area (bin) is close 1.0. It should also be noted that this estimate is inflated due to the assumption that the area covered by communication range of a single node is square rather than circle. In addition to these parameters, the user can also influence the arrangement of nodes in the network. The simulator assumes that nodes are distributed evenly throughout the network (which is the assumption commonly adopted in the literature), however, one can control this distribution by identifying the seed used to generate sequences of random numbers. Using the drop-down list one can specify if the distribution of nodes should be completely random, or random with a seed that is entered by a user - in that case one must select "By Defined Seed" and enter the value of seed in the "Seed" window. Because of this, the same distribution of nodes in the network can be generated repeatedly, and thus one will be able to compare the actions on the same network with various parameters of the simulation and relations settings.

The same window enables to determine which routing algorithm will be used for communication ("Type of algorithm" field). At this moment, the simulator implements three groups of algorithms in seven different variants. The groups are:

- shift register,
- energy balanced,
- HEED,

and differ in the idea of operation, criteria for selecting communication paths (consecutive retransmissions) and the principles of relations ordering. The main difference between the first two groups and HEED is that HEED is a standard hierarchical protocol Younis & Fahmy (2004), which does not use the relationship mechanism. The remaining two groups differ in rules that are used to order nodes within relations. For group of 'Shift register' algorithms ordering takes place only once - after the deployment of nodes, during the initialisation of the network. This distinguishes these algorithms from 'Energy balanced' where ordering takes place after every message sent by a node (sort is made by nodes that have sent, received or heard the message exchanged between neighbouring nodes). For both groups, the ordering concerns part of all WSN nodes. This is determined by setting a percentage of nodes in 'Sorted nodes [%]' window. The value determines what portion of nodes will sort their neighbouring nodes according to their proximity to the growing distance from the base station (for groups 'Shift register') or decreasing amount of remaining energy (for the group 'Energy balanced'). Remaining nodes do not sort their neighbouring nodes, which means that the order neighbours in the relation depends on the order in which node learnt of their existence. Relation for each node is represented in simulator as a vector (Register) of neighbouring nodes. Order of nodes within the vector corresponds to the relation ordering between nodes. Seven routing algorithms available in the current version of the simulator consist of:

- **Shift register** - this is the algorithm in which each node neighbourhood (represented as a vector) behaves like a cyclic shift register, the shift occur only within a subordination relation, and messages are always sent to the first node from the register. The parameter of this algorithm is the intensity of the other subordination relation that determines the number of neighbours who are subordinated to the node. This parameter determines how many neighbours (counting from the beginning of the vector) are taken into consideration when node is about to send the message.
- **Shift register [%]** - an algorithm is similar to the previous one but the intensity of the subordination relation is expressed by specifying the percentage of neighbours that are in a subordination relation rather than the number of nodes.
- Shift register [Card(Π) = k] - in this algorithm the subordination relation includes only neighbouring nodes that are closer to the base station than the current node. Compared with the 'Shift register' algorithm, the difference is that in 'Shift register' subordination relation may consist of nodes that are more

distant from the base station than the current node. In the current algorithm, this situation will never take place, although there is no certainty that the best neighbours (the closest to the base station) will be in a subordination relation. For example, this may happen if the registry (that represents the relation) is not sorted

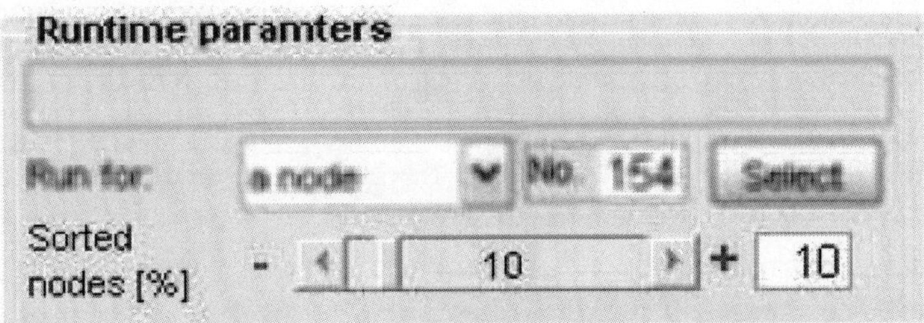

Figure. 4. Parameter Sorted Nodes [%] in the configuration window

- **Energy balanced** - this is an algorithm in which the subordination relation is composed of a number of neighbours in the left part of the vector (either sorted or not) and the number of nodes in relation is an algorithm parameter. The message is sent to the first node from the vector. After each messages sent, the node sorts this vector according to the amount of residual energy in neighbouring nodes - see description of sorting parameter 'Sorted nodes [%] earlier in this section.
- **Energy balanced [%]** - this algorithm is similar to the previous one but the difference is that the intensity of the subordination relation is determined by indicating the percentage of the neighbouring nodes that are in the relation.
- Energy balanced [Card(Π) = k] - similar to 'Shift register [Card(Π) = k]' the algorithm also restricts the subordination relation to only these neighbours that are closer to the base station than the current node.
- **HEED** - this is one of the most popular hierarchical algorithm, which defines how to group neighbouring nodes into clusters and transmit messages in the WSN. This algorithm has been

implemented in order to compare with our proposal of relational based routing and communication.

Neighbourhood Organisation And Network Communication Efficiency

In the self-organisation phase executed prior to the proper operation of the network, each node collects information about its neighbourhood. Then, using the globally defined metric (expressed in number of retransmissions or the Euclidean distance from the Base Station), each node organises (i.e. sorts according to the residual energy in neighbouring nodes) its neighbours. Number of nodes in the network, which make such an arrangement, is determined by one of the parameters and defines the degree of the neighbourhood ordering. We have evaluated the impact of this parameter on the size of the communication area (that is area covered by nodes that take part in message routing), the number of intermediate nodes and energy efficiency of the algorithms used. The 'Sorted Nodes [%]' parameter specifies the percentage of nodes that sort their neighbouring nodes according to their growing distance from the base station. Other nodes do not sort the neighbourhood, which means that the order of neighbours depends on the order in which the node "learnt" of their existence. In the rest of the chapter, results of simulations and conclusions are presented. All simulations were carried out with fixed values of parameters. These are presented in table 1. Changing the number of organised neighbourhoods has a significant impact on the efficiency of all tested algorithms. And so, when the parameter 'Sorted Nodes [%]' had value 10% for both algorithms 'Shift register [Card(Π) = k]' and 'Energy balanced [Card(Π) = k]' then communication area is either very large Fig. 5 or large Fig. 6. It is worth noting that the algorithms from the group of 'Energy balanced', when working with the same parameters, are characterised by a lower

Table 1. WSN and simulation parameters

WSN parameters	
Number of sensors	300
WSN area	100×100
Position of the BS	x=1, y=1
Sensor communication range	20
Initial node energy	300
Energy cost of message sent	5
Simulation parameters	
Number of messages to send	300
Communication to the BS	from one selected node
Number of iterations	300
Deployment of nodes	random with fixed seed equal 10

Principles of Retransmitters Selection and Area of the Communication Size and Energy Efficiency

Algorithms from the 'Shift register' group can be divided due to the selection of successors (the following nodes in the routing path of a message that is transmitted to the base station):

- numerical - the value of the parameter 'Reg. capacity' defines the number of neighbouring nodes, from which the successive node is drawn when messages are about to be send,
- percentage - similar to previous but the value of the parameter 'Reg. capacity' defines the percentage of neighbours that will constitute the set from which the successive node will be drawn,
- directional - the value of the parameter 'Reg. capacity' defines the percentage of neighbours that constitute a set $\hat{\mathrm{D}}\mathrm{es}_{\pi}^{\max}(x)$ - set of nodes subordinated to the actual node (x).

Numeric vs. Percentage Selection

Numerical selection is the least effective method because it allows for the selection of retransmitters without any restrictions; even those nodes can be selected that are outside the desired direction toward the base station. This type of selection of retransmitters does not take into consideration the number of nodes in the neighbourhood that is a property of each node of the network, and may differ significantly throughout the network. Fig. 7 presents how selection of the number of potential retransmitters, appropriate to the number of nodes in the neighbourhood improves the communication efficiency. The 'Reg. capacity'= 10 allows sending the same number of packages, but without reaching the state of energy depletion in some nodes. For example, it follows from Fig. 7 that Card $(Des_{\pi}^{max})=10$ is the best value. However, this may not be true for the other nodes. Our tests show that it is the more favourable approach to use percentage selection, where Card (Des_{π}^{max}) corresponds to the number of nodes

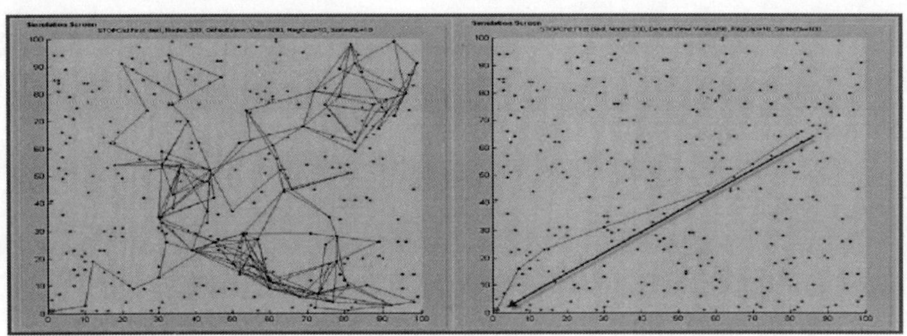

Figure. 5. Algorithm 'Shift register [Card(Π) = k]' with 'Sorted Nodes [%]' parameter equal 10%(left) and 100% (right) - retransmission path view

in the neighbours. Therefore, for each node of the network the number of nodes in Desmax π may differ but when expressed as a percentage, then it is invariant and is adjusted to the local situation of a particular node. This enables us to shape both energy efficiency and the size of the communication area.

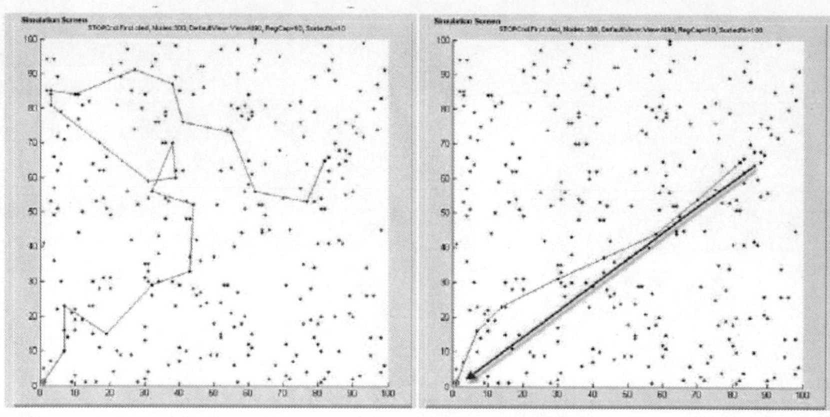

Figure. 6. Algorithm 'Energy balanced [Card(Π) = k]' with 'Sorted Nodes [%]' parameter equal 10% (left) and 100% (right) - retransmission path view

Directional and even energy consumption strategy

Directional selection takes into account the neighbours of the transmitter, but only these that are in subordinate relation with it. This enables to shape WSN communication activity, by setting Card (Desmax π) as a percentage of neighbouring nodes. Hence, it is not possible, regardless of the value of the parameter 'Reg. capacity', to send a message in a different direction, than towards the base station. When energy costs are considered then this is the best approach,

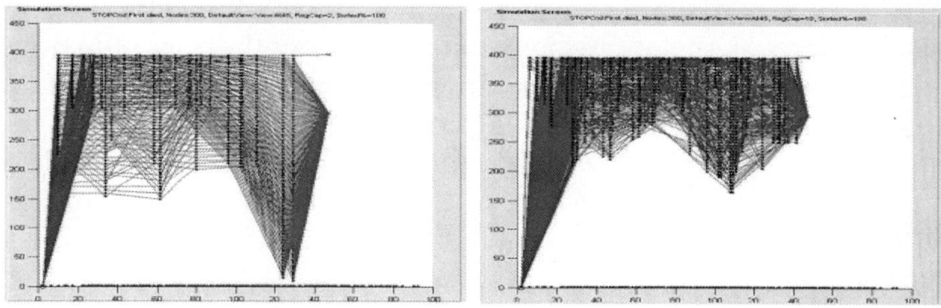

Figure. 7. Energy loses in the network operating according to 'Shift register' algorithm with 'Reg. capacity' parameter set to 2 (left) and 10 (right)

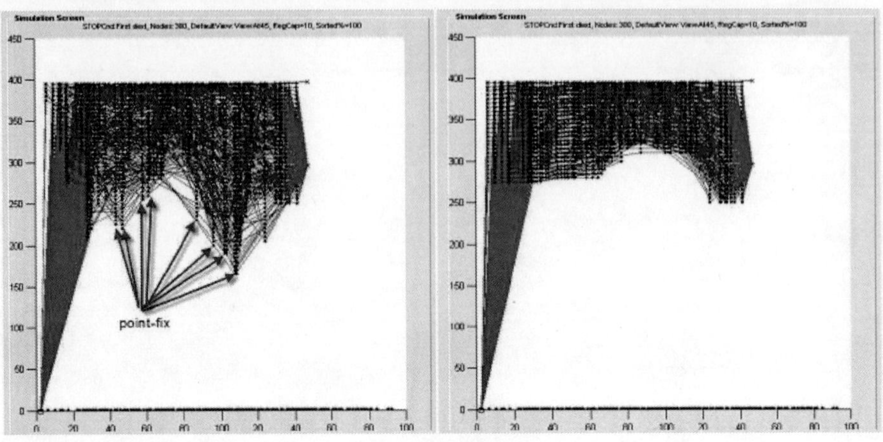

Figure. 8. Energy loses in the network operating according to 'Shift register [Card(Π) = k]' (left) and 'Energy balanced' (right) with 'Reg. capacity' parameter set to 10

however, as it can be noticed from Fig. 8, in the so-formed communication space, pontifixes (i.e. points that collect messages from a number of nodes) become a problem. As nodes that receive messages from a number of nodes they are overloaded (Fig. 8 left). The solution is in such a situation is to draw on even energy cost strategy that provides uniform, depending only on the network structure, balanced energy consumption (Fig. 8 right). The main difference of these algorithms when compared to the 'Shift register' group is the focus on uniform energy consumption throughout the whole network. This is a very important aspect of real life systems, where energy depletion in one sensor may affect the operation of the whole network. Algorithms in 'Energy balanced' group strive for a balanced load of nodes that route messages, that in turn increases the average energy consumption required to transmit a message to the base station. Simplifying the theory we may say that in these algorithms, each node retransmits messages to all its neighbours in turn. During transmission between the nodes neighborhood, only these neighbors are chosen that have the greatest residual energy. The operation of these algorithms allows for excellent energy saving for nodes that otherwise die quickly. These are the 'pontifixes', in which different communication paths converge. Equivalent energy algorithms cope very well with such a situation. Increased consumption of energy for these nodes can be seen very well on left part of Fig. 8. On the other hand there is almost perfectly balanced energy consumption when all nodes are involved in the transmission (Fig. 8 right).

CONCLUSIONS

This article presents a relational approach to model the behaviour of wireless sensor networks. The model draws on relations that enable us to represent general, globally defined goals of the network, as well as describe the operation of a single node that has limited information about the network. Three relations (subordination, tolerance and collision) can be used to model communication activities and to control routing paths that are used to transmit messages from sources to the base station. Although, the best setup of relations parameters is not known yet, simulations present that adjusting the intensity of relations enables to control power consumption and extend network lifetime. This improvement results from the fact that every node of the network can adjust its operation according to the current situation in its neighbourhood, rather than strictly following some predefined routing algorithm. The relational approach is also more general than routing algorithms presented in literature so far. Moreover, it encapsulates all previous proposals, so they can be used when needed.

ACKNOWLEDGEMENT

This paper has been written as a result of realisation of the project entitled "Detectors and sensors for measuring factors hazardous to environment - modeling and monitoring of threats". The project is financed by the European Union via the European Regional Development Fund and the Polish state budget, within the framework of the Operational Programme InnovativeEconomy 2007-2013. The contract for refinancing No. POIG.01.03.01-02-002/08-00

REFERENCES

1. Braginsky, D. & Estrin, D. (2002). Rumor routing algorthim for sensor networks, WSNA'02: Proceedings of the 1st ACM international workshop on Wireless sensor networks and applications, ACM, New York, NY, USA, pp. 22–31.
2. Burmester, M., Le, T. V. & Yasinsac, A. (2007). Adaptive gossip protocols: Managing security and redundancy in dense ad hoc networks, Ad Hoc Netw. 5(3): 313–323.
3. Descartes, R. & Lafleur, L. J. (1960). Discourse on Method and Meditations, New York: The Liberal Arts Press.
4. Dollimore, J., Kindberg, T. & Coulouris, G. (2005). Distributed Systems: Concepts and Design, Addison-Wesley.
5. Jaron, J. (1978). Systemic prolegomena to theoretical cybernetics, Technical report, Inst. of Techn Cybernetics.
6. Manjeshwar, A. & Agrawal, D. P. (2001). Teen: A routing protocol for enhanced efficiency in wireless sensor networks, Parallel and Distributed Processing Symposium, International 3: 30189a.
7. Nikodem, J. (2008). Autonomy and cooperation as factors of dependability in wireless sensor network, Dependability of Computer Systems, International Conference on pp. 406–413.
8. Nikodem, J. (2009). Relational approach towards feasibility performance for routing algorithms in wireless sensor network, Dependability of Computer Systems, International Conference on pp. 176–183.
9. Nikodem, J., Klempous, R., Nikodem, M.,Woda, M. & Chaczko, Z. (2009). Multihop communication in wireless sensors network based on directed cooperation, Selected papers on Broadband Communication, Information Technology & Biomedical Application, BroadBand- Com '09, pp. 239–241.
10. Younis, O. & Fahmy, S. (2004). Heed: A hybrid, energy-efficient, distributed clustering approach for ad hoc sensor networks, IEEE Transactions on Mobile Computing 3: 366 379..

Chapter 2

MULTI-PARAMETRIC CLUSTERING FOR SENSOR NODE COORDINATION IN COGNITIVE WIRELESS SENSOR NETWORKS

Xiao Yu Wang, Alexander Wong*

Department of Systems Design Engineering, University of Waterloo, Waterloo, Canada

ABSTRACT

The deployment of wireless sensor networks for healthcare applications have been motivated and driven by the increasing demand for real-time monitoring of patients in hospital and large disaster response environments. A major challenge in developing such sensor networks is the need for coordinating a large number of randomly deployed sensor nodes. In this study, we propose a multi-parametric clustering scheme designed to aid in the coordination of sensor nodes within cognitive wireless sensor networks. In the proposed scheme, sensor nodes are clustered together based on similar network behaviour across multiple network parameters, such as channel availability, interference characteristics, and topological characteristics, followed by mechanisms for forming, joining and switching clusters. Extensive performance evaluation is conducted to study the impact on important factors such as clustering overhead, cluster joining estimation error, interference probability, as well as probability of reclustering. Results show that the proposed clustering scheme can be an excellent candidate for use in large scale cognitive wireless sensor network deployments with high dynamics

INTRODUCTION

The use of medical sensor systems such as electroencephalography (EEG), electrocardiography (ECG), blood pressure monitors, and glucose monitors for monitor the vital signs of patients have long been a staple of the modern healthcare establishment. However, such medical sensing systems have been largely wired and tethered to a specific location, which results in not only a mess of wires that can affect patient comfort levels, but also requires a wired infrastructure that is inconvenient for clinical personnel as well as restricts patient mobility [1]. This restriction in mobility would be considered particularly disadvantageous in large disaster response situations [2], [3]. With the advent of advanced wireless communication technologies and portable sensing devices, there is now an increasing demand for wireless sensor networks (WSNs) to address some of these limitations. For example, patients within hospitals would be able to move from location to location without having to be reconnected, thus allowing for uninterrupted real-time patient monitoring. In the case of large disaster response scenarios, a large number of victims who are scattered a random locations can be monitored simultaneously at the disaster location. As such, there are a large number of healthcare scenarios where wireless sensor networks can enable a much more robust and versatile health monitoring environment than conventional wired systems. Despite the great number of advantages of such wireless sensor networks for healthcare monitoring, there are still a number of technical challenges that must be resolved, and as such new approaches for the deployment and management of such networks are required.

A key challenge associated with the deployment of wireless sensor networks for healthcare monitoring purposes is the coordination and management of a large number of randomly deployed sensor nodes. Proper coordination and management is necessary for reducing the communication bandwidth and energy requirements, as well as interference of a large number of sensor nodes working simultaneously within a common wireless sensing network. One effective approach to tackling this issue is to group sensor nodes into clusters to facilitate for improved coordination as well as reduced resource usage. For example, it is more efficient resource-wise for designated sensor nodes ("clusterheads") to collect sensing data from neighboring sensor nodes within clusters and then transmit the data back to a central source, than for individual sensor nodes to transmit to a central source in a direct manner. Furthermore, in the case of cognitive wireless sensor networks (CWSNs) [4], [5], clustering also aids in the coordination of cognitive sensor nodes so that the unlicensed spectrum resources can be better utilized for improved coverage and quality of service, while at the same time reducing interference. This is particularly important in a large disaster scenario, where there are a large number of sensing nodes being deployed (as well as other mobile communication devices) that can starve the primary spectrum resources and result in communications failure.

There has been extensive research on clustering techniques in both conventional WSNs and Mobile Ad Hoc Networks (MANETs). In conventional WSNs, clustering is utilized primarily to reduce energy consumption during the data gathering process, which is critical for extending the lifetime of such networks since sensor nodes often have limited available energy [6], [7]. As such, the criteria for clustering in WSNs primarily depends on energy constraints. In MANETs, the main purpose for clustering is to maintain a certain level of system performance in the context of large numbers of high mobility wireless nodes. Given this type of scenario, clustering for MANETs relies more on the overall topology of the network formed by mobile nodes to determine the cluster formation [8], [9].

In this work, we explore the use of clustering to aid in the coordination of cognitive sensor nodes in cognitive wireless sensor networks. The spectrum resource that we utilize in this work is multiple spatially and temporarily available subbands, which is different from the statically assigned single radio channel of conventional WSNs and MANETs. The dynamic nature of spatially and temporarily available subbands introduces challenges of returning legitimate users on the already identified available subbands, and the characteristics of the returning legitimate users may be very different on each subbands and result in interference. Therefore, existing techniques may not work well for such cognitive wireless sensor networks and hence a new approach to designing clustering for cognitive sensor nodes within such a network is required.

The main contributions of this paper are summarized as follows.

- A novel approach for dynamically clustering cognitive sensor nodes based on weighted Fuzzy C-means (FCM) [23] that takes into consideration multiple important network parameters such as channel availability, interference characteristics, and topological characteristics is introduced to allow for more reliable and efficient communication.
- A probabilistic approach to defining cluster membership is employed instead of the conventional deterministic approach of fixed cluster memberships. This approach allows cognitive sensor nodes to join and switch between different clusters for better connection, thus allowing better spectrum efficiency to be achieved.
- A set of cluster formation, cluster joining, cluster switching, and resolution mechanisms is introduced.

Simulation results shows great potential for achieving improved performance when compared with existing clustering algorithms in terms of clustering overhead, cluster joining estimation error, interference probability, and probability of reclustering.

The rest of this paper is organized as follows. First, the related work is reviewed. The system model is then presented, and the proposed clustering scheme is described. Performance evaluation results are then presented and conclusions are drawn.

RELATED WORK

Given the relative infancy of the research area, there are only a few related works on clustering for multichannel ad-hoc networks such as cognitive wireless sensor networks. In general, channel availability is the most popular network parameter for clustering nodes. Most of these schemes [10]–[13] assume or imply that spectrum availability does not change during the cluster formation procedure. In [10], clusters are formed based on a single available channel, where nodes compete to be the clusterhead after detecting no messages on the channel. The successful clusterhead then issues a beacon to control the channel access of the cluster. In[12], [13], a recursive distributed voting scheme is used to dynamically select a common channel, which is labeled with the highest connectivity with a neighborhood. Any new joining nodes eavesdrops the control messages to determine which cluster to join. Since this approach attempts to cluster users through a single common channel, changes in primary user activities on this channel can result in the disconnection of users in the group, which leads to frequent reclustering to ensure full neighborhood connectivity [14].

To reduce the amount of reclustering, Lazos *et al*. formulated the clustering problem as a maximum edge biclique problem, which is solved by a spectrum-opportunity based clustering algorithm [14]. In this approach, the nodes are clustered based on similar channel availability, which allows the nodes to choose a control channel from a group of available channels. Furthermore, the nodes can migrate to another control channel without the need for reclustering if the current control channel becomes occupied due to primary user activities. However, since only channel availability is taken into consideration when determining the clustering of nodes, this approach can potentially be sensitive to the presence of interference between different nodes.

SYSTEM MODEL

In this study, the CWSNs consist of cognitive sensor nodes that collect real-time data over a large area and needs that data to be transmitted reliably in a continuous manner, such as for healthcare applications such as real-time monitoring of patients in hospital and large disaster response environments. While such nodes may operate regularly in the unlicensed industrial, scientific and medical (ISM) bands, as most WSNs do, the ISM band is also used by an increasing number of wireless devices operating on technologies such as Bluetooth, Wi-Fi, and near field communication (NFC). As such, not only is the unlicensed ISM band spectrum resources become increasing scarce, co-existence issues arise between different devices using different protocols and technologies all trying to operate within the unlicensed ISM band. Therefore, in this study, we consider the cognitive sensor nodes being deployed in the CWSNs to be equipped with extra capability for spectrum sensing and opportunistic accessing to already-licensed spectrum bands for other services, such as any television (TV) bands within 400–600 MHz and Ultra High Frequency (UHF) TV bands, which has recently been made available by government regulators such as the Federal Communications Commission (FCC). Therefore, in the situation where the unlicensed ISM spectrum has been consumed by on-going data traffic or results in interference, the cognitive sensor nodes can make use of the additional white space.

In this study, there are a total of n primary users, and N cognitive sensor nodes. The cognitive sensor nodes are not necessary within the radio transmission range of each other. The primary users are designated as the legitimate users and are statically allocated in the TV band. In this same spectrum, each of the cognitive sensor nodes has the additional capability to sense and opportunistically access spatiotemporally available spectrum resources in a secondary manner.

CHANNEL MODEL

The spectrum available for opportunistic access is divided into M non-overlapping subbands, denoted as $C_i, i=1,2,\ldots,M$, with f_i denoting the center frequency of C_i. A channel is a single subband and the unit of spectrum usage. The radio propagation of these channels is assumed to be subject to small scale Rayleigh fading, which has been commonly taken to describe the rapid fluctuation of radio signal over a short period of time or transmission distance[15]. Mathematically, given a transmitter-receiver pair and the transmitter power $\mathcal{P}$, the received signal strength is given as: $\mathcal{P}_r = \frac{\mathcal{P}G}{d^{\xi}}$ **(1)** where d is the distance between the transmitter and the receiver, ξ is the path loss exponent, and G is a comprehensive channel factor including a random value of a chi-square distribution with two degrees of freedom modeling the Rayleigh fading, as well as antenna gain factor. Where the primary users are randomly located around a reference cognitive sensor node, the total received power at the reference cognitive sensor node on channel C_i from primary transmissionsisgivenas[16]:

$$\mathcal{I}_i = \frac{\mathcal{P}_{i,1} G_{i,1}}{d_1^{\xi}} + \frac{\mathcal{P}_{i,2} G_{i,2}}{d_2^{\xi}} + \ldots + \frac{\mathcal{P}_{i,n} G_{i,n}}{d_n^{\xi}} \quad (2)$$

where $\mathcal{P}_{i,1}, \mathcal{P}_{i,2}, \ldots, \mathcal{P}_{i,n}$ denotes the power of ongoing transmission by primary users indexed as $1, 2, \ldots, n$; $G_{i,1}, G_{i,2}, \ldots, G_{i,n}$ denotes the channel factor of corresponding primary users; and$d_1, d_2, \ldots, d_n$ denotes the distance between the cognitive sensor node to the primary users.

Spectrum Sensing Model

In the Rayleigh fading channel model, each cognitive sensor node detects the presence of primary users independently of other cognitive sensor nodes. Since it is very hard to correctly distinguish a faded signal of a primary user from the environmental noise and hence the existence of primary users in the presence of channel fading, a number of feature detection techniques have been proposed to differentiate the noise energy from the signal energy, such as cyclostationary feature detection [17] and pilot signal detection. However, comparing to the widely used energy detection, the main disadvantages of feature detection method are long observation time, computational complexity, and greater energy consumption. Moreover, some primary user signals exhibit no stable and common features, such as wireless microphone signals operating in TV white space spectrum [18]. Therefore, in this work, energy detection is conservatively assumed to obtain the presence of the primary users in a fast but relatively inaccurate manner. Given a certain probability of false alarm, P_f, the average detection probability $\bar{P}_{d,i}$ of channel C_i can be approximated [19]

Interference Model

Branching off interference modeling work in cognitive networks [20], [21], in the interference model, the victim receiver is defined as a primary user which is subject to interference by cognitive sensor nodes. Three of the main causes of such interference are considered. The first cause of interference being considered is that primary users are spatially distributed within the interference range

Ω of the cognitive sensor nodes, following a probability distribution function P_Ω. For example, in the simple case where the primary users are uniformly distributed within Ω, P_Ω, can be defined as the ratio between the area of Ω and the area of primary user network coverage.

The second cause of interference being considered is that that primary users may return to channels that were previously identified as available but is currently being occupied by cognitive sensor nodes. It is assumed that the spectrum usage of primary users on channel C_i follows an M/G/1 model [22], where the primary users arrive on channel C_i according to a Poisson process with rate $\lambda^{(i)}$, and the busy period of usage is on an arbitrary distribution. Therefore, the probability of the earliest returning primary user during the transmission period of cognitive sensor node can be estimated as [22].

$$P_{i,re} = \frac{I_i}{\bar{T}_i} \int_0^{T_{\max}} (1 - e^{-t/I_i}) f_{T_i}(t)dt, \quad (3)$$

where I_i is the average idle period in the primary user network for C_i, $f_{T_i}(t)$ is the probability density function of cognitive sensor node transmission time for C_i, $\bar{T}_i$ is the average transmission time of C_i, and T_{max} is the maximum allowable transmission time.

The third cause of interference being considered is that, technically, due to the detection sensitivity, the cognitive sensor nodes are not able to identify severely faded primary user signals, and thus leading to undesirable access to unavailable channels that are being used by primary users. The corresponding probability can be determined by $1 - \bar{P}_{d,i}$.

Based on these three causes, interference to the primary users by the cognitive sensor nodes can be a result of two scenarios: 1) detection error in the interference range of the cognitive sensor nodes, 2) returning primary users to the successfully identified channel without any false alarm, i.e., $1 - P_f$, within the interference range of the cognitive sensor node; therefore, the probability of interference can be evaluated as

$$P_{i,I} = P_\Omega(1 - \bar{P}_{d,i}) + P_\Omega(1 - P_f)P_{i,re}. \quad (4)$$

Discovery Model

Note that before cluster formation, cognitive sensor nodes do not directly communicate with each other. However, the cognitive sensor nodes can communicate with macrocell base stations wirelessly (though briefly to limit communication overhead). This facilitates the discovery of the other cognitive sensor nodes. Through brief information exchanges with macrocells, the cognitive sensor nodes are aware of information about other cognitive sensor nodes. In particular, the information about a cognitive sensor node k includes its location $\vec{L}=[x,y]$ denoted the spatial coordinates, available channels $\vec{C}_a$ with index a, as well as the corresponding interference characteristics $\vec{P}_a$ of available channels with index a. This information can be represented by the vector $\vec{z}_k=\{\vec{L},\vec{C}_a,\vec{P}_a\}$. The overall information of all cognitive sensor nodes is denoted as $\vec{Z}=\{\vec{z}_k,\forall k\}$. The information of available channels and interference characteristics is time sensitive and is the key to the proper coordination among cognitive sensor nodes. We will take them into consideration while designing the clustering scheme.

METHODS

Overview

The proposed multi-parametric clustering scheme can be divided into four main stages: i)*clustering estimation,* ii) *cluster formation,* iii) *cluster joining,* and iv) *cluster switching*. The interaction of each stage of the proposed scheme is shown in Fig. 1. In the clustering estimation stage, each cognitive sensor node autonomously identifies the possible clusters within the network as well as its membership via weighted Fuzzy C-means clustering (FCM)[23]. Based on the clustering estimation, the selected candidate cognitive sensor nodes enter into the cluster formation stage, and compete for clusterhead that provide service to the individual clusters, as well as identify the common channels upon which the service can be provided. The remaining cognitive sensor nodes enter into the cluster joining stage, where the joining cognitive sensor nodes decide upon which cluster to join and the corresponding mechanism to employ. Finally, in the cluster switching stage, cognitive sensor nodes switch fast to backup clusters based on the cluster membership estimated in the clustering estimation stage to avoid returning primary users.

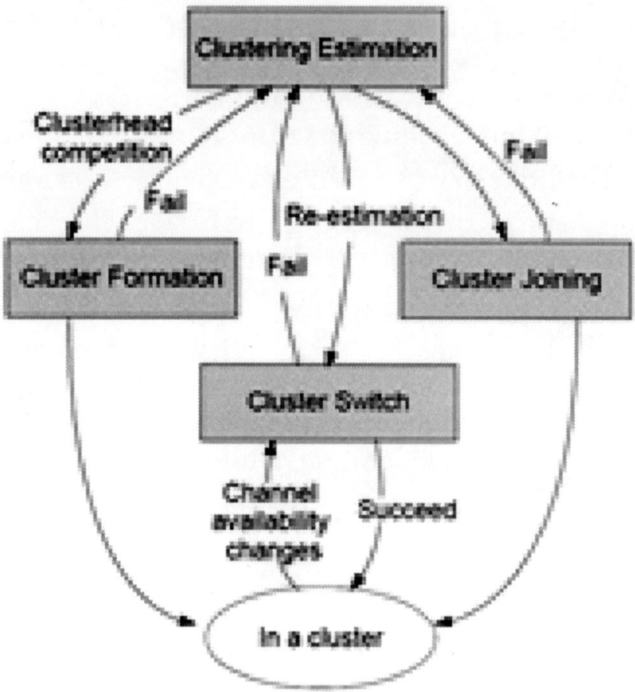

Figure 1. Stages of proposed clustering scheme.

doi:10.1371/journal.pone.0053434.g001

The following subsections describe the detailed mechanisms of clustering estimation, cluster formation, cluster joining, as well as resolution of returning primary users.

Clustering Estimation with Weighted FCM

Clustering with low communication overhead is challenging, especially under the situation where the spectrum resource is scarce and network connectivity are rapidly changing [24]. To make this demand, the proposed scheme employs and modifies Fuzzy C-means (FCM) [23]clustering, which is relatively fast and, not only does it allow for better handling and modeling of imprecise data with large variability by allowing for cluster mixtures in a probabilistic manner, which is important given the set of network parameters being considered, but also can be implemented distributively on individual cognitive sensor nodes to reduce the communication overhead. The information $\vec{z}_k = \{\vec{L}, \vec{C}_a, \vec{P}_a\}$ pertaining to the cognitive sensor node k contains location information $\vec{L}$, as well as time sensitive information about multiple network parameters, such as channel availability $\vec{C}_a$ and the corresponding interference characteristics $\vec{P}_a\}$. Therefore, reliability factors are required to weight the obtained information. In terms of channel availability, it is easy to assume that the use of channels by the primary users does not change during certain period of time, such as a time slot or a cycle of updating period. However, it is often not practical and the reliability of usage information fades as time elapses. To avoid a binary response (e.g. reliable or not), a soft thresholding strategy is employed on a set of available channels $\vec{C}_a$ to ensure tighter estimates based on Poisson process of primary user arrival $\vec{\lambda}_a^{(1)}$ by using $\vec{\omega}(\vec{C}_a, t) = 1 - e^{-\vec{\lambda}_a^{(1)} t}$. **(5)**

Moreover, in terms of interference characteristics, the time sensitivity has been reflected in the estimation of the primary user arrival in Eq. (3). The value of the arrival rate $\vec{\lambda}_a^{(1)}$ on the set of available channels $\vec{C}_a$ can be estimated based on a sliding observation window T_W, where the oldest observations are removed from the system while the latest observations are being recorded. Let b_i be an indicator of primary user arrival on channel C_i, where $b_i(T) = 0$ indicate no arrival and $b_i(T) = 1$ indicate the arrival of the primary users on channel C_i, respectively at observation time instance T. The arrival rate of the available channel set $\vec{C}_a$ can be estimated as

$$\vec{\lambda}_a^{(1)} \approx \sum_{T \in T_W} \vec{b}_a(T) / T_W. \quad \textbf{(6)}$$

Based on the information of the other cognitive sensor nodes obtained via macrocell base stations, denoted as $\vec{Z}$, as well as the weighted reliability factors $\vec{\omega}(\vec{C}_a, T)$ at time instance T, clustering estimation may be conducted at the individual cognitive sensor nodes.

Let $V=[\vec{v}_1,\ldots,\vec{v}_{N_c}]$ denote the unknown cluster centers in a given network area, and let N_c be the number of cluster centers. A cluster center is not a clusterhead but a logical center of the cluster, containing the information about multiple parameters such as common channel availability and the reference interference characteristics of a certain coverage location, all of which indicate similar network behavior such that cognitive sensor nodes can be clustered together. Based on the assumption that a cognitive sensor node can coordinate at least g numbers of neighboring cognitive sensor nodes, the maximum number of N_c can be initially estimated as $N_c=N/g$, where N is the total number of cognitive sensor nodes in the given network area.

Moreover, let U denotes a matrix, whose elements u_{jk} value in $[0,1]$. If $u_{jk}=\alpha$, which indicates the membership, i.e., the probability, of the cognitive sensor node k in cluster j is α. An individual cognitive sensor node obtains the estimates of both the cluster centers and the membership $(\mathbf{V},\mathbf{U})$ by minimizing the weighted FCM objective function:

$$J_m(V,U;\vec{Z})=\sum_{k=1}^{N}\sum_{j=1}^{N_c}(u_{ik})^m\left\|\vec{\omega}(\vec{C}_a,T)^*\vec{z}_k-\vec{v}_j\right\|^2, \quad (7)$$

$$\text{subject to} \quad \sum_{j=1}^{N_c} u_{jk}=1, \forall k,$$

$$\sum_{k=1}^{N} u_{jk}>0, \forall j, \quad (8)$$

where $\vec{z}_k=\{\vec{L},\vec{C}_a,\vec{P}_a\}$ pertaining to the cognitive sensor node k contains location $\vec{L}$, channel availability $\vec{C}_a$ and the corresponding interference characteristics $\vec{P}_a\}$, m is any real number greater than 1, known as *fuzzifier*, $*$ is the transpose, and $\|\cdot\|$ is the Euclidean norm. The estimated cluster centers and the membership of the clusters $(\mathbf{V},\mathbf{U})$ are obtained through loops of estimates for the $\mathbf{U}^{(\ell-1)}\Rightarrow\mathbf{V}^{(\ell)}\Rightarrow\mathbf{U}^{(\ell)}$ and then checks the termination criterion $\|\mathbf{U}^{(\ell)}-\mathbf{U}^{(\ell-1)}\|_{err}\leq\varepsilon$, where ℓ denotes the loop. Accordingly, each element u_{jk} and v_j are updated iteratively based on the following Lagrangian multipliers [25]:

$$u_{jk} = \left(\sum_{i=1}^{N_c} \left(\frac{\left\| \vec{\omega}(\vec{C}_a, T)^* \vec{z}_k - \vec{v}_j \right\|}{\left\| \vec{\omega}(\vec{C}_a, T)^* \vec{z}_k - \vec{v}_i \right\|} \right)^{\frac{2}{m-1}} \right)^{-1}, \forall j,k, \quad (9)$$

$$\vec{v}_j = \frac{\sum_{k=1}^{N} u_{jk}^{m} \vec{z}_k}{\sum_{k=1}^{N} u_{jk}^{m}}, \forall j, \quad (10)$$

until $|u_{jk}^{(\ell+1)} - u_{jk}^{(\ell)}| < \varepsilon$.

The steps for the proposed cluster estimation are summarized in Table 1.

Table 1. Clustering Estimation.

doi:10.1371/journal.pone.0053434.t001

(ESTIMATION)
Initialize $l = 0$, and $\mathbf{U}^{(l)} = [\mathbf{u}_{jk}]$;
if need clustering **then**
Retrieve cognitive sensor node information Z;
Retrieve the updated $\lambda_a^{(1)}$ using Eq. (6);
Update the reliability of the information with Eq. (5) as $\omega(C_a, T)^* Z_k$;
Update the interference characteristics by using Eq. (4) with updated $\lambda_a^{(1)}$;
repeat
Update $l = l+1$;
Calculate the cluster center $\mathbf{V}^{(l)}$ based on $\mathbf{U}^{(l-1)}$ using Eq. (9);
Update $\mathbf{U}^{(l)} = [\mathbf{u}_{jk}]$ based on $\mathbf{V}^{(l)}$ using Eq. (10);
until $\|\mathbf{U}^{(l)} - \mathbf{U}^{(l-1)}\|_{err} \leq \varepsilon$;
Obtain $\mathbf{U} \leftarrow \mathbf{U}^{(l)}$;
end if

doi:10.1371/journal.pone.0053434.t001

Cluster Formation

At the beginning of the cluster formation stage, the obtained matrix **U** provides information regarding the possible formation of the clusters. To avoid having all cognitive sensor nodes within a cluster competing to be a clusterhead, each cognitive sensor node calculates the value of $\left\|\omega(\vec{C}_a,T)^* \vec{z}_k - \vec{v}_i\right\|^2$, which indicates the distance to the logical cluster center. The cognitive sensor nodes with the lowest value effectively act as the clusterhead. It is reasonable since this cognitive sensor node is close to the logical cluster center. In the case where there are several cognitive sensor nodes identifying themselves with the lowest distance values, these selected candidate cognitive sensor nodes compete to be the clusterhead that provides service for the cluster. The most common way to deal with the clusterhead competition is to choose the one with the highest identification (ID) [26]. The clusterhead competition procedure at each cognitive sensor node proceeds according to Table 2.

Table 2. Cluster Formation.

doi:10.1371/journal.pone.0053434.t002

```
State (FORMATION)
Listen on the available channels to gain knowledge of competing cognitive sensor nodes for cluster;
if hear no on-going transmission & never sent HEADCOMPETE message then
  Broadcast HEADCOMPETE[ v_i,ID] message with the cluster ID set as the corresponding value of v_i and cognitive sensor node unique ID;
else
  if hear on-going transmission == HEADCOMPETE message then
    if own cognitive sensor node ID < HEADCOMPETE.ID then
      Stay silence;
    else
      Broadcast HEADCOMPETE[ v_i,ID] message with its own ID;
    end if
  end if
else
  if hear no on-going transmission & sent HEADCOMPETE message then
    Clusterhead competition succeed;
    Broadcast HEAD[ v_i,ID] message with unique cluster ID, and its own ID;
  end if
else
  if hear returning primary users then
    Set to SWITCH state;
  end if
end if
```

doi:10.1371/journal.pone.0053434.t002

The most important aspect of the clusterhead competition process is to have at least one cognitive sensor node being declared as the clusterhead. The winning clusterheads broadcast their own IDs as the unique cluster IDs, while the losing cognitive sensor nodes as well as other cognitive sensor nodes keeps silent and set their cluster IDs with the corresponding clusters.

CLUSTER JOINING

After successful clusterhead competition, the individual cognitive sensor nodes must now join its corresponding clusters within the network. Based on the obtained matrix **U**, the joining cognitive sensor node k proceeds as follows:

- *Step 1*: Pick index J as $u_{Jk} = \max\{u_{1k},...,u_{Nk}\}$;
- *Step 2*: Look up the cluster center $\vec{v}_J$ containing the information of available channels;
- *Step 3:* Find the common available channels of $\vec{v}_J$ and its own spectrum sensing results;
- *Step 4*: Listen to these channels in order to obtain HEAD.[$\vec{v}_j$·ID] message or control messages that contains the cluster ID and cluster head ID; [$\vec{v}_j$·ID];
- *Step 5*: Send a JOIN message on one of the common available channels after identifying no ongoing transmission in the cluster to avoid interference to the cluster members;
- *Step 6:* The joining process succeeds at the $J^{*}th$ highest value of membership, $u_{(J^{*})k}$, after receiving an acknowledgement message from the cluster head; otherwise, choose the next cluster candidate based on the descending value of $u_{(j)k}$ and go back to Step 2.

In the worse-case scenario where a cognitive sensor node fails to join any cluster, the joining cognitive sensor node initializes its own cluster based on the cluster formation process to claim itself as the cluster head.

Cluster Switching

Thanks to the matrix **U**, the cognitive sensor node is able to have information of the cluster membership, i.e., the probabilities of belonging to the cluster, which not only facilitates for joining clusters in the highly dynamic network environment but also provides fast backup resolution of returning primary users. As long as returning primary users are identified on the channels that are currently used by a cluster, the cognitive sensor nodes belonging to this cluster immediately switches to the other clusters according to the descending order of u_{J^*k}.At a same time, a new matrix **U** will be calculated to prepare for the next set of joining attempts. This fast switching process is designed to make time for the cognitive sensor node to update $\vec{Z}$ and calculate the new matrix **U**. If the switching process succeeds before the new results of the membership information, this new matrix **U** can be used as a reference of the next fast switching process. The switching process is summarized in Table 3.

Table 3. Switch.

doi:10.1371/journal.pone.0053434.t003

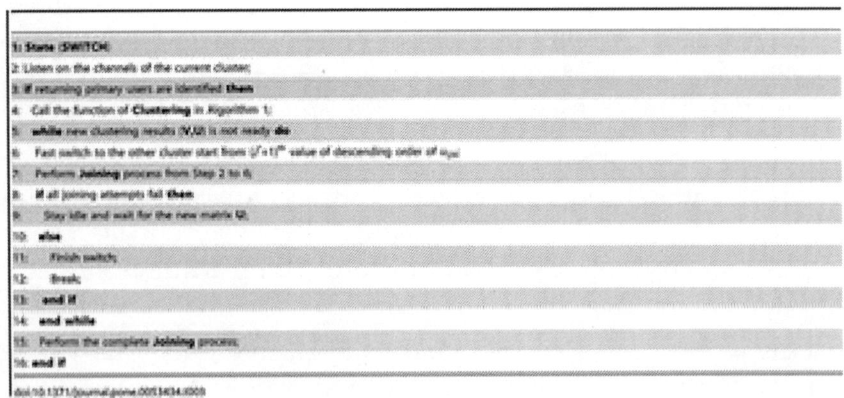

```
1: State (SWITCH)
2: Listen on the channels of the current cluster;
3: if returning primary users are identified then
4:   Call the function of Clustering in Algorithm 1;
5:   while new clustering results (V,U) is not ready do
6:     Fast switch to the other cluster start from (J*+1)th value of descending order of u_{J*k}
7:     Perform Joining process from Step 2 to 6;
8:     if all joining attempts fail then
9:       Stay idle and wait for the new matrix U;
10:    else
11:      Finish switch;
12:      Break;
13:    end if
14:  end while
15:  Perform the complete Joining process;
16: end if
```

doi:10.1371/journal.pone.0053434.t003

RESULTS AND DISCUSSION

In this section, we present a series of simulation results to evaluate the performance of the proposed multi-parametric clustering scheme. For comparison purposes, a number of previously reported clustering schemes were also evaluated, such as a voting-based clustering algorithm [13] and Spectrum Opportunity-Based Clustering scheme [14]. In line with a large disaster response scenario, we simulate a 500 m×500 m network area uniformly distributed with the cognitive sensor nodes, which forms an ad hoc network. Each cognitive sensor node has a radio transmission range radius of 100 m forming a non-fully-connected topology, where not all cognitive sensor nodes are within the transmission range of each other. For every transmission, the one-way propagation delay is set to $0.5\,\mu s$. The primary user network dynamics is simulated as a M/G/1 model on total $M = 20$ channels with primary user packet arrival rate $\lambda^{(1)}$, and the channel availability varies accordingly. Each simulation consists of 10 trials, and the results represent the mean of the trials within a 93% confidence interval.

In the first set of simulations, we study the clustering performance of the proposed scheme. In the second and third set of simulations, we look into the performance of the proposed scheme in the state of cluster formation by comparing with other schemes, as well as the performance of cluster joining, respectively. In the fourth set of simulations, the interference amongst the cluster heads is investigated to give an insightful view of the effectiveness of the proposed scheme. In the last set of simulations, we study the effects on the dynamics of primary users network. The performance measurements are defined as follows:

- Cluster head selection overhead o: average time consumed on cluster head selection.
- Cluster joining estimation error : ratio of the number of failed cluster joining attempts to the number of attempts.
- Interference probability of clusterheads P_c: probability of interference between clusterheads.
- Probability of reclustering P_r: ratio of the reclustering process to the number of instances of network behavior change.

SNAPSHOT OF CLUSTERING

A snapshot of clustering obtained using the proposed scheme for a large scale deployment of cognitive sensor nodes is shown in Fig. 2, where there are $N = 1000$ cognitive sensor nodes and the number of clusters is set to a small number $N_c = 10$ in this set of simulations for the purpose of clarity in the diagram presentation. The cognitive sensor nodes are colored with different colors to indicate that they belong in different clusters, and the corresponding logical centers of the clusters are plotted as small black squares to distinguish them from the cognitive sensor nodes. It can be seen that the boundaries of each cluster are never regular and could be overlapped. It is due to the fact that both of channel availability and interference characteristics are adaptively taken into account in the clustering process. Moreover, the logical cluster centers represent the centers of all the information, denoted as $\vec{v}_j$ in Eq. 10, and they are not necessarily the physical clusterheads. The performance of the selection of clusterhead is presented in the next section.

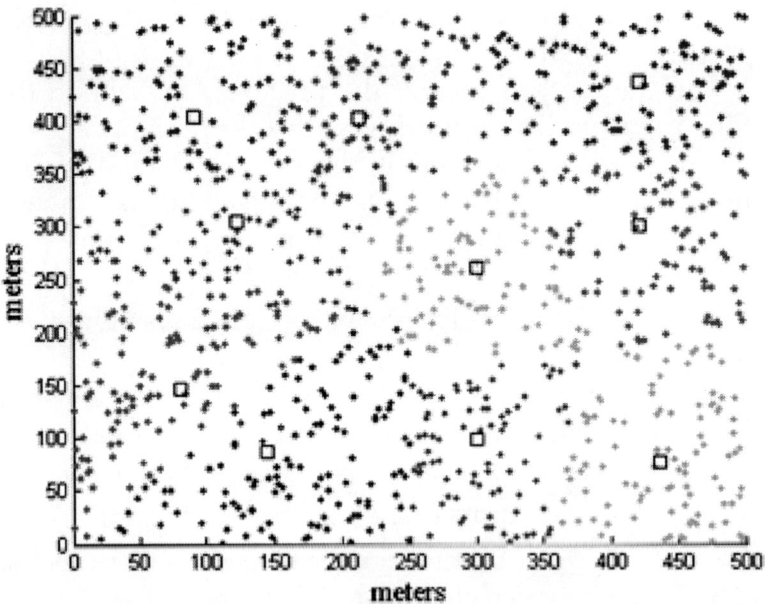

Figure 2. A snapshot of clustering using the proposed scheme for a large scale deployment of cognitive sensor nodes, with different colored dots representing individual cognitive sensor nodes in different clusters, and the small black squares representing the logical centers of the clusters.

doi:10.1371/journal.pone.0053434.g002

Evaluation of cluster formation

In this set of simulations, we compare the performance of the proposed clustering scheme with the other schemes under consideration in the study using the cluster head selection overhead, *o*, which is defined as the average time consumed on cluster head selection for a cluster in the network in the cluster formation process. Fig. 3 shows that the average clusterhead selection overhead with respect to the number of cognitive sensor nodes. It can be seen that the cluster head selection overhead increases as the number of cognitive sensor nodes increase. Furthermore, it can be observed that the proposed clustering scheme achieves lower overhead than that of the spectrum opportunity-based clustering and voting-based clustering schemes. This is due to the fact that the proposed scheme only considers cognitive sensor nodes within close distance of the estimated logical cluster centers as potential candidates for clusterheads, and as such allow for fewer cognitive sensor nodes to enter into clusterheadcompetition. This in turn mitigates a massive communication overhead in the clusterhead selection process. This low overhead is very essential for successful integration into large scale cognitive sensor node deployments in cognitive wireless sensor networks.

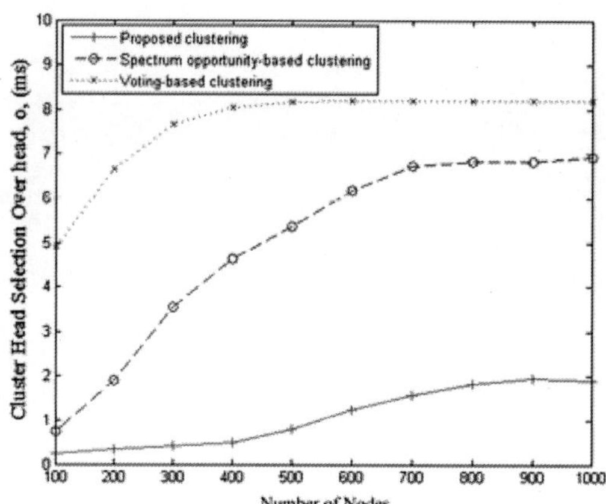

Figure 3. Cluster head selection overhead vs. number of cognitive sensor nodes in comparison.

doi:10.1371/journal.pone.0053434.g003

To provide a better indication of efficiency, we compare the clusterhead selection overhead $o$with different number of clusters and fixed number of cognitive sensor nodes. Note that all the three clustering algorithms dynamically determine the number of clusters and as such the actual number of clusters are difficult to tracked and compared in a parametric analysis manner. Therefore, for comparison purposes, the maximum number of clusters is set to the same for each clustering algorithm. Fig. 4 show the simulation results on o with respect to the maximum number of clusters N_c with number of cognitive sensor nodes set to $N = 100, 500$, and 1000, respectively. It can be seen that the amount of clusterhead selection overhead decreases as the number of maximum number of cluster increases; moreover, the proposed scheme has noticeably lower overhead and the results decrease more slowly. It is due to the fact that less cognitive sensor nodes join cluster head competition after estimating their memberships using the proposed scheme.

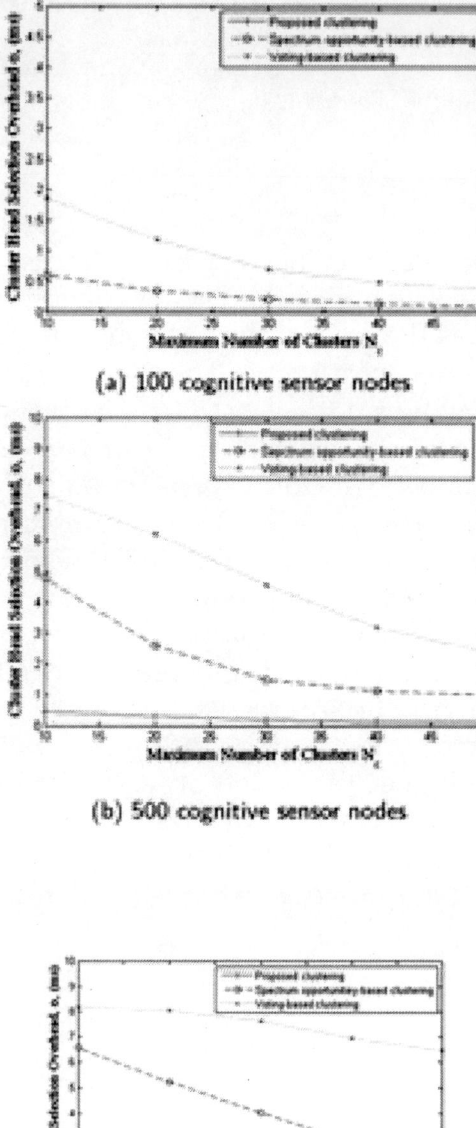

(a) 100 cognitive sensor nodes

(b) 500 cognitive sensor nodes

(c) 1000 cognitive sensor nodes

Figure 4. Cluster head selection overhead vs. maximum number of clusters in comparison.

(a) 100 cognitive sensor nodes, (b) 500 cognitive sensor nodes, and (c) 1000 cognitive sensor nodes.

doi:10.1371/journal.pone.0053434.g004

Evaluations of joining process

To investigate the efficiency of the joining process of the proposed clustering scheme, we study the cluster joining estimation error, which is defined as the ratio of the number of failed cluster joining attempts to the number of attempts. The simulation results are shown in Fig. 5 with total $M = \{10, 20, 30\}$ channels versus the different number of cognitive sensor nodes. It can be seen that with the increase of the number of cognitive sensor nodes, the cluster joining estimation error increase. It is due to the large number of cognitive sensor nodes introducing noise in the clustering estimation process, which may lead to estimation discrepancy. Moreover, the number of total channels has noticeable impact on the performance, since the cluster joining estimation error increases when the total number of channels in the network decreases. It is due to the fact that given the same volume of primary traffic within the network, the fewer the channels the higher the usage on each channels. This results in low probability of channel availability and high probability of returning primary users, which effectively increases the interference characteristics and thus increasing the estimation error in the joining process.

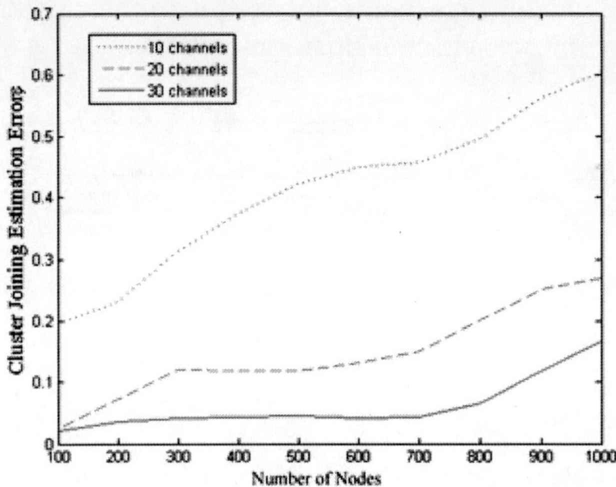

Figure 5. Cluster joining estimation error with different number of channel and different number of cognitive sensor nodes.

doi:10.1371/journal.pone.0053434.g005

Interference

In this set of simulations, we further compare the performance of the proposed scheme with other clustering algorithms under consideration in the study using interference probability of cluster heads P_c, which is defined as the probability of cluster heads interference with each other in the network. Fig. 6 plots the interference probability of cluster heads versus the different number of cognitive sensor nodes in the network area. It can be observed that the interference probability of clusterheads of all three approaches increases as the number of cognitive sensor nodes increases. It can also be observed that the proposed clustering scheme outperforms the other clustering algorithms in the scenario of large scale cognitive sensor node deployments. It is due to two factors: 1) the proposed scheme takes interference characteristics into account as part of the set of network parameters upon which clustering is determined, and 2) unlike the other clustering algorithms, which require each cluster member to be within the transmission range of each other, the proposed clustering scheme only requires the clusterhead to be able to communicate with the cluster members.

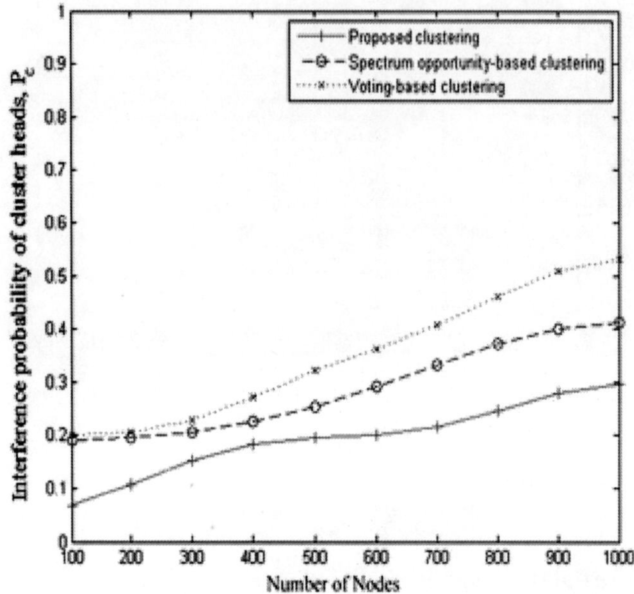

Figure 6. Interference probability of cluster heads with different number of cognitive sensor nodes in comparison.

doi:10.1371/journal.pone.0053434.g006

Impact from Primary Dynamics

Finally, the impact from primary dynamics is investigated in this set of simulations by evaluating the probability of reclustering P_r, which is defined as the ratio of the number of reclustering to the number of instances of network behavior changes which are caused by the primary user arrivals. Fig. 7 shows the probability of reclustering with different number of cognitive sensor nodes versus the primary arrival rate $\lambda^{(1)}$. It can be observed that as the primary arrivals increase the probability of reclustering increases. It is clearly due to the fact that the primary user arrivals cause changes to the channel usage status as well as the interference characteristics in the network. As the primary user arrivals increase, the changes of network status occur more frequently, which resulting in the need for more reclustering. Moreover, it also can be seen that the larger the number of cognitive sensor nodes, the higher the probability of reclustering.

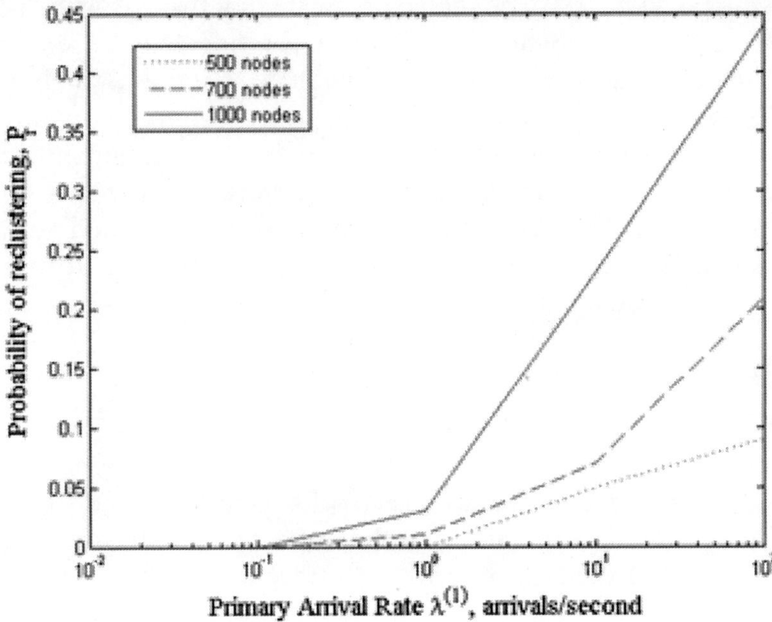

Figure 7. Probability of reclustering with different number of cognitive sensor nodes versus the primary arrival rate .

doi:10.1371/journal.pone.0053434.g007

Relationship to Energy Conservation and Consumption

One of the objectives of employing clustering strategies for aiding in the coordination of cognitive wireless sensor networks is to improve energy conservation by reducing the amount of communication needed by limiting communications to the clusterheads and the central source. Since much of the energy in WSNs is spent during communication, the clustering process itself should be kept to a minimum to minimize energy costs. As such, there is a direct relationship between energy consumption and clustering overhead (the higher the clustering overhead, the more energy is consumed by the sensor node). Furthermore, the amount of energy consumed by sensor nodes is also directly related to the probability of interference, since a higher probability of interference results in a higher packet losses and hence additional energy to be spent at the sensor nodes for resending packets. It can be seen from Fig. 3 that the proposed scheme achieves lower overhead than that of the spectrum opportunity-based clustering and voting-based clustering schemes, which equates to reduced communication and hence reduced energy consumption. Furthermore, it can be seen from Fig. 6 that the proposed scheme results in the lowest probability of interference compared to the spectrum opportunity-based clustering and voting-based clustering schemes, which also results in reduced energy consumption by requiring less packets to be resend due to interference.

CONCLUSIONS

In this paper, a novel multi-parametric clustering scheme designed for cognitive wireless sensor networks is introduced. Extensive performance evaluation studying the impact on clustering overhead, cluster joining estimation error, interference probability, as well as probability of reclustering, demonstrated that the proposed clustering scheme has strong potential for improving performance of cognitive wireless sensor network deployments with high dynamics and heterogeneity. One point of interest for further investigation is the challenges associated with real-world implementation and deployment of the proposed scheme in cognitive wireless sensor networks. As modern healthcare monitoring systems have increasingly powerful low-power embedded microprocessors for processing sensing data, it is of great interest to implement the proposed scheme to work directly with such existing microprocessors.

ACKNOWLEDGMENTS

We thank the Natural Sciences and Engineering Research Council (NSERC) of Canada and the Ontario Ministry of Economic Development and Innovation for supporting this work.

AUTHOR CONTRIBUTIONS

Conceived and designed the experiments: AW XW. Performed the experiments: XW.Analyzed the data: AW XW.Wrote the paper: AW XW.

REFERENCES

1. Ko J, Lu C, Srivastava M, Stankovic J, Terzis A, Welsh M (2010) Wireless Sensor Networks for Healthcare. Proceedings of the IEEE 98: 1947–1960. doi: 10.1109/jproc.2010.2065210
2. Gao T, Pesto C, Selavo L, Chen Y, Ko J, et al.. (2008) Wireless medical sensor networks in emergency response: Implementation and pilot results. IEEE Int. Conf. Technol. Homeland Security: 187–192.
3. Malan D, Fulford-Jones T, Welsh M, Moulton S (2004) BCodeBlue: An ad hoc sensor network infrastructure for emergency medical care. Proc. Workshop on Applied Mobile Embedded Systems: 12–14.
4. Zahmati A, Hussain S, Fernando X, Grami A (2009) Cognitive Wireless Sensor Networks: Emerging topics and recent challenges. Proc. IEEE Toronto International Conference on Science and Technology for Humanity: 593–596.
5. Vijay G, Ben Ali Bdira E, Ibrikahla M (2011) Cognition in Wireless Sensor Networks: A Perspective. IEEE Sensors Journal: 582–592.
6. Deosarkar B, Yadav N, Yadav R (2008) Clusterhead Selection in Clustering Algorithms for Wireless Sensor Networks: A Survey Proceedings of IEEE ICCCN.
7. Kumarawadu P, Dechene D, Luccini M, Sauer A (2008) Algorithms for Node Clustering in Wireless Sensor Networks: A Survey. Proceedings of IEEE ICIAF.
8. Yu J, Chong P (2005) A Survey of Clustering Schemes for Mobile Ad Hoc Networks. IEEE Communications Surveys 7.
9. Chatterjee M, Das S, Turgut D (2002) WCA: A Weighted Clustering Algorithm for Mobile Ad Hoc Networks. Cluster Computing: 5.
10. Chen T, Zheng H, Maggio G, Chlamtac I (2007) CogMesh: A Cluster-based Cognitive Radio Network. Proceedings of IEEE DySPAN.
11. Kim M, Yoo S (2009) Distributed Coordination Protocol for Common Control Channel Selection in Mulitchannel Ad-hoc Cognitive Radio Networks. Proceedings of IEEE WiMob.
12. Zhao J, Zheng H, Yang G (2005) Distributed Coordination in Dynamic

Spectrum Allocation Networks. Proceedings of IEEE DySPAN.

13. Zhao J, Zheng H, Yang G (2007) Spectrum Sharing Through Distributed Coordination in Dynamic Spectrum Access Networks. Wireless Communications and Mobile Computing: 7.
14. Lazos L, Liu S, Krunz M (2009) Spectrum Opportunity-Based Control Channel Assignment in Cognitive Radio Networks. Proceedings of IEEE SECON.
15. Rappaport T (1996) Wireless Communications: Priciples& Practices, Prentice-Hall.
16. Haenggi M, Andrews J, Baccelli F, Dousse O, Franceschetti M (2009) Stochastic Geometry and Random Graphs for the Analysis and Design of Wireless Networks. IEEE J. Sel. Areas Commun. 27.
17. Gardner W (1994) Cyclostationarity in Communications and Signal Processing. IEEE Press.
18. Shellhammer S, Sadek A, Zhang W (2009) Technical Challenges for Cognitive Radio in the TV White Space Spectrum. Proc. Inf. Theory Appl. Workshop.
19. Digham F, Alouini M, Simon M (2007) On the Energy Detection of Unknown Signals over Fading Channels. IEEE Trans. Commun.: 15.
20. Ghasemi A, Sousa E (2008) Interference aggregation in spectrum-sensing cognitive wireless networks. IEEE JSTSP 2: 41–56. doi: 10.1109/jstsp.2007.914897
21. Rabbachin A, Quek T, Shin H, Win M (2011) Cognitive Network Interference. IEEE JSAC: 29.
22. Huang S, Liu X, Ding Z (2008) Opportunistic Spectrum Access in Cognitive Radio Networks. Proceedings of IEEE INFOCOM.
23. Bezdek J (1981) Pattern Recognition With Fuzzy Objective Function Algorithms. New York: Plenum.
24. Baker D, Ephremides A, Flynn J (1984) The Design and Simulation of a Moble Radio Network with Distributed Control. IEEE J. Sel. Areas Commun.: 2.
25. Chintalapudi K, Kam M (1998) A noise-resistant fuzzy c means algorithm for clustering. Proceedings of IEEE International Conference on Fuzzy System.
26. Baker D, Epheremides A (1981) The Architectural Organization of a Moblie Radio Network via a Distributed Algorithm. IEEE Trans. Commun. Com-29.

Chapter 3

PROTOCOLS FOR SELF-ORGANIZATION OF A WIRELESS SENSOR NETWORK

Katayoun Sohrabi, Jay GAO, Vishal Ailawadhi and Gregory J Pottie

Electrical Engineering Department
UCLA Box 951594
Los Angeles, California, 90095-1594
{sohrabi, gao, Vishal, potties} @ ee.ucla.edu

ABSTRACT

Once the nodes have booted up and a network is formed, most of the nodes will be able to sustain a steady state of operation, i.e. their energy reservoirs are nearly full and they can support all the sensing, signal processing and communications tasks as required. In this mode, the bulk of the nodes will be formed into a multi-hop network. The nodes begin to establish routes by which information is passed to one or more sink nodes. A sink node may be a long-range radio, capable of connecting the sensor network to existing long- haul communications infrastructure. The sink may also be a mobile node acting as an information sink, or any other entity that is required to extract information from the sensor network.

Wireless Networking

Given the hardware limitations and physical environment in which the nodes must operate, along with applications level requirements the algorithms and protocols must be designed to provide a robust and energy efficient communications mechanism. Design of physical layer methods such as modulation and source and channel coding also fall in this category. Channel access methods must be devised and routing issues and mobility management must be solved. This paper focuses on a number of design aspects of this category.

Applications

Once the nodes have booted up and a network is formed, most of the nodes will be able to sustain a steady state of operation, i.e. their energy reservoirs are nearly full and they can support all the sensing, signal processing and communications tasks as required. In this mode, the bulk of the nodes will be formed into a multi-hop network. The nodes begin to establish routes by which information is passed to one or more sink nodes. A sink node may be a long-range radio, capable of connecting the sensor network to existing long- haul communications infrastructure. The sink may also be a mobile node acting as an information sink, or any other entity that is required to extract information from the sensor network.

Once the nodes have booted up and a network is formed, most of the nodes will be able to sustain a steady state of operation, i.e. their energy reservoirs are nearly full and they can support all the sensing, signal processing and communications tasks as required. In this mode, the bulk of the nodes will be formed into a multi-hop network. The nodes begin to establish routes by which information is passed to one or more sink nodes. A sink node may be a long-range radio, capable of connecting the sensor network to existing long- haul communications infrastructure. The sink may also be a mobile node acting as an information sink, or any other entity that is required to extract information from the sensor network.

General Operational Scenario

Once the nodes have booted up and a network is formed, most of the nodes will be able to sustain a steady state of operation, i.e. their energy reservoirs are nearly full and they can support all the sensing, signal processing and communications tasks as required. In this mode, the bulk of the nodes will be formed into a multi-hop network. The nodes begin to establish routes by which information is passed to one or more sink nodes. A sink node may be a long-range radio, capable of connecting the sensor network to existing long- haul communications infrastructure. The sink may also be a mobile node acting as an information sink, or any other entity that is required to extract information from the sensor network.

Once the nodes have booted up and a network is formed, most of the nodes will be able to sustain a steady state of operation, i.e. their energy reservoirs are nearly full and they can support all the sensing, signal processing and communications tasks as required. In this mode, the bulk of the nodes will be formed into a multi-hop network. The nodes begin to establish routes by which information is passed to one or more sink nodes. A sink node may be a long-range radio, capable of connecting the sensor network to existing long- haul communications infrastructure. The sink may also be a mobile node acting as an information sink, or any other entity that is required to extract information from the sensor network.

There are instances when there is need for collections of nodes to cooperate together in detection of signals or events, as described in [1]. When a cooperative function is required to extract information about a specific target, a local network is built to facilitate the necessary signaling and data transfer tasks. Typically, cooperative functions involve a small set of nodes near the target location and operate for relatively short time span. They are required to adapt quickly and efficiently to the appearance of target and the nature of the signal processing techniques required. Although the multi-hop network can operate in the sensor-to-sink or sink-to-sensor (broadcast or multi-cast) modes, the bulk of traffic will belong to the former. This will put significant strain on the energy resources of the nodes near the sink, making that neighborhood more susceptible to energy depletion and failure. Nodes may fail due to other reasons such as mechanical failure.

When many nodes have failed, the MAC and routing protocols must accommodate formation of new links and routes to the sink nodes. This may require actively adjusting transmit powers and signaling rates on the existing links to reduce energy consumption, or rerouting packets through regions of the network where nodes have more energy left.

Wireless Sensor Networks are a New Family of Networks

To illustrate the impact of the physical limits of sensor networks on the design of our wireless networking algorithms we briefly discuss related wireless network models, namely mobile ad hoc networks, cellular networks, and a number of short range wireless local area networks.

A Mobile Ad-hoc NET work (MANET) is a peer-to-peer network which is usually comprised of tens to hundreds of communicating nodes which are able to cover ranges of up to hundreds of meters. Each node is envisioned as a personal information appliance such as a Personal Digital Assistant (PDA) outfitted with a fairly sophisticated radio transceiver. The nodes are fully mobile. The MANET aims to form and maintain a connected multi-hop network capable of transporting multi-media traffic between the nodes. In order to provide QoS in the face of mobility a MANET must do the following:

a. Organize the nodes in such a way that they are able to access the shared communications medium efficiently. This is called forming an infrastructure in some cases, and includes the function of providing a means of channel access for the nodes as well.

b. Performing routing in the network

c. Maintain the network organization and routing in the face of mobility

In a MANET the three-pronged tasks of Organization-Routing-Mobility-management (ORM) are done to optimize for QoS. That is, the network is designed to provide good throughput/delay characteristics in the face of high node mobility. Although the nodes are portable battery powered devices, energy consumption in this system is of secondary importance, since each device is always attached to a person, and presumably the depleted battery will be replaced when needed (the same way batteries are changed on Laptops). A cellular network is a vast network consisting of both stationary and mobile nodes. The stationary nodes, or base stations, are connected among them in a sub-network with a wired backbone, forming a fixed infrastructure. The mobile nodes greatly outnumber the stationary nodes (tens to hundreds of mobiles per base station) which are usually situated quite sparsely. The base stations are usually placed to cover a large region with little overlap. The issue of organization is only encountered in terms of cell-to-cell handoffs as the mobile navigates the region. Each mobile node will be only one hop away from any base station. The primary goal here is of providing a high QoS, along with high bandwidth efficiency. The base stations themselves effectively have an unlimited power supply, while the mobiles are battery operated. Bluetooth [7] is a short-range wireless networking system which is intended to replace the cable between electronic consumer devices and provide RF connection between them. The Bluetooth topology is a star network where a master node is able to have up to seven slave nodes attached to it to form a picante each picante uses a centrally assigned TDMA schedule and frequency-hopping pattern. The raw signaling rate in this system is 1 Mb/s. All nodes are synchronized to the master. There are mechanisms in place for multiple picante to interconnect and form a multi hop topology. Typical transmission power is about 1 mW. It is expected to achieve a 10 m range. Another short-range commercial system under development is the Home RF [8]. The goals of this system are very similar to those of Bluetooth. However the networking model is based on the IEEE 802.11 standard. The system is able to handle single hop ad-hoc networks. The radio is a frequency-hopping module. Channel access is possible under TDMA and CSMA modes. Raw data rates of up to 2 Mb/s are possible. Transmission power levels are at 100 mW. Typical ranges are distances encountered in the house and the yard.

By contrast to all of these networks, our sensor network is potentially comprised of hundreds to thousands of nodes. These nodes are generally stationary after deployment, with the exception of a very small number of mobile sensor nodes. The traffic will likely have statistical properties unlike the multi-media data streams of conventional wireless networks. Although exact sensor data traffic properties are not known yet, it is clear that, due to the nature of the observed phenomena, the required bandwidth for sensor data will be low, on the order of 1-100 kb/s [1].

The main goal in conventional wireless networks is providing high quality of service (i.e. high throughput low delay) and high bandwidth efficiency when mobility exists. For a sensor network, by contrast, we are interested in prolonging the lifetime of the network. To this end we must conserve energy, and we are willing to give up performance in other aspects of the operation such as QoS and bandwidth utilization. Each node depends on small and low capacity batteries as energy sources, and cannot expect replacement when operating in hostile or remote regions.

For networks with a fixed infrastructure, loss of connectivity is a statistically rare event and independent of energy usage. On the other hand, in mobile networks, topological changes are mostly attributed to the mobility of the nodes, not the energy depletions caused by the execution of various networking protocols. Therefore, in order to raise system performance, mobility management and failure recovery assumes more importance than energy conservation in protocol design. For ad hoc sensor networks, however, energy depletion is the primary factor in connectivity degradation and length of operational lifetime. Therefore, overall performance becomes highly dependent on the energy efficiency of the algorithm

Energy Conserving Techniques in Sensor Networks

Energy consumption occurs in three domains: sensing, data processing, and communications. In the wireless sensor network communications is the major consumer of energy. To better grasp this idea let us compare energy costs of data transmission via radio and data processing. Taking the example described in [1], for ground to ground transmission, it costs 3 J of energy to transmit 1Kb of data a distance of 100 meters. On the other hand a general-purpose processor with the modest specification of 100 MIPS/W processing capability executes 3 million instructions for the same amount of energy. Fortunately it is possible to make tradeoffs between data processing and wireless communications. The sensor nodes will do more local processing, as opposed to exchanging raw data over the air. In the same vein the protocols responsible for ORM must reduce their messaging overhead as much as possible. This leads to the need for highly localized and distributed algorithms for data processing and networking.

Our Protocols

In this section our algorithms, which will perform ORM for sensor networks, are described. Specifically we will describe the Self-organizing Medium Access Control for Sensor networks (SMACS) for the network startup and link layer organization. Next the Eavesdrop-And-Register (EAR) algorithm will be presented. This algorithm enables seamless interconnection of mobile nodes in the field of stationary wireless nodes, and represents the mobility-management aspect of the protocol. Finally we present a Sequential Assignment Routing (SAR) algorithm that facilitates multi-hop routing and the Single-Winner Election (SWE) and Multi-Winner Election (MWE) algorithms that handle the necessary signaling and data transfer tasks in local cooperative information processing. For in-depth detail about the internal mechanisms of the SMACS, SAR, SWE, and MWE, see [9,10].

Link Layer Issues

The two major services which the link layer provides to higher layers are formation of a link layer topology (or infrastructure) and regulation of channel access among the nodes. In most of the existing or proposed ad-hoc networks, channel access is done by two different methods, namely by contention or explicit organization in time/frequency/code domains. The various flavors of MACA and MACAW reported widely in literature are examples of the former. The MAC layer design for 802.11 standard is an example.

The second class of channel access schemes which we term "organized" channel access, attempt to determine the network radio connectivity first, i.e. discover the radio neighbors of each node, and then assign collision-free channels to links. The task of assignment of channels, i.e. TDMA slots, frequency bands or spread spectrum codes, to links between radio neighbors such that they do not collide is a hard problem. To ease the assignment problem a hierarchical structure is formed in the network to localize groups of nodes and make the task of channel assignment more manageable. The problem in this approach is how to determine the cluster memberships and cluster heads such that the entire network is covered while the nodes move. Some examples of solutions are given in [11, 12, 13].

The contention based channel access schemes are clearly not suitable for sensor networks, due to their requirement for radio transceivers to monitor the channel at all times. This is a particularly expensive proposition for the low radio ranges of interest for sensor networks, where transmission and reception have almost the same energy cost. We would like to turn off the radios when no information is to be sent or received.

The organized methods of channel access require nodes in the network to be synchronized with each other at some level (usually at the slot boundary epochs for TDMA systems). In organized schemes, usually a period is set aside for neighbor discovery. If a centralized channel assignment algorithm is to be used, the entire connectivity information along with any bandwidth requirements for specific links are passed to a single node in the network for calculation of a schedule. There are distributed assignment methods in place where nodes exchange connectivity data only with some local neighborhood. This network-wide synchronization is again expensive for sensor networks, because it requires extensive message passing over the air to synchronize all the nodes.

Description of the stationary MAC and Startup Procedure

In our system we assume the nodes are able to turn their radios on and off. They are also able to tune the carrier frequency to different bands. It is assumed that the number of available bands is relatively large1 In This is not an unreasonable assumption. If we assume the radios operate in the 902-928 ISM band, and that the data rate on each hop is no more than 10Kb/s, then we may have something in the order of 2600 distinct frequency bands available to choose from

Our protocol, a channel is defined as a pair of time intervals, similar to slots in a TDMA schedule. We assume nodes are deployed by hand or remotely such that they are covering some area randomly.

After deployment, each node wakes up at some random time according to some distribution.

The Self-organizing Medium Access Control for Sensor networks (SMACS) is an infrastructure building protocol that forms a flat topology (as opposed to a cluster hierarchy) for sensor networks. SMACS is a distributed protocol which enables a collection of nodes to discover their neighbors and establish transmission/reception schedules for communicating with them without the need for any local or global master nodes.

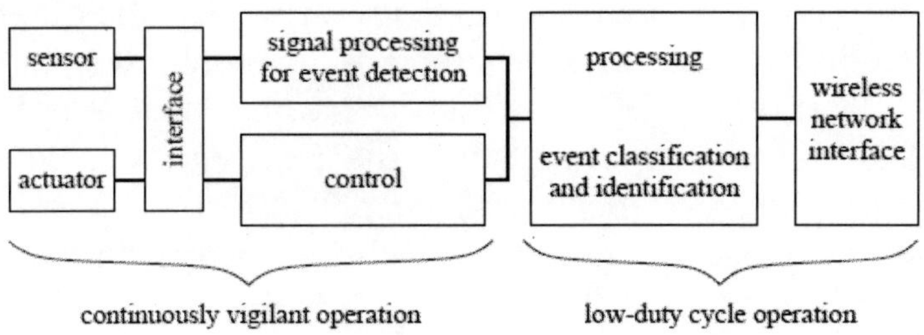

Figure 1. The architecture of a sensor node

In order to achieve this ease of formation, we have combined the neighbor discovery phase with channel assignment phase in the SMACS protocol. Unlike methods such as the Linked Clustering Algorithm (LCA) [12], in which a first pass is performed on the entire network to discover neighbors, and then another pass is done to assign channels, or TDMA slots, to links between neighboring nodes, in SMACS, we assign a channel to a link immediately after the existence of the link is discovered. This way links begin to form concurrently throughout the network. By the time all nodes hear all their neighbors; they will have formed a connected network. In a connected network, there exists at least one multi-hop path between any two distinct nodes.

Since only partial information about radio connectivity in the vicinity of a node is used to assign time intervals to links, there exists a potential for time collisions with slots assigned to adjacent links whose existence is not known at the time of channel assignment. To reduce the likelihood of collisions, we require each link to operate on a different frequency. This frequency band is chosen at random from a large pool of possible choices when the links are formed.

This idea is described in figure 2.b. Nodes A and D wake up at times Ta and Td. After they find each other they agree to transmit and receive during a pair of fixed time slots. This transmission reception pattern will be repeated periodically every T frame. Nodes B and C wake up later at times Tb and Tc respectively After they find each other they will assign another pair of slots for transmit ion and and reception. Note that if all the nodes operate on the same frequency band, then there is the possibility that some transmissions will collide in the given schedule. For example, a transmission from D to A will collide in time with a transmission from B to C. On the other hand if different frequency bands are assigned to different links, for example fx to AD link and fy to BC link, then the time schedule of figure 2.b will work without collisions2 When there are many frequencies to choose from, and frequencies are chosen uniformly at random, the likelihood that the same frequency is chosen by two links which are in each other's ear shot is small.

T frame as described above is fixed for all nodes, and is a parameter of the MAC. T frame is the length of the super frame for our MAC. As new neighbors are found and new links are formed, the super frame of each node will start to be filled. From figure 2.b we see that T frame epochs for node A and B, for example, do not coincide. Now if we call each transmission or reception period a slot, we see from the same figure that the protocol will result in slot assignments that do not need to be aligned throughout the entire network. Again, the reason this non-synchronous assignment is possible, is assignment of different frequencies to links. The ability to assign non-synchronous slots in the network is the key issue that enables the nodes to form links on the fly. We call this concept the Non-synchronous Scheduled Communication or NSC. This spontaneity enables a quick method for scheduling of links throughout the network.

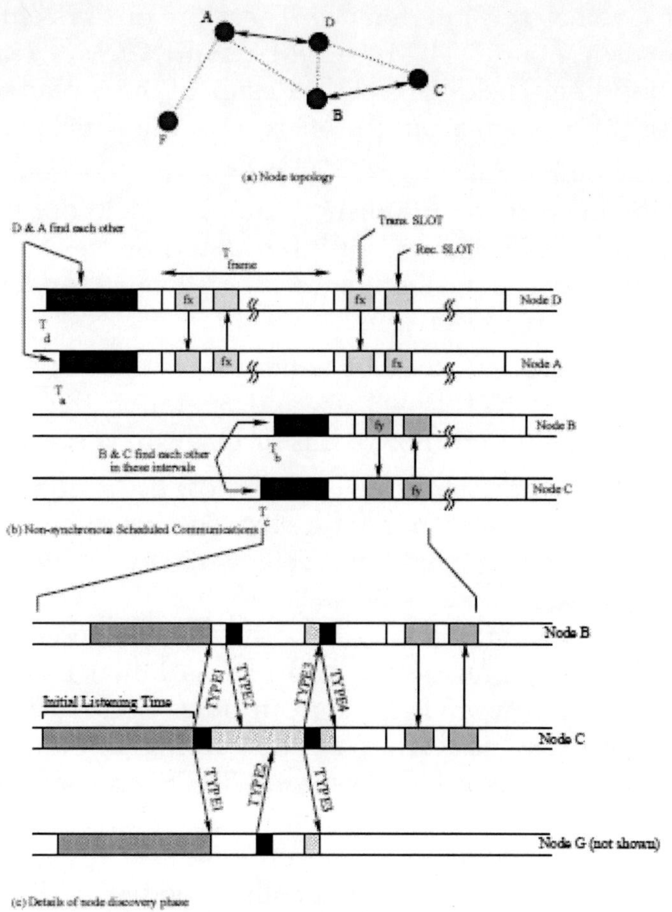

Figure 2 Link layer self-organizing procedures

After a link is established, a node knows when to turn on its transceiver ahead of time to communicate with another node. It will turn off when no communications are scheduled. This scheduled mode of

In a more general case, in order to combat channel degradations, instead of a fixed frequency, each link will be assigned a distinct frequency-hopping pattern. Using frequency hopping will separate transmissions in the frequency domain, and at the same time reduce vulnerability of the links to channel degradations due to intentional and unintentional jamming, such as channel fades and hostile jamming, as well as self-interference. Therefore our system is really a variation of a hybrid TDMA/CDMA with CDMA realized as frequency hopping. The details of the design of the spread spectrum signaling for this system is out the of scope of this article.

Communication enables energy savings for the node. As the link assignment was accomplished quickly, without requiring accumulation of global connectivity information, or even connectivity information that reaches farther than one hop away, the overall effect will be significant energy savings.

We now discuss the method by which nodes find each other, and the mechanism by which time slots and operating frequencies are determined. A brief description of this mechanism was given in [14].

To illustrate this mechanism we will follow the actions of a set of nodes, B, C, and G, as shown in figure 2.c. These nodes are engaged in the process of finding neighbors. They wake up at random times. Upon wakeup, each node will listen to the channel on a fixed frequency band, for some random time duration. A node will decide to transmit an invitation by the end of this initial listening time if it has not heard any invitations from other nodes. This is what happens to node C, which will broadcast an invitation message, or TYPE1 message. Nodes B and G hear this TYPE1 message. Each one will broadcast a response, or TYPE2 message, addressed to node C, during the interval following the reception of TYPE1 at a random time. If the TYPE2 messages do not collide, node C will hear both. Node C must choose only one of the respondents. It will choose node B, because, its response arrived first. Other selection criteria for choosing a respondent may also be used, such as choosing a node with higher received signal levels, or choosing a node with more attached neighbors. Node C will send a TYPE3 message immediately after the end of the interval following TYPE1 message, to notify all respondents which one was chosen. Node G, which was not chosen, will turn off its transceiver for some time and then start the search procedure.

If node C is already attached, it will transmit its schedule information, along with the time its next super frame will start, in the body of TYPE3. Node B will read this information, compare the two schedules and time offsets, and arrive at a set of two free time intervals as the slots assigned to the link between C and B.

Node B will then send the location of these time slots along with the randomly selected frequency band of operation to node C in the body of a TYPE4 message. At this point the two nodes have a pending link between them. Once a pair of short test messages is successfully exchanged between the two nodes using the newly assigned slots, the link is added to the nodes' schedules permanently.

We define a sub-net to be a subset of nodes that form a connected graph and have coinciding super fame epochs. There are two or more nodes in each sub-net. For example, in figure 2.b nodes, A and D form a sub-net and B and C form another As time goes on, these sub-nets grow in size, by attaching new nodes. They will eventually become attached to other sub-nets, until finally almost all the nodes in the network are connected together3 The case when two nodes find each other and attempt to form a link, while they are already members of different sub-nets is the most challenging scenario in our startup procedure. As long as the super frame of both nodes has enough overlap in unassigned regions to allocate a pair of slots for the new link, there is no need for the two nodes to re-organize their respective schedules in order to make room for the new link. If there is no room left, the two nodes will simply give up and search for other nodes.

List of Startup messages

The following messages are exchanged between nodes when they are searching for new neighbors:

- TYPE1: short invitation containing node's id and number of its attached neighbors. The node which sends it, is the inviter during the search transaction.
- TYPE2: response to TYPE1. The node that sends it, will be an invitee. There may be more than one invitee for each inviter. This message gives the inviter and invitee's addresses, and invitee's attached state.

Note that it is possible for some of the nodes in the network to never find a neighbor, and not attach to the wireless network at all. This is an acceptable phenomenon. The goal of the startup algorithm is to automatically form an infrastructure that will support local and long distance transport of sensor information. The percentage of the nodes which will not get connected is a function of the node density, transmit powers and terrain type.

- TYPE3: response to TYPE2. Indicates which invitee was chosen. It contains the following additional information depending on the node's attached state:
  i. Inviter not attached: none.
  ii. Invitee, inviter attached: inviter's schedule and frame epoch.
  iii. Invitee not attached, inviter attached: proposed channel for the link, calculated by inviter.
- TYPE4: response to TYPE3. Message contents are as follows:
  i. Invitee not attached, inviter not attached: channel determined by the invitee.
  ii. Invitee not attached, inviter attached: none.
  iii. Invitee attached, inviter not attached: channel determined by the invitee.
  iv. Invitee attached, inviter attached: channel determined from own and inviter's schedule information.

Mobile MAC Issues

As the stationary network becomes fully formed, it is possible that mobile nodes will begin to interact with the network. While adding to the overhead accompanying topological variability, mobile nodes further the functionality of the network, and thus their existence is desired. The goal of the mobile MAC protocol presented here is to provide the required connectivity to mobile sensors as they interact with the static network, while adhering to the constraints for the entire stationary network.

Mobility management within wireless networks has been studied extensively, with each network manifestation resulting in new methods of handling the ORM tasks. The mobile management issues in MANETs, for example, have classically been oriented towards routing issues within the network. As the network consists of solely mobile nodes, the task of Routing and Mobility within the MANET are generally handled jointly. One way that has been devised to handle these networks is to group the mobile nodes into small clusters, electing a cluster-head to route information to in a local neighborhood [16, 17]. The group of cluster-heads in the entire network in turn forms a sub-network. Information is then routed through this sub-network. As mobile nodes move from one area to the next, they may decide to register within a new cluster, and continue operation as usual.

Cellular systems are structurally quite different than conventional MANETs. The wired backbone on stationary nodes facilitates routing, as the wireless channel is avoided. Consequently, it is only the single hop from a mobile node to the stationary base station that needs to be considered. Thus, mobility management is primarily considered here from the point of view of forming connections with the best base station. As mobile users travel from the vicinity of one base station to the next, the desired connection is simply updated using handoff techniques and communication continues as normal [18, 19] As the base stations are assumed to have a large energy reservoir, they take up much of the responsibility of the mobile management task (i.e. setting up new routes to the mobile nodes, informing mobile nodes of handoffs, etc.)

Although studies have been done to explain the handling of the ORM tasks for various networks, the properties of the networks are vastly different than those being investigated here. MANETs, in particular, are in the true sense Ad-Hoc networks, but the absence of stationary nodes makes it difficult to simply use their algorithms for handling our mobility management. The nodes themselves are assumed to have a large range (on the order of hundreds of meters), focusing less on power consumption and more on network connectivity as the topology changes quite rapidly. Cellular systems, though, do introduce a stationary infrastructure, but the mobile nodes greatly outnumber the stationary base stations. This implies that the base station will assume many of the tasks in maintaining the required connectivity between the mobile nodes and their serving base station. Figure 3 shows typical scenarios for each of the three system types mentioned here.

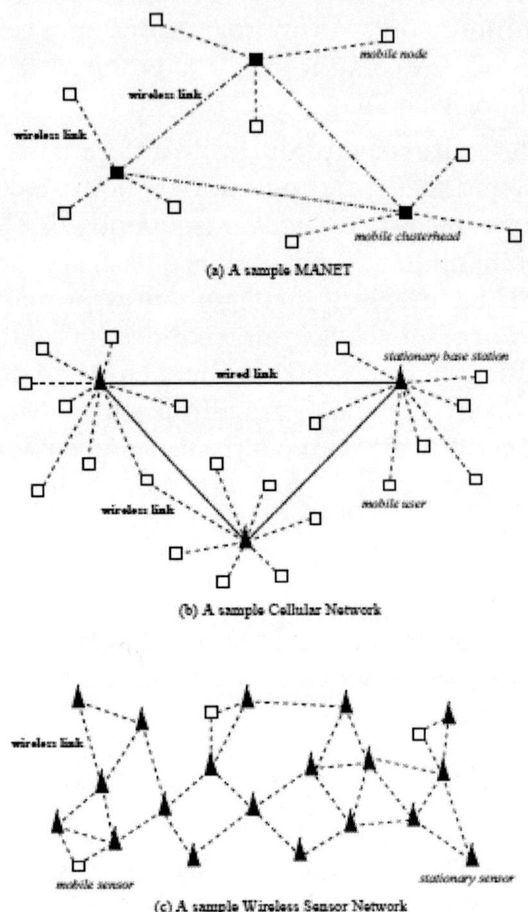

Figure 3 Various Wireless Networks

The EAR Algorithm Motivation

Mobiles that have been introduced into the system function as extensions to the stationary sensor network. It cannot be assumed that each mobile node is aware of the global network state and/ or node positions. Also, it may not be the case that a mobile node is able to complete its task (data collection, network instruction, information extraction) while remaining motionless. Thus, the EAR protocol attempts to offer continuous service to these mobile nodes under both mobile and stationary node constraints.

Mobile connections to a vast wireless sensor network can arise in many scenarios where either energy or bandwidth is a major concern. In situations where there is the constraint of limited power consumption, small, low bit-rate data packets can be exchanged to relay data to and from the network whenever necessary. In this way, the low power EAR protocol allows for operations to continue within the stationary network while intervening at desired moments for information exchange.

Network Constraints

As the primary limitation is that of the battery power on the stationary nodes, the communication channels between the mobile and stationary sensors must be established with as few messages transmitted by the stationary sensors as possible. This can be accomplished by allowing the mobile node to determine when to invite the stationary node as a connection, as well as when to drop a connection.

The network is assumed to consist of primarily stationary nodes, with few mobile nodes, all of which are randomly distributed. Such an assumption leads to the notion that only a select few stationary sensors will be within the vicinity of a mobile sensor at any given time. Giving the ability to form connections to the stationary nodes would result in the constant specialized signaling with the intent of inviting mobile nodes to join the network. To avoid the unnecessary use of power associated with lost messages, the mobile nodes assume full control of the connection process. Furthermore, the overhead associated with acknowledgements can be eliminated. This is possible as the proximity between sensors almost surely ensures message reception.

In many situations, a handoff may not even be required. By exploiting the tight stationary sensor packing (within 10-20 meters of each other), the mobile sensor can maintain its connections while being aware only of the sensors in the near field, handing off when one of the received SNR values along a current connection drops below a predetermined threshold. Thus, the mobile sensor will keep a registry of the surrounding nodes, selecting a new connection only when absolutely necessary.

As there will be few stationary nodes that are aware of the presence of the mobile nodes, the EAR protocol will be transparent to the existing stationary protocol. This allows the functionality of the stationary protocol to remain fixed, until the interjection of a mobile node. Also, by placing the mobile MAC protocol in the background, very few specialized messages need to be invented to establish, or drop, connections. Also, we consider, here, the prospect of giving the mobile nodes a higher priority of forming connections. We assume that the stationary nodes are using a TDMA-like frame structure, within which slots are designated for inviting neighboring nodes into the network. By reserving the first slot following an invitation for mobile sensor connections, we can effectively assign a higher priority to the mobile nodes.

The EAR Algorithm

During some predetermined slot in the TDMA-like frame structure in the stationary MAC algorithm, the stationary node should transmit some type of invitation message to the surrounding neighborhood, with the intent of inviting new stationary nodes to join the local network. This message need not occur in every epoch of the TDMA structure; it is only needed at some semi-regular interval, and serves as the "pilot signal" for the mobile nodes. Thus, no specialized message is required to initiate the connection procedure. As the stationary node does not require a response to this message (although it will wait for a predetermined time for a response), the mobile node is simply "Eavesdropping" the control signals in the stationary MAC protocol. It must then decide the best course of action regarding the transmitting stationary sensor; hence this invitation message will act as the trigger for the EAR algorithm.

In order to keep a constant record of neighboring activity, the mobile node will form a registry of neighbors. This registry will hold only the required information for forming, maintaining, and breaking connections. As the registry will only be comprised of stationary nodes corresponding to signals that are received by the mobile, the mobile will node will have information about the stationary nodes in the immediate neighborhood. From the transmitted invitation message, the mobile can extract the received SNR, the node ID, the transmitted power (in a power controlled scheme), etc. Making, or breaking, a connection is based on the status of connections, as well as the location and mobility information inferred from the entries in the registry. Figure 4 depicts a typical situation of a mobile node, showing current, as well as future, connections.

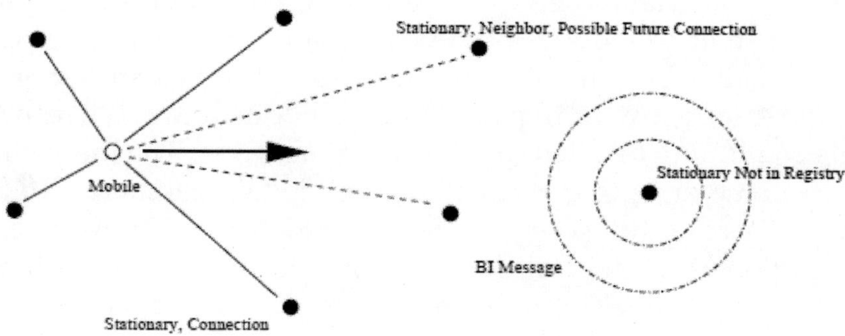

Figure 4. General Mobile Activity

The stationary node will maintain a registry as well, although its role is minimal compared to that of the mobile node. The stationary node simply will register mobiles sensors that have formed connections and remove them when the link is broken, effectively limiting participation in the connection procedures.

To design a system in which the mobile assumes full responsibility of making and breaking connections, a novel signaling method must be defined. If the invitation message, which is inherently part of the stationary MAC algorithm, is included as a shared message, the EAR algorithm makes use of the following 4 primary messages:

Broadcast Invite (BI) The stationary node invites other nodes to join. Mobile Invite (MI) The mobile responds to BI to request a connection. Mobile Response (MR) The stationary node accepts the MI request. Mobile Disconnect (MD) The mobile informs the stationary node of a disconnect; no response is needed.

Acknowledgements are avoided by taking appropriate precautions, such as timeouts, to prevent lost messages from incorrectly identifying connections and neighbors. The stationary nodes are only responsible for the transmission of one specialized message within the EAR algorithm. This reduces the power expense in forming and breaking connections between mobile and stationary nodes.

A newly introduced mobile node will begin its connection protocols upon the reception of the stationary node's BI message. The stationary node is registered, and a decision is made, depending on the present connection status of the mobile node, as well as the potential link quality between the mobile node and the stationary node, whether to request a new connection. If a connection is not requested, the associated stationary node is simply held in the registry. If a connection is, in fact, requested, the mobile node awaits a response, while continuing to listen for invitation messages. The mobile node will continue to register every stationary node encountered, until its registry becomes full (a registry size is predetermined). At this time, new stationary nodes will have to contend for a place within the registry by a simple comparison scheme, possibly replacing a node with an inferior channel quality.

Upon receipt of the MI message, the stationary node will determine if a connection is possible. If so, slots are selected along the TDMA frame for communication, and a reply is sent to the mobile node accepting the connection. Simultaneously, the stationary node will enter the mobile node in its own registry. It is possible, however unlikely, that the stationary node will reach the entry limit in its own registry (again, the size of which is predetermined). Similarly, it may not have a communications slot available that coincides with those presented to it by the mobile node. In such cases, a decline is sent to the mobile node.

It is likely that the mobile node will receive many BI's from registered stationary nodes. Instead of simply dropping the message, the mobile node uses this new information to extract information about the channel quality, and thus its general proximity to the stationary sensor. As the received SNR along the channel improves, or degrades, the mobile sensor may wish to request a connection, or a disconnection (with a MD). The mobile decides which nodes to request connections to, and which nodes to disconnect from, based on predetermined thresholds. In the EAR algorithm, two threshold values are used to avoid the "ping-pong" effect, a connect and disconnect threshold. As an unconnected stationary sensor's received SNR rises above the connection threshold, a connection is considered. Similarly, as a connected stationary sensor's SNR drops below the disconnection threshold, a MD is sent. A high connection threshold will generally yield an overall higher

As it is sometimes difficult to adjust the registries due to inconsistencies in signal reception, the mobile node employs a set of timeouts to limit registry errors. When a connection to a stationary node is requested, the mobile node updates the connection status to "PENDING." It is possible that this invitation message is lost in transmission, resulting in the mobile maintaining the PENDING status indefinitely. Thus, if a response is not received within a specified time frame, the mobile node will downgrade the stationary node's status to "NOT-CONNECT." Furthermore, once a connection has been established, if information is not readily available for extraction from the network, the mobile node will rely on reception of the BI messages to update the connection status. As the BI messages are not sent regularly, it is possible that the mobile node will quickly move out of range of a neighboring stationary node. If this happens, the mobile sensor will drop the connection, after a predetermined waiting period.

MAC/TDMA/Bandwidth Utilization

As the mobile node will primarily use its schedule for mobile-stationary communications, it will be inefficient to use similar TDMA schedules for each type of node. A possible solution is to allow the mobile node's frame length to be an integer fraction (N) of that of the stationary node. The mobile node may offer R slot pairs for communication, resulting in R*N options for the stationary node, any number of which may be chosen. Although communications may not occur during each of the mobile node's N frame repetitions, the associated slot is always reserved. Figure 5 depicts a typical request for a connection by a mobile node, with N = 4 and R = 2. Here, only one slot pair is accepted, causing the mobile node make the reservation, and communicate during every 4th instance of its frame period.

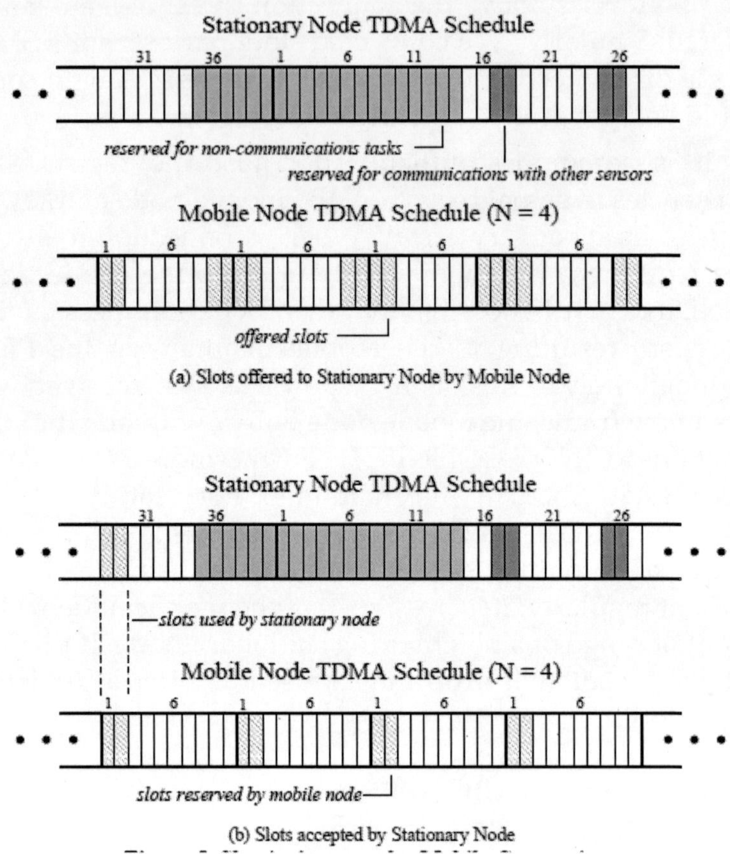

Figure 5. Slot Assignment for Mobile Connections

Routing

As the mobile nodes interact with the network, it is possible that they become involved in the routing paths calculated at the network layer. For information sources, such as robotic data collectors and instructional personnel, routing is not an issue as the only goal is to place the information on the network, allowing the stationary nodes to route the information to the required destinations.

If the mobile node is used as an information sink, though, routing tables have to be devised to allow information to efficiently reach the user. If the degree of mobility is relatively slow, new routing trees can be calculated as the mobile moves from location to location. To avoid unnecessary re-computations, though, it is possible to simply recompute the routing trees in the locale of the mobile node. As this tends to become inefficient when the mobile moves some distance from its original location, a new complete routing tree will be calculated only when necessary. For both multi-hop as well as cooperative network routing, efficiency can be improved in three different areas:

(1) Route setup,

(2) Route maintenance, and

(3) Service.

However, there is generally a trade-off among them. Complex route computations may find energy efficient paths, but they are expensive to maintain as network topology changes. Therefore energy efficiency should be emphasized in each area to the degree that appropriately matches its importance in meeting the overall objective. For multi-hop routing, the objective is to provide priority service with robustness on a long-term basis; therefore, more energy will have to be spent on route setup and route maintenance to meet these requirements. On the other hand, for a non-coherent cooperative function network, where data traffic is light, optimization of energy cost on each route is not nearly as important as reducing overhead during route setup phase

Multi-Hop Routing

Two multi-hop routing algorithms have been proposed for MANET: Ad Hoc On Demand Distance Vector (ADOV) routing and Temporally Ordered Routing Algorithm (TORA). Both are examples of demand-driven system that eliminated most of the overhead associated with table update in high mobility scenario. However, it has high energy cost during the route setup (path discovery) phase. Since our system does not deal with high mobility, it is in the interest of energy efficiency to go with a table driven system. Another algorithm, called Power-Aware Routing [20], finds the minimum metric paths on two different power metrics:

(1) Minimum energy per packet

(2) Minimum cost per packet.

The first metric is intuitive and produces substantial energy saving while the network retains full connectivity; however, performance degradation due to node/link failure is not accounted for. The minimum cost metric is obtained by weighting the energy consumption by the energy reserve on each node. It has the nice property of delaying failures by steering traffic away from low energy nodes; however overhead for path maintenance could be high.

To improve energy efficiency in a low mobility network, we turn to a table-driven, multi-path approach. The degree of failure protection is directly related to the degree of disjoint-ness k, of the paths joining a node to a data sink (that is, the number of paths with no common branches). A k-disjoint structure can protect against failures of k links or nodes. As a rule of thumb, to generate a k-disjoint structure requires about k times the overhead complexity of a shortest path algorithm [21] However, the disjoint property creates strong coupling between routing tables that makes a localized recovery scheme nearly impossible. The key to reduce overhead is to loosen up this coupling effect by relaxing the disjoint requirement outside the 1-hop neighborhood of the sink. Although the degree of failure protection is lower, it can be compensated by localized path restoration procedure at much lower energy cost

To create multiple paths from each node to the sink, multiple trees, each rooted from a 1-hop neighbor of the sink, are built. Each tree will be forced to grow outward from the sink by successively branching, whenever possible, to neighbors at higher hop-distance from the sink while avoiding nodes with very low QoS and energy reserve. At the end of the tree building procedure, most nodes will belong to multiple trees and thus having multiple paths that are disjoint inside the 1-hop neighborhood of the sink. The advantage of this structure is that it allows each sensor indirect control of which 1-hop neighbor of the sink will relay a message. For each node, two parameters are associated with each path: (1) energy resource estimated by maximum number of packets that can be routed without energy depletion if it has exclusive use of the path, (2) additive QoS metric where higher metric implies lower QoS.

Having multiple paths to the sink node, each sensor uses a Sequential Assignment Routing (SAR) algorithm for path selection.

It takes into consideration the energy resource and QoS on each path and the priority level of a packet. Path selection is made by the node that generates the packet, unless topology change down the path requires the packet be diverted. Each link contributes an energy cost and delay, and thus a resistance to packet flow that can be captured in an additive metric for any given path. Against this a packet will have credits so that it can achieve priority in using for example paths that are low latency but traverse nodes with depleted energy. For each packet routed through the network, a weighted QoS metric is computed as the product of the additive QoS metric and a weight coefficient associated the priority level of that packet for purpose of performance evaluation. The intuitive interpretation of this weighted QoS metric is that it measures the QoS provided to each packet relative to the priority level of the packet. Therefore, to maintain the same weighted QoS metric, higher QoS(lower QoS metric) will be used for higher priority(higher weight coefficient) packets. The objective of the SAR algorithm is to minimize the average weighted QoS metric throughout the lifetime of the network.

As each path is used over time, the available energy resource will change. There are also possible changes in the QoS on each path. These changes will be accounted for by periodic metric update triggered from the sink node. Simulation study [15] shows SAR has better performance than the minimum metric algorithm , which optimize performance by focusing, very singularly, on lowering energy consumption for each packet, without considering its priority.

Failure recovery is implemented by a handshaking procedure that enforces routing table consistency between the upstream and downstream neighbor on each path, so that any local failure will automatically trigger a re-computation procedure locally. This procedure will converge as long as a path exists in the network topology [10]. In order to prevent the possibility of slow convergence (i.e., counting to infinity problem), a threshold method detects rapid increase of path metric and speeds up convergence to infinity, which effectively marks the erasure of a path. This can conserve energy for nodes that are separated from the sink but may later re-establish connection again.

Adaptive Local Routing for cooperative signal processing

We assume that an application level algorithm or outside agent will determine what cooperative function is needed and trigger the network formation process. In the following section, the term ``network`` refers specifically to a connected set of sensors that detected a common target. Before describing the network formation algorithm, a few remarks on the basic categories of environmental stimuli and cooperative functions are warranted. In general, environmental stimuli can be separated into two major categories: (1) near-field (NF) and (2) far-field (FF). Near-field stimuli have short range relative to the baseline width of sensor groups within detectable distance. Signal propagation is dominated by the line-of-sight component; therefore SNR of sensor data can be modeled in the form: k d-r, where d is the distance between the sensor and the signal source and k and r are constant determined by the propagation medium. Accurate localization and identification are possible if the target is located inside the convex hull of the network. Far-field targets are located at much farther distance relative to the baseline width of the network. For these targets, source localization and range estimation are much more challenging. Due to greater physical distance from the network, signals encounter both increased dispersion and attenuation

There are two types of cooperative signal processing techniques:

(1) Non-coherent

(2) Coherent

For non-coherent processing, raw sensor data will be preprocessed at each node to extract a small set of parameters to be forwarded to a central node (CN) for further processing; for coherent processing like blind beam-forming [22], raw sensor data, after minimal pre-processing, will be tagged with a time stamp and uploaded through the local network to the CN for more intensive computations. Although energy efficiency is the ultimate goal, different approaches can be used depending on what cooperative functions are used. Non-coherent functions have fairly low data traffic loading; therefore we will focus our effort on improving algorithmic efficiency. On the other hand, since coherent processing generates long data streams, energy efficiency must be achieved by path optimality. For clarity of presentation, we separately discuss coherent and non-coherent processing networks.

Non-coherent cooperative function:

In general, there are three phases in the processing network formation process:

I. Target Detection, Data Collection, and Pre-Processing
II. Membership Declaration
III. Central Node Election

During phase I, a target is detected, its data collected and pre-processed. Although the sink node can override any decision made on the local level, the results of pre-processing can serve as good indicators whether a node should participate in a cooperative function. One such indicator is the Signal-to-Noise Ratio(SNR). When a node decides to participate in a cooperative function, it will enter phase II declare this intention to all neighbors. This should be done as soon as possible so that each sensor has a local understanding of the network topology. Phase III of the formation process is the election of the Central node (CN). Since CN is selected to perform more sophisticated information processing, it must have sufficient energy reserve and computational capability. It can also be selected based on SNR, which is a good estimator for distance to the target in NF case. The CN election algorithm has two components:

(1) Single Winner Election (SWE) algorithm,
(2) Spanning Tree (ST) algorithm.

The first component handles the necessary signaling that facilitates the exchange of candidate information; the second component computes a minimum hop spanning tree rooted at CN. By piggybacking election and routing information together in an Elect message, it is possible to execute both algorithms concurrently.

Each Elect message identifies a potential CN candidate and a set of parameters that serve as the election criteria by which candidates are compared. In the initial stage of the SWE process, each node may impose a voluntary delay of varying length before announcing itself as a CN candidate by broadcasting Elect messages. In response to the first batch of Elect messages, those nodes that received them will start comparing the proposed CN candidates with itself and respond with a second batch of Elect messages, which carries the result of this initial comparison. The second batch of message passing will likely spawn further exchange of messages. During this process, for each message that presents a better candidate, its information will be recorded in the registry and then be forwarded to all neighbors; otherwise the message is discarded. Figure 6 shows how the continuing exchange, forwarding and discarding of Elect messages allows the winning candidates' information to ``diffuse`` throughout the network. Together with this diffusion process, a minimum-hop spanning tree rooted at the winning candidate will gradually increase its coverage. By the end of the SWE process, a minimum-hop spanning tree will completely cover the network.

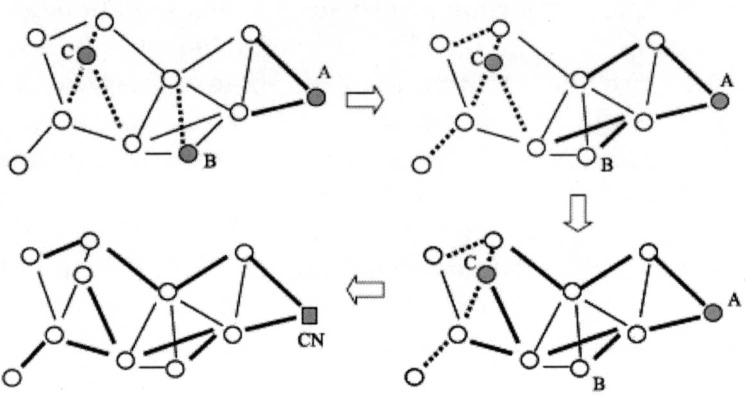

Figure 6. Diffusion of Candidates Information under SWE

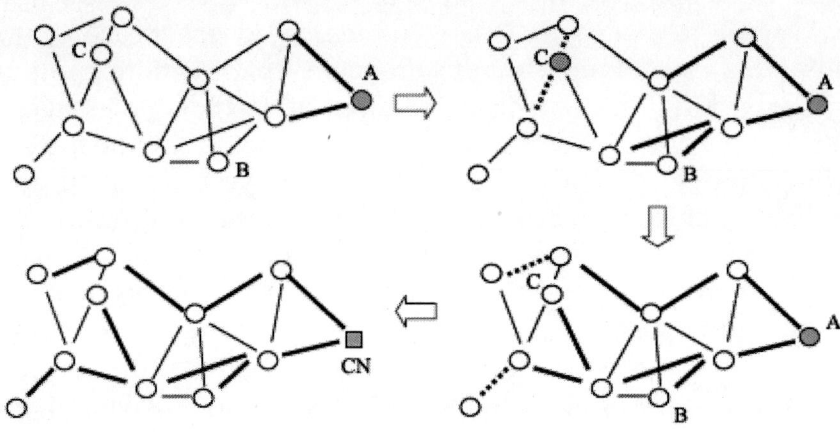

Figure 7. Another SWE Election Process

An overhead-delay trade-off exists such that if each candidate voluntarily delays itself based on its likelihood to win the election (i.e., value of the election criterion used,) the diffusion process of the Elect messages for the better candidates will have a head start. This simple mechanism can eliminate many local Elect message exchanges among losing candidates, and greatly reduce overhead (compare Figure 6 and 7). When sufficient delay difference exists between the best candidate and the rest of the network, Elect messages of the winner can cover the entire network without opposition, thus achieving minimum overhead. Simulation experiments showed that the local network formation process is quite scalable when some formation delay can be tolerated.

Coherent cooperative function:

The coherent algorithm differ the non-coherent case in two respects:

(1) Limited number of sensors generating data;

(2) Explicit computation of minimum energy paths.

Since the energy cost of uploading long data stream to the central node is high, a Multi-Winner Election (MWE) process is used to limit the number of sensor source nodes (SN) that will provide the data. The MWE process is a simple extension of the SWE process.

Instead of keeping record of one best candidate, each node will now keep up to n of them. Just as in the non-coherent case, for each winning SN candidate, a minimum-energy path can be computed by piggybacking link power information on the Elect messages. At the end of the MWE process, each sensor in the network has a set of minimum energy path to each SN. Then the total energy consumption to upload data from each SN to each node in the local network can be computed. Using this energy consumption figure as the election criterion, a SWE process can be used to find the node that yields the minimum energy consumption. This node can then serve as the CN for the coherent cooperative function. In general the formation process has longer delay, higher overhead, and lower scalability than for non-coherent processing networks. Figure 8 illustrates the formation process.

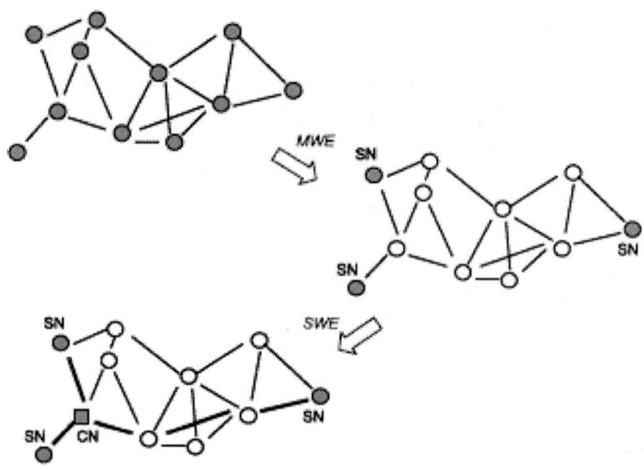

Figure 8. Formation Process for Coherent Routing

Simulation Implementation

A simulation testbed for the above protocols was implemented in Parsec [23]. In this simulation, a radio propagation model complete with shadowing and path-loss is used. The simulation is capable of running packet level experiments, to test the behavior of the algorithms. The simulation is able to accommodate simulations of hundreds of nodes at the moment. The simulation environment models each node as a separate Parsec entity. The functionality of each layer, namely MAC, mobile MAC, and the network layer, is implemented as a function inside the node.

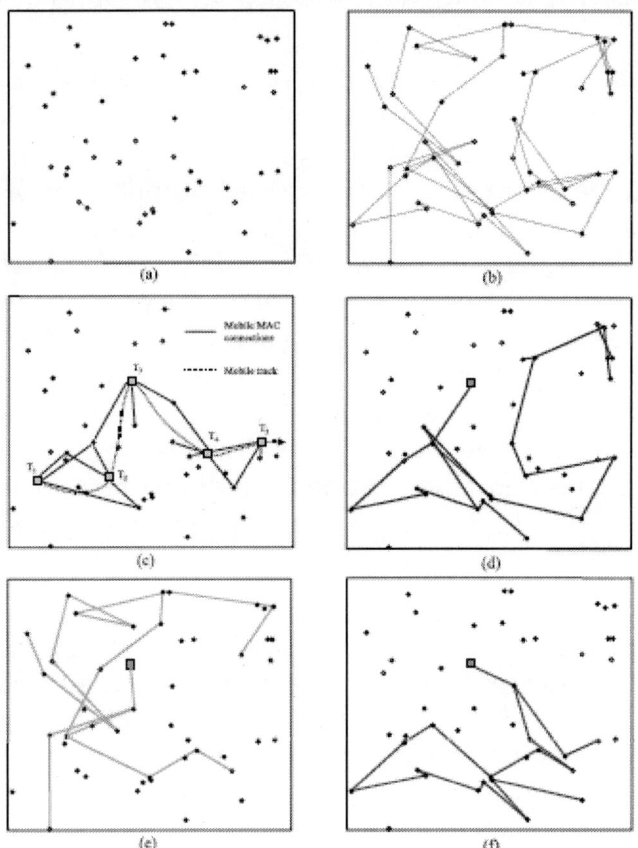

Figure 9. Simulation of behavior of various protocols

A network consisting of 45 nodes, scattered randomly in space, with density λ=0.04 nodes/m2 was simulated, as shown in 9.a. In this simulation, the sensor nodes are using 1mW transmit power, T frame=8.0 sec, and 100 frequency bands are available. Path loss follows a fourth power drop off with distance law, and the shadowing variance is 8 db. Figure 9.b gives the state of the network links at the moment it has become connected. In figure 9.c the behavior of the mobile MAC is shown. The mobile node is travelling at a velocity of 0.1 m/s, with the capability of having 10 neighbors registered, but limited to only 3 connections. The connection threshold is set at a received SNR level of 12 dB, with the disconnection threshold at 7dB. The figure shows the track of a mobile and its link level connections maintained by the Mobile MAC protocol at five sample points {T1, T2, T3, T4, T5}.

Figure 9.d, 9.e, and 9.f show three spanning trees connecting the sensor to the mobile which has declared itself as a sink node at time T3. Each spanning tree is created from a distinct 1-hop neighbor of the sink, and the required to branch to higher hop-distance is relaxed when the tree is small. At such an early stage of network formation, when the average network degree is only 2.13 (as depicted in Figure 9.b), only 14 out 45 (roughly 31%) of the sensors have multiple paths to the sink. However, as the self-organizing MAC algorithm continues to pick up new link level connections, the average degree, as well as the multi-path coverage will continue to improve until the topology becomes stabilized. Note that in all these cases, in order to keep the diagrams clear, the existing underlying links are not shown.

CONCLUSION

We have presented a set of algorithms for establishing and maintaining connectivity in wireless sensor networks. The algorithms exploit the low mobility and abundant bandwidth, while coping with the severe energy constraint and the requirement for network scalability. The algorithms further accommodate slow mobility by a subset of the nodes. However, many important research questions remain, including for example bounds on the minimum energy required for network formation especially taking into account the interactions with the signal processing functions. Another issue is the extent to which the algorithms can efficiently deal with more extensive mobility in the nodes and the targets

The most fundamental open question is that of hierarchy in the distributed signal processing and networking functions. It is clear that some layering of signal processing functions is required to produce energy-efficient operation. We cannot afford the most expensive signal processing algorithms to be constantly running, nor can we afford the poor decision quality that results from relying only on the simplest procedures. Since communications dominates the energy cost when cooperative functions among nodes are needed, the question naturally arises as to the extent that the signal processing hierarchy demands a corresponding networking hierarchy. We have developed substantially different algorithms for setting up sub-networks to perform cooperative signal processing functions, with the effort involved and the scalability depending quite strongly on the signal processing function. However, this is only the first venture in exploring a very rich space of problems. Hardware testing of alternative algorithms in large networks is certain to yield many interesting challenges

REFERENCES

1. G. J. Pottie and W. J. Kaiser,`` Wireless Integrated Network Sensors'', Communications of the ACM, vol. 43, no. 5, May 2000, pp. 51-58.
2. May 2000 Issue of Communications of the ACM.
3. D. Estrin, R. Govindan, and J. Heidemann,``Embedding the Internet'', Communications of the ACM, vol. 43, no. 5, May 2000, pp.39-41.
4. G. Asada, M. Dong, T. S. Lin, F. Newberg, G. Pottie, W. J. Kaiser, and H. O. Marcy, ``Wireless integrated network sensors: Low power systems on a chip'', Proceedings of the 1998 European Solid State Circuits Conference, 1998.
5. F. Bennet, D. Clark, J. Evans, A. Hopper, A. Jones, and D. Leask ,` Piconet: Embedded mobile networking'', IEEE Communications Magazine, pp.7-15, October 1997.
6. G. J. Pottie, ``Hierarchical Information Processing in Distributed Sensor Networks,`` ISIT, Cambridge, USA. August 1998, pp. 163.
7. K. Sohrabi, "On Low Power Wireless Sensor Networks," Ph.D. Dissertation, Department of Electrical Engineering, UCLA, June 2000.
8. J. L. Gao, ``Energy Efficient Routing for Wireless Sensor Networks," Ph.D. Dissertation, Department of Electrical Engineering, UCLA, June 2000.
9. M. Gerla and J. T. Tsai, ``Multicluster, mobile, multimedia radio network,`` Wireless Networks, vol. `, 1995, pp. 255-265.
10. D. J. Baker and A. Ephremides, "The architectural organization of a mobile radio network via a distributed algorithms", IEEE Transactions

on Communications, no. 11, pp. 1694-1701, November 1981.

11. A. D. Amis, R. Prakash, T. H. P. Vuong and D. T. Huynh, "Max-Min D-Cluster formation in wireless ad-hoc networks", IEEE INFOCOM, March 2000.
12. K. Sohrabi, G. Pottie, "Performance Of A Novel Self-Organization Protocol For Wireless Ad-Hoc Sensor Networks," Proceedings of IEEE Vehicular Technology Conference, September 1999, Amsterdam, Netherlands.
13. K. Sohrabi, J. Gao, V. Ailawadhi, G. Pottie, ``A Self-organizing Wireless Sensor Network," Proc. 39th Annual Allerton Conference on Communication, Control, and Computing, Urbana, Illinois, October 1999.
14. wata, A. et al., "Scalable Routing Strategies for Ad Hoc Wireless Networks," IEEE Journal on Selected Areas in Communications, vol. 17, no. 8, pp 1369-79, August 1999. [17] Pei, G. and Gerla, M., "Mobility Management in Hierarchical Multi-hop Mobile Wireless Networks," Proceedings Eight International Conference on Computer Communications and Networks, Piscataway, NJ,
15. USA: IEEE, 1999. p.324-9. [18] Viterbi, A. et al., "Soft Handoff Extends CDMA Cell Coverage and Increases Reverse Link Capacity,"
16. IEEE Journal on Selected Areas in Communications, vol. 12, no. 8, pp 1281-8, October 1994. [19] Wong, D. and Lim, T. J., "Soft Handoffs in CDMA Mobile Systems," IEEE Personal Communications, pp 6-17, December 1997. [20] S. Singh, M. Woo, C.S. Raghavendra, ``Power-Aware Routing in Mobile Ad Hoc Networks," MOBICOM'98, Dallas Texas. Pp. 181-190.
17. J.W. Suurballe, Disjoint Paths in a Network," Networks, 4:125-145, 1974, John Wiley & Sons.
18. K. Yao, R.E. Hudson, C.W. Reed, D. Chan, F. Lorenzelli, ``Blind Beamforming on a Randomly Distributed Sensor Array System,`` IEEE Journal On Selected Areass in Communications, vol. 16, no. 8, October 1998.

Chapter 4

COMMUNICATION STRATEGIES FOR STRIP-LIKE TOPOLOGIES IN AD-HOC WIRELESS NETWORKS

Daniele De Caneva, Pier Luca Montessoro
|and Davide Pierattoni

University of Udine Italy

INTRODUCTION

Many routing protocols have been designed for wireless sensor networks considering nodes that operate in a mesh topology. For specific application scenarios, however, a mesh topology may not be appropriate or simply not corresponding to the natural node deployment. Bridge (Kim et al., 2007) or pipeline (Jawhar et al., 2007) monitoring applications are examples where the position of sensor nodes is predetermined by the physical structure and application requirements. In this applications, where is clearly present a privileged dimension, it is quite natural to take advantage of it. Similar consideration can be made in more dynamic applications like the one of vehicular communication since the network can be approximated to have a linear topology without loss of accuracy.

This chapter will go through a description of the strategies developed so far to handle the problem of communication in strip-like topologies. For this specific problem several studies can be found in literature. Few research directions can be outlined: strip oriented routing, physical device design and specific MAC protocols. In the following four approaches are presented in order to describe how each direction can be investigated. The first two are related to the network layer of ISO/OSI protocol stack, the third one proposes use of devices with directional antennas while the fourth one designs a MAC protocol based on synchronous transmit-receive patterns. These approaches are somewhat complementary, each better suited for different scenarios.

ROUTING LAYER STRATEGIES

MERR

MERR (Minimum Energy Relay Routing) is a routing protocol which aims to address the problem of an economical use of power in wireless sensor networks. The goal is to minimize power consumption during communications in order to build networks for long-lasting operations. Its reference scenario is that of networks where sensors are deployed over a linear topology and have to send data to a single control center.

Assuming homogeneous sensor nodes deployed in an arbitrary linear sensor network, MERR permits every node to independently find a route to the base station that approximates the optimal routing path. Finding a route means selecting appropriate relays between a sensor and the base station.

The problem of relaying data from nodes to the control center can be approached in two ways. The first is direct transmission, where every node transmits its packets directly to the base station. This approach suffers from important problems: first of all, in an environment with many obstacles or if the distance is too large, successful reception at the base station might not be feasible. Secondarily, with direct transmission, since the effort related with transmission increases as a power function of the distance, nodes far away from the base station will suffer greater power consumption and thus exhaust quickly their battery. From this considerations becomes clear that direct transmission is ideal only for scenarios where nodes are close to the base station or when the energy required for reception is large. In that case transmitting data directly to the control center, limits energy dissipation due to reception at the base station (which usually have unlimited power supply).

The second approach consists in taking advantage of the other nodes by using them as routers to forward data packets to the control center. MERR follows this method and in particular states the rules for router choice. MERR authors (Zimmerling et al., 2007) take distance from the MTE policy of routing where routers are chosen in order to minimize transmit energy. Minimizing transmit energy means choosing the nearest neighbor as router, with the evident drawback that a huge amount of energy is wasted if nodes are close to each other or the energy required for reception is high. MERR tries to respond to the question concerning which node must be chosen as router in order to obtain an energy efficient network. Zimmerling et al. based their work on that presented by Bhardwaj et al. (2001) where it is demonstrated that the optimal number of hops to reach a base station situated at a distance D is always:

$$K_{opt} = \left\lfloor \frac{D}{d_{char}} \right\rfloor \text{ or } K_{opt} = \left\lceil \frac{D}{d_{char}} \right\rceil \quad (1)$$

where d_{char} is the characteristic distance, given by

$$d_{char} = \sqrt[n]{\frac{\alpha_1}{\alpha_2(n-1)}} \quad (2)$$

where a1, a2 and £ are parameters related to node's transceiver circuitry such that the power consumption involved in relaying r bit per second to a distance d meters onward (assuming a path loss of 1/dn) is

$$P_{relay}(d) = (\alpha_1 + \alpha_2 d^n)r \quad (3)$$

These results show that best performances are reached when packets perform $(K_{opt} - 1)$ relays by means of nodes equally spaced in intervals of D/Kopt.

Based on these assumptions, MERR states that every node should decide independently which will be its relay node. The choice is made seeking the down-stream node within the maximum transmission range whose distance is closest to the characteristic distance. After this decision is made by every node in the network, transmission power is independently reduced to the lowest possible level so that the radio signal can be received by the next-hop node without any errors. During normal functioning, a node will transmit data always to

the chosen relay node, regardless that this data comes from internal sensors or from another node.

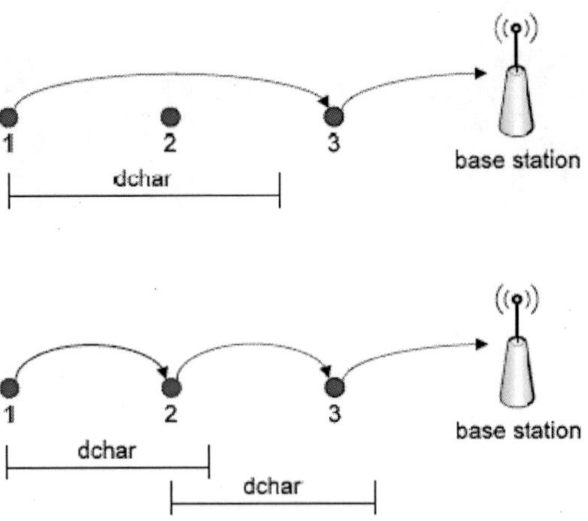

Figure 1. Characteristic distance influences packets routing path

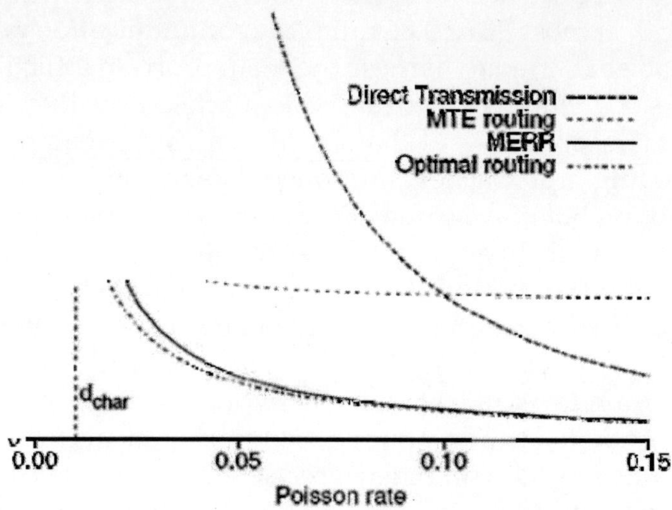

Figure. 2. Expected power consumption depending on Poisson rate 'A for a constant number of sensors (n = 100) and path loss exponent 2.

In order to chose its own relay node, every sensor must know the characteristic distance (which is the same for all node if they are of the same kind) and the distance of all its neighbors (which can be manually measured during deployment or estimated using one of the methods present in literature such as Received Signal Strength or Time of Arrival). Zimmerling et al. offer a comparison in terms of expected power consumption between MERR, optimal transmission, MTE and direct routing. For the sake of generality, the comparison is made using a one-dimensional homogeneous Poisson process with constant rate 'A to model the distribution of nodes. The comparison, drown from a stochastic analysis made by the authors of MERR, clearly shows that energy consumption of MERR is always upper bounded by that of MTE. In particular MERR require less energy if the mean distance between nodes is lower than the characteristic distance.

Load Balanced Short Path Routing

Although not directly focused on strip-like topologies, the work presented by Gao et al. (2006) is worth mentioning because it covers the special case of a network where nodes are located in a narrow strip with width at most -J3/2 0.86 times the communication range of each node. Gao et al. tried to harness the main problem afflicting wireless networks, i.e. energy constraints. In particularly they focused on routing layer pointing out that, by minimizing path length, shortest path routing approaches minimize latency and overall energy consumption but may ignore fairness. In fact a protocol that searches the shortest path to route packets, will tend to abuse of some set of hops not exploiting all network resources. This behavior will quickly drain the batteries of involved nodes, causing the creation of holes within the network. On the other hand load balanced routing strategies aim to use all available network resources in order to even the load, not regarding about communication performances. Gao et al. in their work combined greedy strategies used to minimize path length and those used to evenly distribute load with the aim to achieve good performances in both metrics of latency and load balance. The problem of finding the most balanced routes is NP-hard even for a simple network and that is why Gao et al. firstly concentrated their efforts on a particular topology. The basic idea of their work is to maintain for each node a set of edges, called bridges, that are guaranteed to make substantial progress. In addiction their paper shows that, when a node has many neighbors, by distributing a collection of binary search trees on the nodes, memory needed on each node and routing/update cost can be reduced significantly.

The routing algorithm relies on two assumptions. The first is that each node knows its location, the second is that the rough location of the destination is known such that the source node knows whether it should send the packet toward its left or right.

For each node p, bc is a right (left) bridge if b and c are a couple of nodes visible to each other such that b is directly reachable by p, while c lies outside the communication range in a position that is right (left) to that of p (see Fig. 3). The load associated to the bridge is defined as maximum between the loads of b and c.

The routing is organized as follows: when p receives a packet, it first checks if the destination is a direct neighbor. In that case, it sends the packet to the destination. Otherwise, p chooses the lightest bridge, say bc, that forward the packet toward the destination. Then p send the packet to b, where the process is repeated and so on till the destination is reached. Gao et al provided a thorough demonstration that the algorithm works under the condition that strip width is equal or minor times the communication range of nodes. Additionally they presented simulation results over different network and traffic conditions

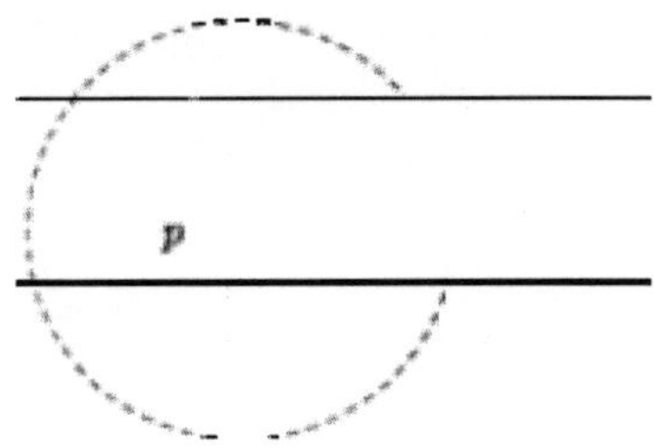

Figure. 3. Communication over a bridge

MAC LAYER STRATEGIES

DiS-MAC

DiS-MAC (Directional Scheduled MAC) has been developed for wireless sensor networks that show a linear topology. It bases its functioning on a particular use of antennas. The premises that lead to this protocol is that directional or smart antennas have the potential to offer increased spatial reuse, longer communication ranges and the ability to point the radio beam toward a desired direction, properties that if properly exploited could potentially lessen the problem of interferences between nodes. Authors of DiS-MAC (Karveli et al.,2008) pointed out that current advances in antenna miniaturization techniques will open the doors of wireless sensor networks world to this kind of radiating systems. The reference scenarios is that of highway and roadside monitoring sensors networks. Since roadsides and highways can be approximated to have a linear topology without loss of accuracy, Karveli et al. concentrated their effort on a sensor network deployed in such topology and consisting of N static nodes generating data packets of equal length with an arbitrary traffic rate. Every node is equipped with a directional antenna that can concentrate the main-beam to a particular direction and presents a some low gain side-lobes in other directions

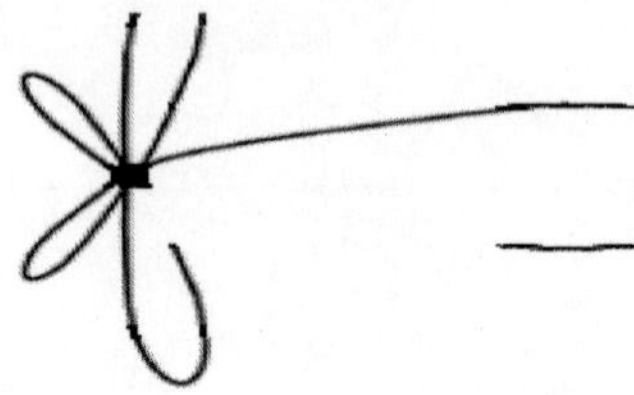

Figure. 4. Model of the antenna system radiation pattern

Figure 4 shows the model for the radiation pattern used to develop the protocol. Other assumption for this protocol are that nodes are synchronized and that the traffic flows only in one direction. Network synchronization permits to divide channel access in two phases of equal length. In the first phase every node occupying a odd position (2n - 1) directs its radiation beam in order to point to the subsequent node and then transmits its data. In this phase nodes occupying a even position (2n) switch their transceiver in reception mode. During the second phase roles are inverted: this time even nodes transmit data to their next node, while odd nodes perform reception. The alternation of phase I and phase II will continue indefinitely.

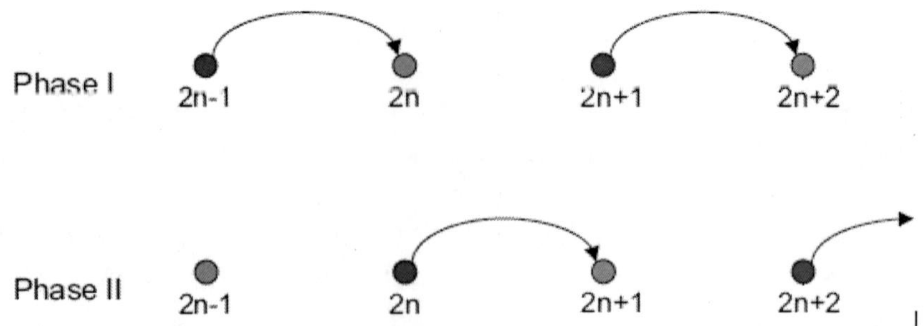

Figure. 5. Two phases scheduling

This scheduled system provides a great efficiency, since it remove the possibility of collisions and the hidden terminal problem. In fact, since there is no contention, there is no need of control packets and thus it doesn't suffer from the overhead produced by them. This neatly configured system deterministically reaches a channel utilization equal to 1/2. This is quite impressive since in literature (Li et al, 2001) it is shown (both by simulations and experiments) that the capacity of a IEEE 802.11 network deployed in chain topology is limited to only 1/7. Additionally, thanks to the absence of channel contention, per hop latency, i.e. the time spent from packet generation at one node to its reception at the next node, is minimized and can be approximated by the duration of two phases.

Moreover the protocol is intrinsically robust because it limits interference between nodes, in fact when a node transmits, the first downstream node that can eventually suffer from this transmission is 3 hops ahead. Thus even considering the common assumption that the interference radius is twice the nominal transmission one, as shown in Fig. 6, DiS-MAC grants the avoidance of intra-network interference problems. Authors of DiS-MAC outlined two extensions for their protocol. The first is a minor one, which states that if a node has no packet to transmit, it can enter into a sleeping mode. If another node have to transmit a packet to this sleeping node, it have to generate a short wake up radio signal in order to warn about the imminent transmission. The second enhancement consist in the introduction of ACK packets to confirm that the transmitted packet has reached its destination without errors. Thanks to the contention-free nature of DiS-MAC, the repeated absence of ACK reception can be used as a marker of node failure. In this case, Karveli et al. have thought a strategy to react to the topology change. If node 2n fails, neither node 2n - 1 nor node 2n + 1 will receive its packets (the first one will receive no ACK packet, while the second will receive no data packet). After a predefined counter expires, node and node will consider their neighbor failed and will start a recovery procedure. The first will extend its transmission range in order to reach the second one and then it will send a phase change request, which will propagated to all subsequent nodes. Phase change request is made through a special control packet and warns a node that its position into the chain is changed (e.g. node is become node) and that it have to modify its behavior according to new topology. To avoid false failure detection, this protocol extension requires the transmission of periodical keep-alive packets.

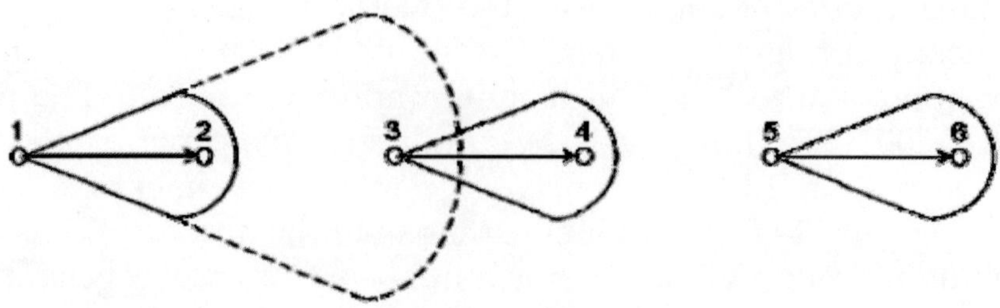

Figure. 6. Interference radius (dashed line) and transmit radius (solid line).

WiWi

The purpose of WiWi (De Caneva et al., 2008) is to emulate a wired link by means of an ad hoc network constituted by nodes distributed along a strip. The purpose of this wired link virtualization is that to handle scenarios where a single hop wireless link is not feasible and a wired link is not practical. An example could be given by a speleologist going deep down into the bowels of the earth, which can deploy the wireless network while it goes further with the exploration in order to maintain a communication channel with the outside world. Other examples can be found in all those situation where a multi-hop link is required. Moreover WiWi can be successfully used in monitoring applications.

Results presented in (Min & Chandrakasan, 2003) regarding power consumption over multi- hop networks demonstrated that the number of hops used to route a packet from source to destination should not be too high. In fact in such situation the portion of power consumption which is independent by the transmission distance becames predominant, thus causing energy saving obtained by shorter transmission hops to be nullified. Moreover, the higher the hops number, the higher the latency. Nevertheless, the coverage range is limited by nodes' architectural characteristics and this define a lower bound for the hops number. This considerations led WiWi developers to choose a non-uniform node displacement and thus a cluster chain topology.

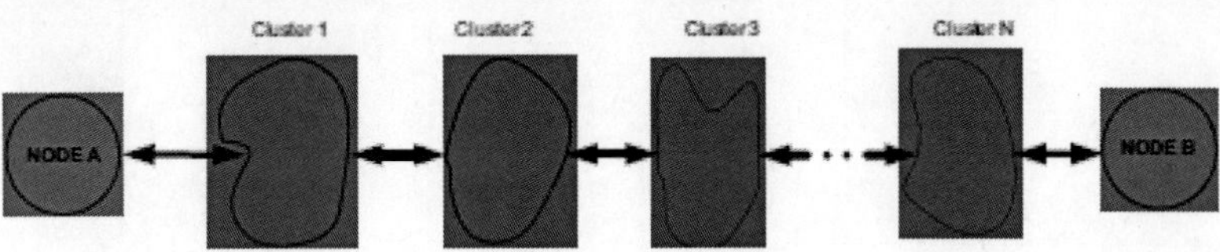

Figure. 7. WiWi topology

De Caneva et al. made no assumptions over node deployment within the clusters, but full inter-cluster graph connection as well as complete radio coverage between nodes belonging to adjacent clusters. WiWi protocol follows a synchronous full-duplex communication with fixed-side packets where clusters act as single nodes. In particular there exists two data stream which proceed along the chain in two different manners, depending on the direction. The first is a downward stream that relays packets from the head of the strip to the tail (gray packets in Fig. 8). This stream, which is responsible of maintaining network synchronization, follows a staggered pattern, i.e. a cluster sends a packet to the next cluster, which in turn immediately forwards it further down along the chain. This stream shows a latency equal to Downlink hops Ts , where Tr is the length of a time slot. The throughput associated with this stream can be expressed as the ratio between the number of bits forming a packet and the time interleaving two consecutive downstream transmissions (i.e. () Ts , where o is the number of slots by which spaces two consecutive transmissions).

The opposite stream follows the same principle of passing messages along the cluster chain, but between the reception of the packet and its forwarding, the cluster waits four time slots in order not to collide with the downward (Fig. 8 shows in different colors the steps taken by different upward packets). The latency affecting the upward stream is ()- 1 times the one of the downward, while the throughput is the same. WiWi protocol is based on datagram transmission, in fact does not provide ACK packets to guarantee the correct packet exchange. Authors of WiWi point out that, if needed, the use of error correction codes could be introduced as well as acknowledgement mechanisms at higher level protocols.

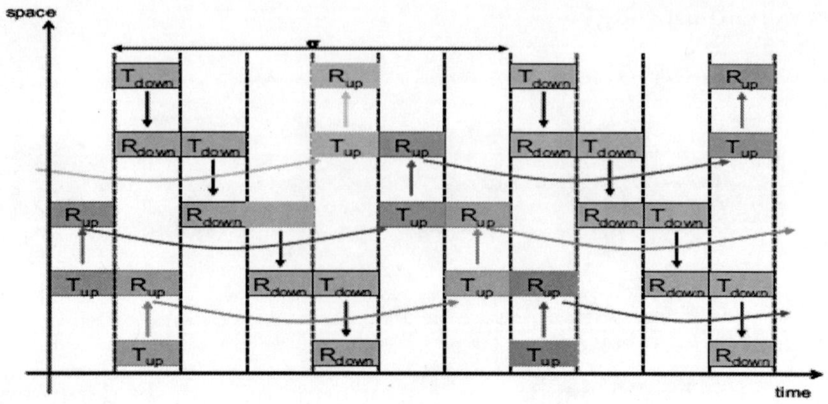

Figure. 8. Bidirectional, staggered transmission with symmetric throughput and asymmetric latency over a WiWi link

As previously mentioned WiWi clusters act as a single node. This is done in order to reach redundancy as well as load balance. In fact WiWi requires that each cluster independently organize itself by ordering its nodes. By ordering a node belonging to the cluster can be elected as node on duty, i.e. the node that have to perform the packet relaying operations that compete to the cluster. The other nodes act as backup nodes. Operatively, during the reception slot every node of the cluster receives and stores the packet arriving from the previous cluster in the chain. In the subsequent transmission slot, the node on duty forwards the packet, while at the same time all backup nodes perform a sensing of the wireless channel. If the backup nodes perceive the loss of the duty node, they react autonomously by redefining their order within the cluster. This way the backup node, which would have its turn next to the current duty node, takes the role of forwarding the packet. The remaining backup nodes perform the sensing again in order to be sure that a backup node has reacted and the forwarding has occurred (Fig. 9). WiWi protocol grants an immediate redundancy equal to the number of backup nodes, which is the total number of active nodes in a cluster minus one. This means that the slot time upon which WiWi is based must have a duration capable to conserve this redundancy mechanism, which lead to a minor loss in throughput and latency performances. In the packet header could be inserted a notification flag to inform subsequent clusters of the failure event. Clearly the node on duty is burdened with a higher power consumption, that is why nodes in turn cover this role following a round robin schedule. Additionally the scheduling of the duty evenly shares the load among cluster nodes extending the network lifetime and opening the door to the use of energy scavenging techniques. The bandwidth unused by the redundancy mechanism, in normal conditions could be periodically exploited to reorganize each cluster on the run, in order to take care of the post- deployed nodes, if any.

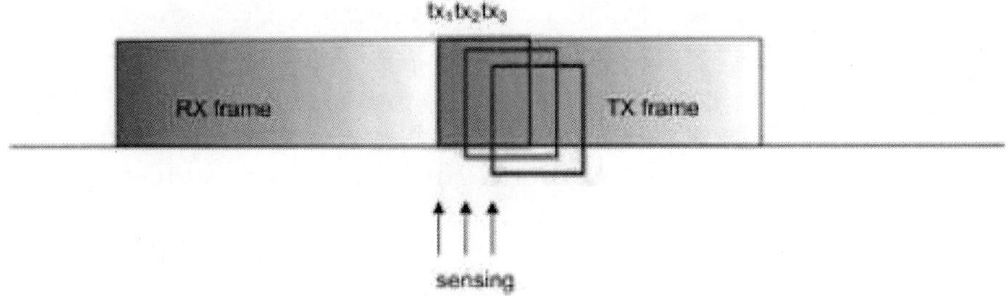

Figure. 9. Cluster redundancy management.

CONCLUSION

In this chapter were presented four algorithms whose aim is to manage packet relaying within an ad-hoc wireless network formed by nodes deployed over a strip. This algorithms are not exactly competing, instead they are focused on somewhat different scenarios which are related to different applications and hardware capabilities. In a field like the one of wireless sensor networks, where hardware constraints and application needs arise extremely challenging problems, taking every possible advantage is crucial. From this point of view it is clear that research have to develop new algorithms and protocols which exploit network topology. Algorithms for linear and strip topologies represent the first steps toward this new trend of topology-oriented protocols.

REFERENCES

1. Bhardwaj, M.; Garnett, T., Chandrakasan, A., "Upper bounds on the lifetime of sensor networks", Proceedings of IEEE international conference on communications(ICC 2001), pp. 785-790, Jun. 2001.
2. De Caneva, D.; Montessoro, P.L.; Pierattoni, D., "WiWi: Deterministic and Fault Tolerant Wireless Communication Over a Strip of Pervasive Devices", , Proceedings of Wireless Communications networking and Mobile Computings 2008 WiCOM 08 4th International Conference on, pp.1-5, 12-14 Oct. 2008.
3. Gao, J.; Zhang. L., "Load-balanced short-path routing in wireless networks", Parallel and Distributed Systems, IEEE Transactions on , vol.17, no.4, pp. 377-388, April 2006
4. Karveli, T.; Voulgaris, K.; Ghavami, M.; Aghvami, A.H., "A Collision-Free Scheduling Scheme for Sensor Networks Arranged in Linear Topologies and Using Directional Antennas", Proceedings of Sensor Technologies and Applications, 2008. SENSORCOMM '08. Second International Conference on, pp.18 - 22, 25-31 August 2008.
5. Kim, S.; Pakzad, S.; Culler, D.; Demmel, J.; Fenves, G.; Glaser, S; Turon, M, Health "Monitoring of Civil Infrastructures Using Wireless Sensor Networks", Proceedings of Information Processing in Sensor Networks, 2007. IPSN 2007. 6th International Symposium on, pp. 254-263, 25-27 April 2007.
6. Jawhar, I.; Mohamed, N.; Shuaib, K., "A framework for pipeline infrastructure monitoring using wireless sensor networks", Proceedings of Wireless Telecommunications Symposium, 2007. WTS 2007, pp. 1-7, 26-28 April 2007.
7. Li, J.; Blake C.; De Couto D.S.J.; Imm Lee, H.; Morris, R., "Capacity of Ad Hoc Wireless Networks", Proceedings of Mobile Computing and Networking, 7th ACM International Conference on, pp. 61-69, July 2001.
8. Min, R. & Chandrakasan, A., "Top Five Myths about the Energy Consumption of Wireless Communication", ACM SIGMOBILE Mobile Computing and Communications Review, Vol. 1, No. 2, 2003.
9. Zimmerling, M.; Dargie, W.; Reason, J.M., "Energy-Efficient Routing in Linear Wireless Sensor Networks", Proceedings of Mobile Adhoc and Sensor Systems, 2007. MASS 2007. IEEE International Conference on, pp. 1-3, 8-11 October 2007.

Chapter 5

RODENT SCOPE: A USER-CONFIGURABLE DIGITAL WIRELESS TELEMETRY SYSTEM FOR FREELY BEHAVING ANIMALS

David Ball[1*], Russell Kliese[2], Francois Windels[3], Christopher Nolan[3], Peter Stratton[3], Pankaj Sah[3], Janet Wiles[4]

[1]School of Electrical Engineering and Computer Science, Queensland University of Technology, Queensland, Australia,

[2]TOPTICA Photonics AG, Lochhamer Schlag 19,

Gra¨felfing, Germany,

[3]Queensland Brain Institute, The University of Queensland, Queensland, Australia,
[4]School of Information Technology and Electrical Engineering, The University of Queensland, Queensland, Australia

ABSTRACT

This paper describes the design and implementation of a wireless neural telemetry system that enables new experimental paradigms, such as neural recordings during rodent navigation in large outdoor environments. RoSco, short for Rodent Scope, is a small lightweight user-configurable module suitable for digital wireless recording from freely behaving small animals. Due to the digital transmission technology, RoSco has advantages over most other wireless modules of noise immunity and online user-configurable settings. RoSco digitally transmits entire neural waveforms for 14 of 16 channels at 20 kHz with 8-bit encoding which are streamed to the PC as standard USB audio packets. Up to 31 RoSco wireless modules can coexist in the same environment on non-overlapping independent channels. The design has spatial diversity reception via two antennas, which makes wireless communication resilient to fading and obstacles. In comparison with most existing wireless systems, this system has online user-selectable independent gain control of each channel in 8 factors from 500 to 32,000 times, two selectable ground references from a subset of channels, selectable channel grounding to disable noisy electrodes, and selectable bandwidth suitable for action potentials (300 Hz–3 kHz) and low frequency field potentials (4 Hz–3 kHz). Indoor and outdoor recordings taken from freely behaving rodents are shown to be comparable to a commercial wired system in sorting for neural populations. The module has low input referred noise, battery life of 1.5 hours and transmission losses of 0.1% up to a range of 10 m.

INTRODUCTION

Since the first recordings of single neurons in anaesthetised animals [1], [2], technological advances have enabled electrophysiological recordings with greater recording precision, less noise and in progressively more natural conditions. Extracellular recordings in animals, made using wire implants within the brain, detect changes in the extracellular voltage when neurons discharge action potentials (APs) or groups of neurons generate low frequency local field potentials (LFPs). Recording from multiple cells simultaneously and discriminating the activity of each cell over time requires high signal to noise recordings at high bandwidth. Moreover, for these recordings to be ecologically significant, animals need to be awake and behaving in natural environments. However, animals are typically tethered to a neural recording system, limiting research to within simple, small indoor environments.

Wireless neural telemetry systems have been in development for decades [3] and are typically designed with particular types of scientific research questions in mind, each with their own requirements and limitations. See [4] for a good review of recent advances and challenges. Our target research involves high fidelity neural recording as one or more rodents perform navigation tasks in outdoor environments. We have identified two complementary sets of criteria that an experimentally-useful wireless solution for outdoor recordings must satisfy: (1) verifiable fidelity - neural recordings must be high fidelity, quantify any interference, record entire waveforms, and permit offline verification of results; and (2) useability - to facilitate practical experiments the channels must be user-configurable, provide sufficient battery power for a complete recording session, and must not interfere with an animal's normal movements. No single rodent neural telemetry device, including currently available commercial solutions, addresses the criteria above including error quantification in noise-prone environments and configurable settings.

In this paper we describe a digital neural telemetry system, Rodent Scope (RoSco), that addresses these criteria. It records 16 channels of neural signals at 8 effective bits, and is a head-mounted module that weighs 22 g and is ideally suited to rodent experiments in outdoor-like environments. Due to the digital design, RoSco has verifiable fidelity and system parameters can be configured in real time. Prior to transmission each channel can be independently grounded to disable noisy electrodes, be amplified in 8 factors from 500 to 32,000 times, and can be filtered for either LFPs or APs. We present results from both our wireless system and an Axona tethered recording system. Both recordings were made in a single session from a freely behaving rat in a laboratory setting, demonstrating similar SNR between the systems and the same number of spike clusters. We also present results from our wireless module from a rat foraging in a 3.5×2.5 m caged outdoor arena. We have made the schematics [5] and firmware [6] for RoSco freely available online to allow other researchers to reuse or modify our design.

Verifiable fidelity is crucial for trust in novel experimental paradigms, and requires measuring the accuracy of the recorded neural signal. Popular commercial solutions such as the Triangle BioSystems W-Series are analog systems. To facilitate experiments in more natural conditions, analogue system require careful attention to remove any possible sources of radio interference that can compromise the integrity of the recording. Analog modules, though lighter and more power efficient than their digital counterparts, cannot quantify transmission noise. Since signal quality is a key requirement in novel experiment settings, we diverged from much of the wireless field in opting for digitisation before transmission. Digitisation also confers other advantages, such as higher spectral efficiency and bi-directional communication as discussed below.

Continual miniaturisation of analog-to-digital and digital transmission components has recently led to the development of a number of digital wireless neural telemetry systems [7]–[14]. The design of these systems varies considerably. Wireless systems can opt to reduce transmission bandwidth requirements by performing spike detection on the wireless module, transmitting only spike times and the spike waveform [10], [14]. However, this design decision can adversely impact later signal analysis. Spike detection is not a simple process as the threshold for detection of single units can affect the classification of these spikes and for many research purposes, complete source waveforms are required for offline analysis.

Usability is a design criterion that covers all aspects of the telemetry system that supports its ease of use in practical experiments by electrophysiologists, and is an essential factor in adoption of new technology. Existing tethered systems have a large set of features to support typical recording tasks. In particular, they allow online, real time configuration of the individual channels, previously recognised as important for a variety of tasks such as detecting and disabling noisy channels, selecting ground reference, and recording at maximum gain without saturation of the signals [7]. The RoSco system has what we consider the minimum set of the online configuration options, including:

- user-selectable independent gain control of each channel in 8 factors from 500 to 32,000 times,
- two selectable ground references from a subset of channels,
- selectable channel grounding to disable noisy electrodes, and
- selectable filters suitable for action (300 Hz–3 kHz) and low frequency (4 Hz–3 kHz) potentials.

Finally, any module must not unduly interfere with the mobility of the animal such that its range of normal behaviour is disrupted, and must operate for long enough to be of practical experimental use.

The device therefore is limited in weight and in its possible mounting configurations. Several existing wireless systems for rodent neural telemetry employ a combined head-stage and backpack, together weighing 50 g or more (excluding the weight of the microdrive used for the implants) [10], [12], [14], [15]. However, behaviour can be impacted by the body harness. Smaller and lighter devices can be mounted entirely on the head of the animal with much less impact on the mobility and range of movements of the animal.

System Description

This section begins with an overview of how the neural signal is processed followed by a description of each part in detail. A block diagram of the RoSco system is given in Figure 1.

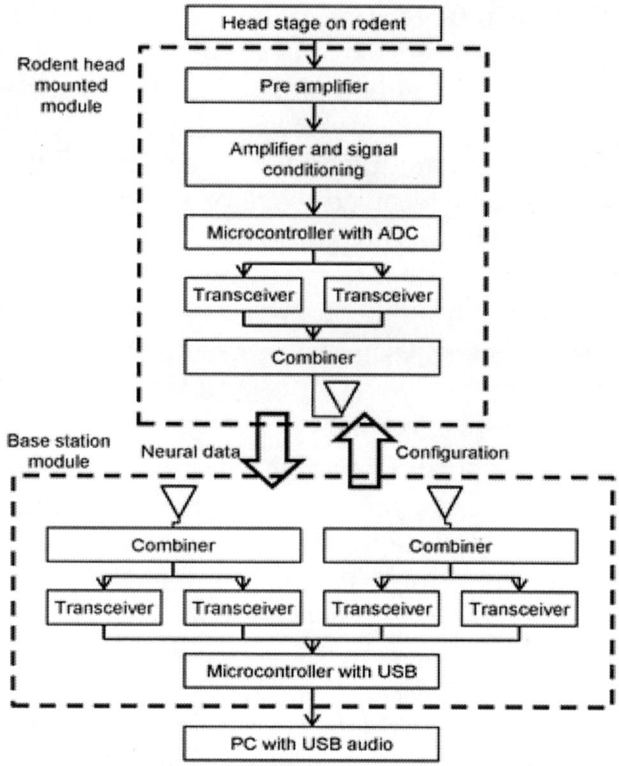

Figure 1. Block diagram of RoSco.

The head mounted module connects to the rodent's head stage. The base station module connects to a PC running USB audio software. Bidirectional communication allows transmission of neural data to the PC, and configuration data to the rat mounted module. The RoSco has one communication module which includes two transceivers that simultaneously operate in parallel to transmit the neural waveform through a single combiner and antenna. The base station module has diversity reception with two communication modules that simultaneously receive the same entire neural waveform in parallel. This provides redundancy and if data packets are missing from one stream the base station can still reconstruct the full neural waveform.

doi:10.1371/journal.pone.0089949.g001

The RoSco system acquires the signal from a head-stage with fixed electrode implants. This signal is first pre-amplified, and then filtered using a configurable band-pass filter to capture the band of interest. These pre-amplified signals are then further amplified and digitised. The digitised waveforms are wirelessly transmitted from the head mounted module to the base station. Finally, the base station re-assembles the received waveforms which are streamed to the PC formatted as USB audio packets [16]. To provide immunity to noise and fading the base station uses diversity reception where two pairs of transceivers simultaneously receive the neural data stream in parallel. This means that if data packets are missing from one stream the microcontroller can reconstruct the full neural waveform using the redundant data from the other stream.

The base station transmits neural data to the PC as a USB audio stream, thus no custom operating system drivers are required to operate the device. Module configuration is managed via the USB audio configuration settings. Where possible, RoSco configuration parameters are mapped to conceptually similar USB configuration parameters, such as RoSco gain to USB audio volume. Using a well-supported open standard such as USB audio, opens the potential for interoperability between telemetry systems and user interfaces giving researcher the freedom to customise recording software to fit into their particular experimental workflows.

The system is built entirely from commercially available components populated across four custom printed circuit boards

(PCBs). Figure 2 shows a picture of the head mounted module on a Long-Evans rat. The rat head mounted module is composed of three PCBs: a stack of two 35×35 mm PCBs and a smaller PCB that provides the unity gain amplifier stage. Power is provided by a 3.7 V 210 mAh lithium-ion cell weighing 3 g placed between the PCBs. Charging is facilitated by a standard micro-USB socket.

Figure 2. The RoSco head mounted module shown on a Long Evans rat.

The head mounted module consists of three PCBs and a small battery. While appearing relatively large in this photo, the head mounted module is light weight. The blue wire is the antenna. The red LEDs are for motion tracking using an overhead camera system.

doi:10.1371/journal.pone.0089949.g002

A common method to record the pose of an animal is to track the motion of LEDs. RoSco has four LEDs, one located on each edge of the top PCB (two green and two red). These LEDs can be individually enabled and disabled online.

Signal amplification and conditioning

Two frequency ranges are of particular interest in neural recordings: APs in the range 300–3000 Hz (as in [17]) and LFPs at lower frequencies. Filtering is used to remove noise outside the range of interest and amplification is used to boost the signal to a level that can be digitized. The filter's lower cut-off frequency is selectable to allow the acquisition of APs or LFPs. It is only necessary to reduce the lower cut-off frequency to acquire LFP signals because they have higher signal amplitudes [18]. Figure 3 shows a block diagram of one of the 16 analog amplification and signal conditioning stages used in the rat head-mounted module.

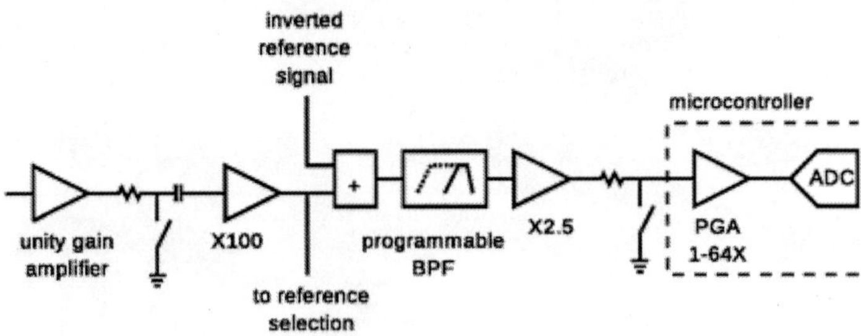

Figure 3. Diagram of one signal amplification and conditioning channel.

The diagram shows how the reference, band pass filter and gain can be configured. Note the programmable gain amplifier (PGA) is a part of the microcontroller saving a large number of external components and electronic complexity.

doi:10.1371/journal.pone.0089949.g003

The unity gain amplifier is implemented using a low-power, low-noise FET input op-amp (Linear Technology LTC6082) which provides a high input impedance to avoid loading the signal from the recording electrodes. Unity gain, rather than a higher gain, is used to cope with large DC offsets which can be of the order of 1 V [19]. To prevent crosstalk from a noisy input (which may occur when a recording electrode wire breaks) to other channels, the outputs of the unity gain amplifier can be disabled via a digitally controlled analogue switch. Broken wires are relatively common in chronic recordings so the ability to selectively disable channels is essential for practical studies.

The output of the unity gain amplifier is AC coupled to a 100× gain stage (Linear Technology LTC6082) which boosts the signal to provide noise immunity and immunity to cross-talk in subsequent stages. This stage, along with the unity gain amplifier stage, is in close proximity to the electrode connector to reduce the effects of external interference on the weak signals.

After the 100× gain stage a reference signal is added. The 16 input signals are divided into two banks of 8 channels. The reference signal can be chosen from any of the inputs within each bank. This reference signal is then inverted and added to all of the other signals in the bank.

The referenced signal is then passed through an op-amp based (Analog Devices AD8544) active bandpass filter which incorporates an additional 2.5× gain. The lower cut-off frequency has a first-order response and is programmable to cut-off at 4 or 300 Hz. A sharper upper cut-off frequency (third-order) at 3 kHz was implemented to minimize the signal power above 10 kHz that would lead to additional noise (signals above the Nyquist frequency cause aliasing). While it would be possible to design the cut-off frequency closer to 10 kHz, this would be at the expensive of a more complicated filter network with minimal benefit.

Programmable gain and digitisation

The rat head mounted module has a microcontroller (Atmel ATxmega256A3) with 16 analog to digital converter (ADC) and programmable gain amplifier (PGA) channels. The PGAs were important due to the limited bandwidth which only accommodates 8 bits sample resolution, and the high dynamic range of the neural signals. The high dynamic range is due to the variation in signal strength as the distance between the electrode and spiking neuron changes. The PGAs allows adjusting the neural signal amplitude to cover a large portion of the ADC's limited 8 bit sampling resolution while avoiding signal clipping. The overall gain levels provided are 500, 1000, 2000, 4000, 8000, 16000 and 32000. Lower values are typically used for LFPs and higher values (4000–16000) are typically used for APs. The ADC has a very low Differential Non-Linearity (DNL) of less than ±1 bit.

Wireless communication

A custom half-duplex wireless communication protocol streams the neural signal from the rat-mounted module to the base station, and sends configuration commands from the base station back to the rat-mounted module. Half-duplex was preferred over full-duplex communication as the configuration data sent back to the rat-mounted module is of very low bandwidth. The bandwidth required for 16 full signal waveforms at 20 kHz with an 8 bit resolution is 2.56 MB/s. Eight bit resolution is adequate for typical neural signals acquired using tetrodes *in vivo* where the signal to noise ratio is typically less than 10:1 as no additional useful information would be gained from higher resolution. In order to achieve the required bandwidth, a pair of highly integrated ultra-low power half-duplex transceivers (Nordic Semiconductor nRF24L01) communicate simultaneously on separate channels. The pair of transceivers provide a maximum user payload data rate of approximately 3.2 MB/s (after accounting for internal protocol overheads) in simplex operation.

The periodic switching between transmission and reception required to implement half-duplex communication further limits the available data throughput. Even though the configuration data sent back to the rat-mounted module from the PC only occupies one 32-byte packet, significant dead-time limits the total available bandwidth for the neural signal to a value slightly above the 2.56 MB/s required. The cycle time for the half-duplex system is 5 ms. This duration was chosen based on the maximum transmit duration of the Nordic transceivers of 4 ms, after which time the transmit frequency can drift out of tolerance. After the data for one block of 5 ms has been transmitted from the rat-mounted module (which takes approximately 4 ms), the transceivers then listen for commands from the base station until the next block of data is ready to be transmitted. The module configuration options – gain selection, reference channel selection, input grounding and tracking LED toggling – are sent wirelessly to the rat-mounted module from the base station. All configuration settings can be changed while recording is in progress so that the effect of the changes can be observed in real-time.

The radio-frequency output power from each transceiver is 1 mW at 2.4 GHz. On the rat-mounted module the two transceivers are connected to a power combiner to drive a single quarter-wave monopole antenna. The base station has two antennas each connected to their own transceiver pair to provide redundancy in receiving neural data through antenna diversity. This antenna diversity provides immunity to fading such as interference caused when signals arrive from multiple paths due to walls and obstacles.

The modules operate on the international 2.4–2.5 GHz unlicensed industrial, scientific and medical (ISM) band. This provides the two-fold benefits of a fixed band which reduces the need to support a wide range of carrier frequencies and an unlicensed band which avoids the costly approval process required for operation on other bands.

PC communication

The base station microcontroller (Atmel AT32UC3A3256) reformats the incoming packets from the transceivers into the USB audio protocol. The microcontroller also receives commands from the PC to vary USB audio properties, which are converted into appropriate RoSco commands and transmitted to the head-mounted module.

A digital phase-locked-loop (PLL) provides synchronisation between the head-mounted module and the base-station module. The PLL makes it possible to detect missing packets based on packet timing and to transmit commands to the rat module at the appropriate times. Missing packets are indicated in the USB audio stream using a reserved sample value. (Valid samples containing the reserved missing-packets value are replaced with the next-nearest value.)

Experimental Procedure

We ran a series of bench tests to measure the performance of the signal conditioning stage including: the bandwidth and gain response, the noise levels, the ground reference selection and the common mode rejection ratio (CMRR). The antenna radiation profile was measured in an antenna range with a vertically polarised horn antenna located in the far-field (~4 m from the module). The module was mounted on a rotary stage and set to transmit a continuous wave 2.45 GHz signal. The radiation pattern was acquired using a network analyser (HP8530A). The filter transfer functions, CMRR, and noise performance were measured using a National Instruments multifunction data acquisition card (NI PCI-6251, 16 bits/sample, 1 M samples/s). Following bench testing, we measured the wireless performance and battery life of the RoSco system.

For functional performance testing we obtained *in vivo* results from a rat implanted as discussed in the following section, recording using both the RoSco system and a commercially available wired system; the Axona dacqUSB Recording System. Ideally these two recordings would be performed simultaneously, however recording in this manner introduced interference in both systems. Data for these comparisons were therefore recorded consecutively, Axona immediately followed by RoSco. Finally, as an example of real-world use of the wireless system, we recorded from a freely behaving rodent in a large, roofed outdoor enclosure located in Brisbane, Australia (Figure 4).

Figure 4. Outdoor rodent test enclosure located in Brisbane, Australia.

The enclosure is 7×5 m, has a translucent roof and wire mesh walls. A rodent wearing RoSco can be seen towards the top of the arena.

doi:10.1371/journal.pone.0089949.g004

The Axona system was configured with 8000 gain, 16 bit at 48 kHz recording with the bandpass filter at 300–7000 Hz enabled. The RoSco system was configured for APs with 8000 gain, 8 bit at 20 kHz recording with a bandpass filter of 300–3000 Hz and LFPs with 1000 gain at 20 kHz recording with a bandpass filter of 3–3000 Hz.

Electrophysiology procedure

Two adult male Long-Evans rats (~370 g at surgery) were implanted with four tetrode Versadrives (Neuralynx) using standard surgical procedures as described in [17]. The electrodes were made of Nichrome (diameter 13 μm metal core; California Fine Wire) insulated with formvar. Electrode tips were electroplated with gold to achieve an impedance of 400–600 kΩ. The electrodes were implanted above the CA1 field of the left hippocampus. After a week of recovery each electrode was individually advanced along the dorso-ventral axis (60–80 μm) on a daily basis until neuronal activity was detected with a signal to noise ratio sufficient to allow for spike sorting. All indoor recordings were obtained while one animal was freely exploring a circular open-field (diameter: 0.8 m). The animals were then transferred to the outdoor facility and handled daily for 3 days. Following this period, recordings were obtained while the animals were foraging for one hour every day in a 3.5 m×2.5 m subsection of the outdoor recording enclosure and an elevated 0.8 m circular arena similar to that used indoors.

Ethics statement

This study was performed in strict accordance with the recommendations in the Australian National Health & Medical Research Council Guidelines to promote the wellbeing of animals used for scientific purposes. The protocols were approved by the animals ethic Committee of The University of Queensland (Permit Number: QBI 049 11 NHMRC ARC).

RESULTS

This section describes comprehensive results for the RoSco. Sections V.A to V.E provide electrical characteristics: amplifier transfer function, CMMR, noise, and wireless performance. Section V.F provides sample neural recordings and comparisons to the Axona wired system.

Filter and Gain Response

The signal conditioning stage described in III.A has a user-selectable filter and gain for LFP and AP recording. Figure 5 shows a measured transfer function for a representative electrode channel. The transfer function was measured using a frequency sweep technique [20]. The LFP and AP mode bandwidths are approximately 4–3000 Hz and 300–3000 Hz respectively. The output of this filter stage is further amplified in the microcontroller by a programmable gain amplifier.

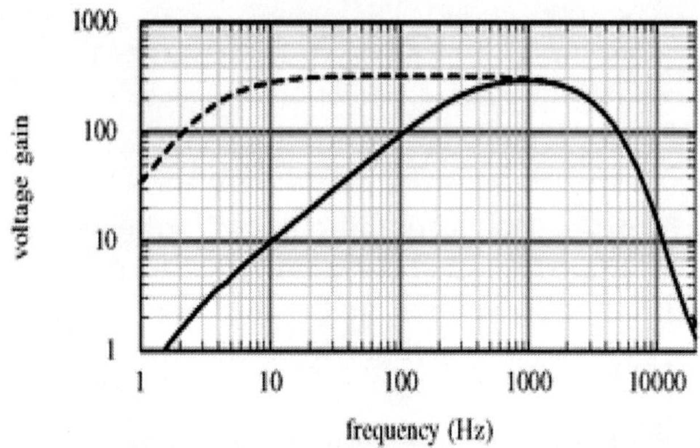

Figure 5. Measured transfer functions of the programmable bandpass filter.

The filter can be configured for both a narrow-band mode for AP recording (solid line) and a wide-band mode for LFP recording (broken line). The output of this filter stage is further amplified by a programmable gain amplifier.

doi:10.1371/journal.pone.0089949.g005

Common-mode rejection ratio

The CMRR characterises the rejection of signals common to the channel of interest and the reference channel. A CMRR plot for a representative channel is shown in Figure 6. The downward spike in the CMRR at 50 Hz is a measurement artefact caused by interference from the Australian 50 Hz mains power used in the measurement instrumentation. The CMRR is in excess of 1000× (60 dB) over most of the band of interest. The CMRR is primarily limited by resistor tolerances of 0.1%.

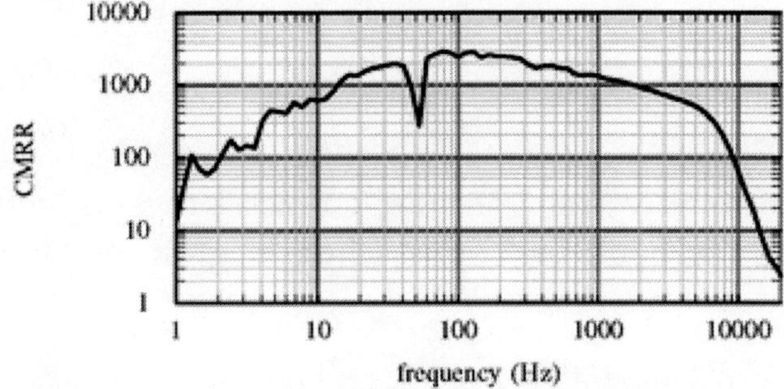

Figure 6. Measured common-mode rejection ratio.

The CMRR measured for a representative channel and the selected reference. The rejection ratio is high over most of the band of interest.

doi:10.1371/journal.pone.0089949.g006

Noise

Figure 7 shows the noise power spectral density measured on one of the channels with the programmable band-pass filter span set to the 4–3000 Hz range. The noise power is approximately 40 $nV/\sqrt{Hz}$ over the 300–3000 Hz pass-band used to record APs. This corresponds to an input referred noise of approximately 2.2 μV RMS. This noise level is insignificant compared to noise levels typically observed in neural signals acquired using tetrodes *in vivo*.

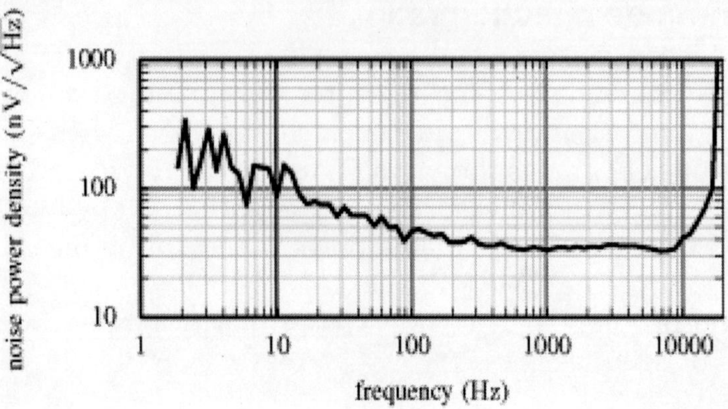

Figure 7. Measured noise power spectral density.

This figure shows the measured noise power spectral density with the programmable band-pass filter programmed with the wide pass-band.

doi:10.1371/journal.pone.0089949.g007

Wireless Performance

Antenna radiation profile

As shown in Figure 8, the radiation from the rat head mounted module is excellent in all directions. The measured profile shows that an omnidirectional radiation pattern has been achieved with some ripple caused by the off-center antenna positioning and the square ground-plane geometry formed by the upper PCB. This omnidirectional radiation pattern allows reliable wireless transmission regardless of the rodent's head direction relative to the base station.

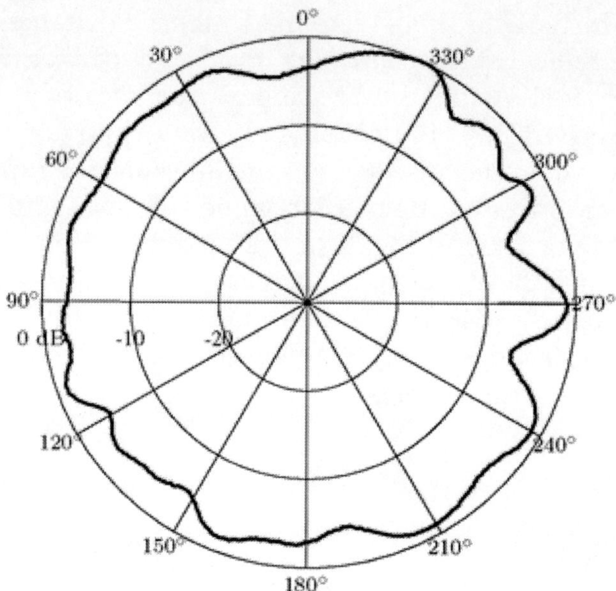

Figure 8. Antenna radiation profile.

Measured horizontal plane radiation profile of the rat head-mounted module (vertical polarization).

doi:10.1371/journal.pone.0089949.g008

The range of the system was evaluated with the RoSco placed at a number of distances, *d*, from the central point between two base station antennas placed 3 metres apart. This geometry is similar to the geometry that was used to record the neural signals for freely behaving rats in the outdoor arena. The omnidirectional base station antennas each had a gain of 5 dBi and were connected to the base station via 10 m cables which had a loss of 2.5 dB.

At each distance considered, the rate of missing packets was evaluated. Packets are automatically dropped by the transceivers when errors are detected, or when the signal is too weak. Errors are detected by first checking that the packet has a valid header, then by a CRC. The base station is phase-locked to the rat module, so the absence of packets is reliably noted. The percentage of lost packets was calculated by recording one second of data and counting the number of missing packet values compared to the total length of the recording. Thirty recordings were made at each distance in order to estimate the typical statistical range of missing packet rates. Figure 9 is a box plot showing the missing packet rate over a range of distances. (The whiskers indicate the minimum and maximum rates, the extent of the box corresponds to the interquartile range, and the horizontal bar indicated the median value.) The missing packet rate remains of the order of 0.1% from the zero distance position up to 10 m after which there is a sharp increase in the missing packet rate. This makes 10 m the practical limit for the system in the configuration tested, but longer range could be achieved with higher gain antennas and lower loss antenna cables.

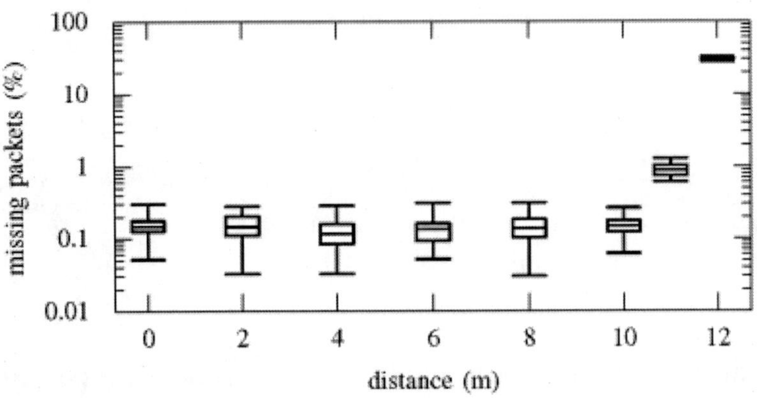

Figure 9. Wireless transmission error rate.

Box plot of the error rate versus the distance between the rat module and the midpoint between the antennas. The figure shows that the practical limit for this wireless system with the given antenna configuration is 10

doi:10.1371/journal.pone.0089949.g009

Antenna diversity

An example of the improvement in error rate that can be achieved using antenna diversity is given in Figure 10. The error rates were recorded under the same conditions as previously described at a fixed distance of 10 m, except that measurements were made with each of the antennas connected individually, then with both antennas connected. The median error rate drops from approximately 0.4–0.5% with one antenna connected (when diversity is effectively disabled) to less than 0.2% with both antennas connected.

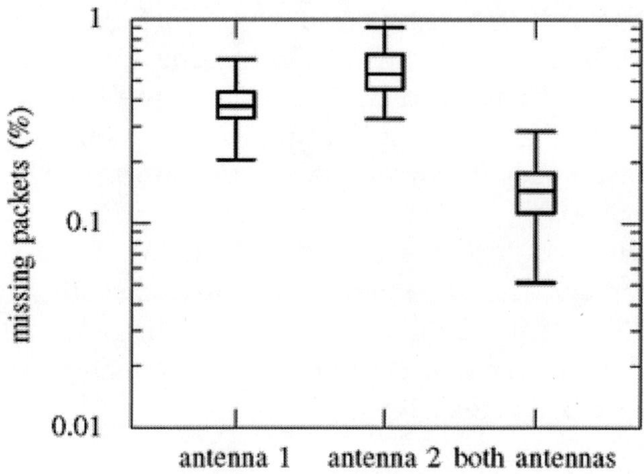

Figure 10. Wireless transmission error rate with diversity reception.

Box plot of the error rate at 10

doi:10.1371/journal.pone.0089949.g010

Battery Life

The battery life is approximately 1.5 hours which is sufficient for most experiments. It is important to note that battery life scales directly to the battery mass and size. For example, if the RoSco system needed to record for 3 hours then the mass would increase by 3 grams. Increasing the RoSco's mass by 3 grams would not significantly affect the rodent's mobility.

Neural Recording

The RMS SNR for detected spikes ranges from approximately 2.0 to

3.1 for RoSco, on average slightly greater than the RMS SNRs of 1.8–2.8 recorded from the Axona system. Examples of these raw signals are shown in Figure 11. After spike detection and clustering, similar units are visible on both the wired and wireless systems (Figure 12). These units are more similar across systems (Axona vs RoSco) than within systems (unit 1 vs unit 2), as measured by their correlations (Axona unit 1 to RoSco unit 1 = 0.851, Axona unit 2 to RoSco unit 2 = 0.855, Axona unit 1 to Axona unit 2 = 0.723, RoSco unit 1 to RoSco unit 2 = 0.722). The difference in the same units across systems (correlations of 0.85 instead of 1) is due to the lower filter cut-off in the Rosco system causing the spikes to be somewhat broader. The small differences in correlations between the same units across systems (0.855–0.851 = 0.004) and between different units in the same system (0.723–0.722 = 0.001) indicates that these differences are systematic and that the spike detection and sorting has not been affected by RoSco's lower bit depth and sampling rate; a result which is supported by theory (i.e. the Nyquist theorem and the required bit depth given the expected SNR).

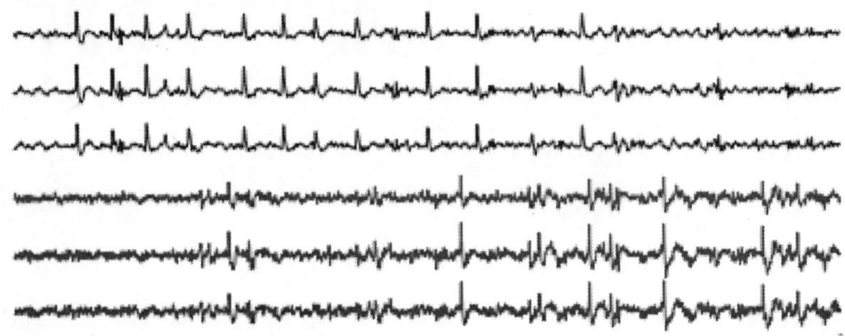

Figure 11. Sample neural waveforms from the RoSco and Axona system.

100(top three traces, blue) and Axona (bottom three traces, red). The RoSco signal has been digitally filtered with a high-order high-pass filter at 300 Hz. The increased detail of the Axona signal is due to the difference in sample rate: RoSco at 20 kHz and Axona at 48 kHz. Scale bars at bottom right are 10 ms and 50 μV for x-axis and y-axis respectively.

doi:10.1371/journal.pone.0089949.g011

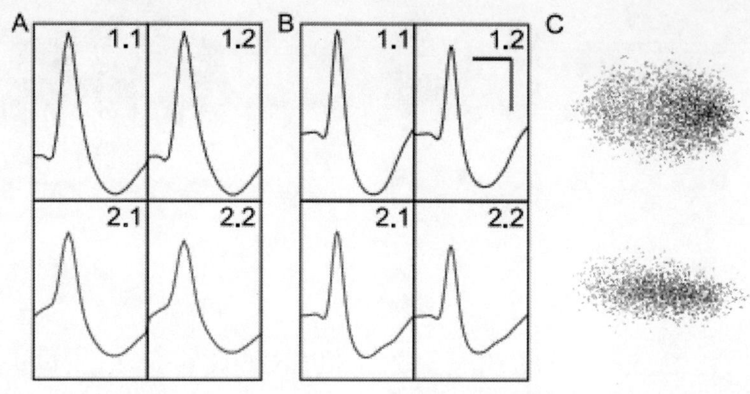

Figure 12. Comparison of characteristic unit spikes from the RoSco and Axona systems.

(a, b) Waveforms were isolated from two units (blue - unit 1; red - unit 2) using (a) RoSco (RMS SNR range 2.0–3.1) and (b) Axona (RMS SNR range 1.8–2.8). Scale bars at top right are 500 μs and 50 μV for x-axis and y-axis respectively. (c) Example dimensions from the unit clustering, for the two units in a and b, obtained using the WaveClus package for the RoSco (top) and Axona (bottom) data. Both dimensions are unitless feature space.

doi:10.1371/journal.pone.0089949.g012

Neural implants were in the dentate gyrus and the CA1 hippocampal subregion (see Section 4), where unit activity is often correlated with a 6–10 Hz oscillation in the LFP [21], [22]. Low frequencies are attenuated by the band-pass filter to only a fraction of one percent of the total signal power in the spike frequency range. The remaining low frequency power is sufficient to be detected and isolated with a low-pass filter, but is too small to have a material effect on spike detection. Analysis of the theta-band LFP shows that spikes are correlated with certain phases of theta (Figure 13). Note that all filters are applied bi-directionally so there is no net phase distortion.

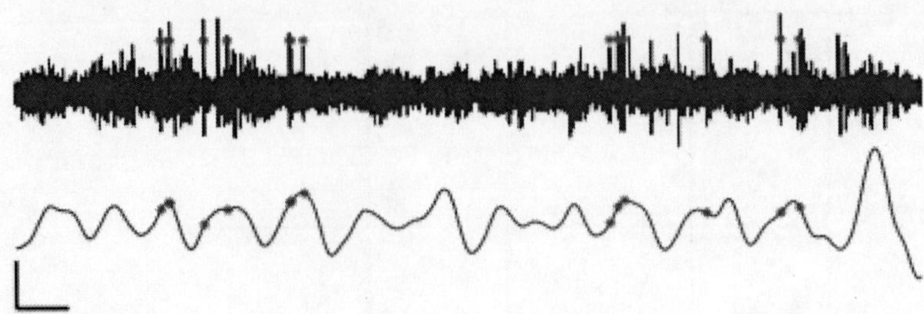

Figure 13. Electrical recording and identified spike times from two units.

One unit from the dentate gyrus is shown with red stars in: (a) the raw trace and (b) a theta-filtered 4-12 Hz LFP. Unit activity appears more often on particular phases of the theta cycle, as expected from many earlier hippocampal studies [19], [20]. Scale bars at bottom left are 100 ms for x-axis and 50 μV/250 μV for top/bottom y-axes. doi:10.1371/journal.pone.0089949.g013

One of the primary purposes of the wireless system is to allow animals to explore larger, more natural environments. Wireless samples were collected while a rat foraged in a subsection of a large 5 m×7 m roofed outdoor cage (shown in Figure 4), for approximately 45 minutes. Unit activity was similar to that collected indoors (Figure 14).

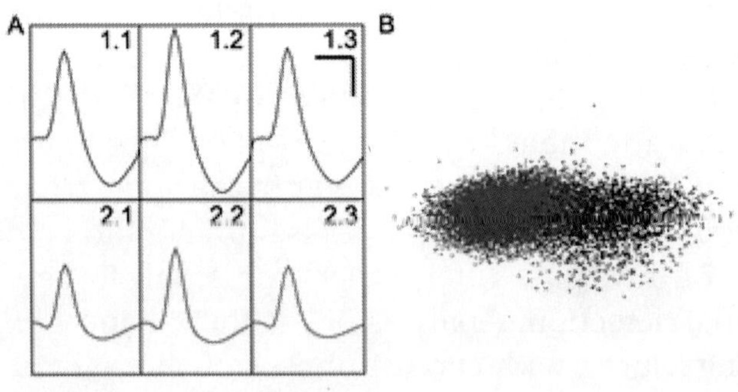

Figure 14. Characteristic unit spikes captured by RoSco in the outdoor enclosure.

The unit spikes were taken from three wires on one tetrode. (a) The characteristic spike waveforms of two units. SNRs (RMS) are between 1.3 and 2.8 depending on the unit and the wire. Scale bars in top right are 500 μs and 50 μV for x-axis and y-axis respectively. (b) Example dimensions from the unit clustering obtained using the WaveClus package. Both dimensions are unitless feature space.

doi:10.1371/journal.pone.0089949.g014

DISCUSSION

We have described the design and operation of RoSco, a wireless telemetry recording system designed for single unit and field potential neural recordings from freely moving animals. This telemetry system has quantifiable fidelity through the use of digital transmission, and has the minimal set of expected user-configurable options. We demonstrate that the recording, and signal-to-noise ratios and action potential traces are comparable to an existing commercial wired system. This telemetry system extends current available tools available for experimental neuroscience into new areas, allowing recording and tracking of rodent navigation in natural outdoor environments.

The design of small lightweight recording systems for rodent studies required several tradeoffs. See Table 1 for a comparison between RoSco and state-of-the-art existing wireless solutions. There are many other analog wireless systems, including several commercial solutions, however they have similar performance to the analog wireless modules shown in the table. The choice between analog or digital design is one of the most fundamental decisions for a wireless system. It affects all other aspects of the design, including the size, weight, and power requirements of the device, the ability to control the device remotely, which affects user configuration, and the ability to quantify the quality of the transmitted signal.

Table 1. Comparison between RoSco and existing systems.

doi:10.1371/journal.pone.0089949.t001

	RoSco	Fan et al.	Szuts et al.	HermesD*
Transmitter type	Digital	Analogue	Analogue	Digital
Battery life	1.5 hrs	6 hrs	6 hrs	Not reported
Bandwidth	4–3000 Hz or 300–3000 Hz	0.8–7000 Hz	10–4000 Hz	Not reported
Size	35×35×35 mm	2.2 cm^3	100 cm^3	38×38×51 mm
Mass	22 g	4.5 g	52 g	Not reported
Gain	500–32,000×	800×	1800×	Not reported
Configurable gain	7 options	No	No	No
Input referred noise	2.2 μV RMS	10 μV RMS	Not reported	Not reported
Range	10 m	4 m	60 m	>20 m
Channels	14/16 channels @ 20 kHz @ 8 bit OR 7/8 channels @ 40 kHz @ 8 bit	Variable	64 channels @ 20 kHz	32 channels @ 30 kHz @ 12 bit

Analog recordings are familiar to all electrophysiologists, since most commercial neural recording systems are wired and transmit the neural signals over the tethered link in analog form (e.g. Axona, Plexon, Neuralynx). Similar to wired systems, the majority of wireless systems use analog transmission. Such systems are smaller and lighter than comparable digital systems and power consumption is significantly lower for equivalent data transmission, as demonstrated in existing commercial analog wireless system solutions [15], [23]. Transmission fidelity in such analog systems is typically taken for granted and not quantified, since recordings are made in shielded rooms with careful control of all sources of RF noise, enabling high SNR. However, even in wired systems in such environments, noise can be introduced through the tether itself, which can act as an antenna, or the commutator that enables the animal to move without tangling the cable.

Outside shielded environments, RF noise cannot be controlled and for signals to be trusted, signal quality needs to be monitored as a matter of routine. None of the analog systems published to date (wired or wireless) have methods for quantifying the fidelity of the signals as they are transmitted.

Our decision to digitize before transmission followed directly from the requirement that RoSco be functional in an uncontrolled outdoor-like environment, where interference is prevalent, and needs to be routinely identified and managed. RoSco's digital system enables transmission without error under ideal conditions, and with routine reporting of dropped packets when noise interferes with signal transmission. Another design issue that impacts on confidence in signal quality is whether spikes are processed on the headstage prior to transmission or whether full waveforms are transmitted allowing offline analysis. While primitive spike detection can be achieved using a manual thresholding technique, current leading automatic detection algorithms rely on long-term signal characteristics, requiring the full waveforms in post-processing [24]. Full waveforms require more bandwidth, however they are essential for the confidence that offline computation provides in particular while recording in new experimental paradigms.

Per-channel bandwidth is determined by the sampling rate and the bit-depth. Theoretically, the required sampling rate is determined by the high frequency cut-off of the signal. The Nyquist theorem defines that the sampling rate with perfect filters and transformations needs only be twice the maximum frequency [25]. In practice filters are not perfect and higher sampling rates are required to ensure aliased signals are acceptably small. The required bit-depth is dependent on the signal-to-noise ratio of the signal. In the case of action potentials, the signal is the action potential waveform, and the noise is all other electrical activity.

Theoretical data transmission rates of existing systems range from a few hundred Kbps [9] to 90 Mbps [11], though experimentally-verified implementations to date have been limited to 24 Mbps [8]. Designs such as [4] were intended to enable full configurability of these factors, albeit with increased hardware complexity. RoSco's setting of 20 kHz at 8 bits per sample is sufficient for its filter cut-offs and the expected signal to noise ratio of APs. Beyond this theoretical argument, 48 kHz is a typically sampling frequency of wired systems. For comparison studies, RoSco provides a setting to double the sampling rate to 40 kHz at the cost of halving the number of recorded channels. However in preliminary studies, spike sorting with the 48 kHz signal did not produce any noticeable benefit to the 20 kHz recordings. Recently, Multichannel Systems have released the W-System range of digital wireless neural recording systems, although without the range of configurable settings available in our system.

The useability set of design decisions for RoSco impacts on practical experiments, in particular, the configurability of the system.

Commercial wired systems support a high level of reconfiguration needed for extended studies using animals with chronically implanted electrodes. A wire in a region with little activity is typically selected as a reference for the other wires, but the reference can change over time, as electrodes can move with respect to the cells they record, requiring higher or lower levels of gain, with new cells appearing and previously recorded ones disappearing and disabling needed for broken wires.

Online configuration is supported in RoSco. Reconfiguration of parameter settings after the head stage has been attached to the animal enables online control of settings for gain, bandwidth, grounding, and reference. In addition four LEDs on the headstage can be individually configured, enabling tracking and also wireless control of synchronization signals during an experiment. These features are particularly useful for practical experiments, making configuration of the module efficient and enabling adjustment to the neural conditions in the moment. No other system (digital or analog) matches the breadth of online configuration supported by RoSco. In fact, most analog systems are limited to simplex communication that cannot support online configuration at all.

In summary, criteria for wireless telemetry systems result in a spectrum of designs: RoSco is a digital system enabling quantifiable high fidelity, and user configuration. RoSco's module is heavier than analog systems but still of suitable size and mass for mounting on the head of rat. A single battery provides 1.5 hours of operation, sufficient for outdoor foraging experiments. Additional batteries can be added with linear increase in performance. For example, recording time can be increased to three hours by using two batteries, and would increase the mass to 25 g and the height of the head mount by 6 mm. This would still be suitable for use on a rodent's head.

The reported 10 m range for 0.1% loss is sufficient for a wide range of experiments in large indoor and outdoor environments. The antenna was designed for general purpose use and hence has an omni-directional radiation pattern. It proved effective for the studies in this paper and will be used in future large arena foraging studies. However, it is important to note the radial range is dependent on the antenna design. A different antenna design, with higher gain or different radiation profiles, could extend the range further.

Natural social interactions require animals to have multiple degrees of freedom of movement which are impossible with tethered systems. For future studies involving social interactions, up to 31 RoSco systems can be used simultaneously, each controlled by an independent interface.

The RoSco is designed for use as part of a larger system that records from multiple rodents and tracks their motion. Motion tracking is via LEDs on the module and an overhead camera system. The base station transmits the neural waveform in the standard USB audio protocol that can use standard methods and containers for combining and playing multiple sources of audio and video, such as for movies. These methods include the ability to maintain synchronisation of the streams during data loss.

CONCLUSION

Wireless telemetry systems are as varied as the empirical studies used to investigate neural signals. The RoSco telemetry system was specifically designed for outdoor rodent navigation and behavioural studies, with primary design criteria being quantifiable fidelity and usability. The system has been demonstrated to be empirically useful in animal studies, with 8 bit, 20 kHz signals successfully providing full waveform recordings amenable to spike sorting.

Digital transmission in large scale environments resulted in low noise over a 10 metre range. The small head mounted module was well-tolerated by the animals, enabling freedom of movement beyond anything possible with a tethered system, with battery life enabling experiments to extend over 1.5 hours. The user-configurable settings for remote gain control, LFP filtering, reference selection and channel muting enabled an experimental workflow similar to commercial wired systems.

Wireless systems will continue to expand the range of environments in which recordings can be made, and extend the possibilities for studies in natural and enriched environments. RoSco provides a useful addition to the current range of wireless systems, providing new capabilities compared to published and commercially available modules and enabling new science in the field of small animal behaviour.

AUTHOR CONTRIBUTIONS

Conceived and designed the experiments: DB RK FW CN JW. Performed the experiments: RK FW CN. Analyzed the data: RK CN P. Stratton. Contributed reagents/materials/analysis tools: FW P. Sah. Wrote the paper: DB RK FW CN JW.

REFERENCES

1. Renshaw B, Forbes A, Morison BR (1940) Activity of Isocortex and Hippocampus: Electrical Studies with Micro-Electrodes. Journal of Neurophysiology 3: 74–105.
2. Hubel DH, Wiesel TN (1959) Receptive fields of single neurones in the cat's striate cortex. The Journal of Physiology 148: 574–591.
3. kutt HR, Beschle RG, Moulton DG, Koella WP (1967) New subminiature amplifier-transmitters for telemetering biopotentials. Electroencephalography and Clinical Neurophysiology 22: 275–277. doi: 10.1016/0013-4694(67)90234-9
4. Gosselin B (2011) Recent Advances in Neural Recording Microsystems. Sensors 11: 4572–4597. doi: 10.3390/s110504572
5. Kliese R, Ball D (2013) RoSco Schematics. figshare (http://dx.doi.org/10.6084/m9.figshare.881900).
6. Kliese R, Ball D (2013) RoSco Firmware and Documents. figshare (http://dx.doi.org/10.6084/m9.figshare.881900).
7. Fenton AA, Jeffery KJ, Donnett JG, Vertes RP, Stackman J (2011) Neural Recording Using Digital Telemetry. Electrophysiological Recording Techniques: Humana Press. pp. 77–101.
8. Miranda H, Gilja V, Chestek CA, Shenoy KV, Meng TH (2010) HermesD: A High-Rate Long-Range Wireless Transmission System for Simultaneous Multichannel Neural Recording Applications. IEEE Transactions on Biomedical Circuits and Systems 4: 181–191. doi: 10.1109/tbcas.2010.2044573
9. Chestek CA, Gilja V, Nuyujukian P, Kier RJ, Solzbacher F, et al. (2009) HermesC: Low-Power Wireless Neural Recording System for Freely Moving Primates. IEEE Transactions on Neural Systems and Rehabilitation Engineering 17: 330–338. doi: 10.1109/tnsre.2009.2023293
10. Hampson RE, Collins V, Deadwyler SA (2009) A wireless recording system that utilizes Bluetooth technology to transmit neural activity

in freely moving animals. Journal of Neuroscience Methods 182: 195–204. doi: 10.1016/j.jneumeth.2009.06.007

11. Chae MS, Yang Z, Yuce MR, Hoang L, Liu W (2009) A 128-Channel 6 mW Wireless Neural Recording IC With Spike Feature Extraction and UWB Transmitter. IEEE Transactions on Neural Systems and Rehabilitation Engineering 17: 312–321. doi: 10.1109/tnsre.2009.2021607
12. Chen H-Y, Wu J-S, Hyland B, Lu X-D, Chen J (2008) A low noise remotely controllable wireless telemetry system for single-unit recording in rats navigating in a vertical maze. Medical and Biological Engineering and Computing 46: 833–839. doi: 10.1007/s11517-008-0355-6
13. Harrison RR, Kier RJ, Greger B, Solzbacher F, Chestek CA, et al.. (2008) Wireless neural signal acquisition with single low-power integrated circuit; May. pp. 1748–1751.
14. Farshchi S, Pesterev A, Guenterberg E, Mody I, Judy JW (2007) An Embedded System Architecture for Wireless Neural Recording; May. pp. 327–332.
15. Szuts TA, Fadeyev V, Kachiguine S, Sher A, Grivich MV, et al. (2011) A wireless multi-channel neural amplifier for freely moving animals. Nature Neuroscience 14: 263–269. doi: 10.1038/nn.2730
16. Knapen G (1997) Universal Serial Bus Device Class Definition for Audio Devices. USB Implementers Forum.
17. Windels F, Kiyatkin EA (2006) General anesthesia as a factor affecting impulse activity and neuronal responses to putative neurotransmitters. Brain Research 1086: 104–116. doi: 10.1016/j.brainres.2006.02.064
18. Baranauskas G, Maggiolini E, Vato A, Angotzi G, Bonfanti A, et al. (2012) Origins of 1/f2 scaling in the power spectrum of intracortical local field potential. Journal of Neurophysiology 107: 984–994. doi: 10.1152/jn.00470.2011
19. Bashirullah R, Harris JG, Sanchez JC, Nishida T, Principe JC (2007) Florida Wireless Implantable Recording Electrodes (FWIRE) for Brain Machine Interfaces. pp. 2084–2087.
20. Muller S, Massarani P (2001) Transfer-Function Measurement with Sweeps. J Audio Eng Soc 49: 443–471.
21. O'Keefe J, Recce ML (1993) Phase relationship between hippocampal place units and the EEG theta rhythm. Hippocampus 3: 317–330. doi: 10.1002/hipo.450030307
22. Skaggs WE, McNaughton, Bruce L, Wilson MA, Barnes CA (1996) Theta phase precession in hippocampal neuronal populations and the compression of temporal sequences. Hippocampus 6: 149–172. doi:

10.1002/(sici)1098-1063(1996)6:2<149::aid-hipo6>3.0.co;2-k

23. Fan D, Rich D, Holtzman T, Ruther P, Dalley JW, et al. (2011) A Wireless Multi-Channel Recording System for Freely Behaving Mice and Rats. PLoS ONE 6: e22033. doi: 10.1371/journal.pone.0022033

24. Quiroga RQ, Nadasdy Z, Ben-Shaul Y (2004) Unsupervised Spike Detection and Sorting with Wavelets and Superparamagnetic Clustering. Neural Computation 16: 1661–1687. doi: 10.1162/089976604774201631

25. Nyquist H (1928) Certain Topics in Telegraph Transmission Theory. Transactions of the American Institute of Electrical Engineers 47: 617–644. doi: 10.1109/t-aiee.1928.5055024

Chapter 6

CALL ADMISSION CONTROL IN MOBILE AND WIRELESS NETWORKS

Georgios I. Tsiropoulos, Dimitrios G. Stratogiannis and Eirini Eleni

Tsiropoulou National University of Athens Greece

INTRODUCTION

The increasing demand for advanced multimedia services combined with the resource constraints of the wireless networks indicate the need of efficient admission control schemes to achieve a competent resource management combined with adequate Quality of Service (QoS) levels for end users. QoS provision in wireless networks is closely related to the exploitation of available network resources and the maximization of the number of users. Call Admission Control (CAC) is one of the key issues in wireless mobile communications, concentrating great interest in research work about QoS. CAC algorithms are employed to ensure that the admission of a new call into a resource limited network does not violate the Service Level Agreements (SLAs) concerning ongoing calls.

CAC schemes for wireless networks have been widely studied under different network architectures and network administrator policies. The objectives of the chapter are to present thoroughly the mainconcepts of CAC design and QoS provision in wireless and mobile networks. The study will focus on system and traffic analysis employed tomodel the complexity of communication traffic. In next generation networks where multiple Service Classes (SCs) with different QoS characteristics are supported, the various call types are classified into SCs with precise characteristics and QoS demands. Each SC call is treated differently depending on the criteria set accordingto the operating principles adopted for the admission procedure. CAC schemes handle multiple call stream flows corresponding to different priority levels providing an efficient mechanism to deal with different QoS necessities. The demanding environment of wireless communications poses numerous challenges in CAC design concerning the resource constraints, the connection quality, QoS requirements, SC prioritization, mobility characteristics and revenueoptimization. Another critical issue in admission control is the performance evaluation, through appropriate metrics of the proposed schemes to assess the provided QoS. The metric studied most is Call Blocking Probability (CBP).

Finally,the last section of the chapter provides abroad classification of different design approaches and strategies considered for efficient admission control. CAC schemes are classified upon differentrationales, used to apply call admission policy, aiding to an elucidatorysynopsis of CAC under different network parameters. The majority of CAC schemes base their admission criteria on an efficient resource management, accounted for either in terms of channels or bandwidth units. The methods proposed usually set thresholds related to the desirable QoS for high priority SCs and handoff calls. Other CAC schemes examine Signal to Noise Ratio (SNR) levels to determine an admission criterion satisfying the QoS demands of end users. Such schemes have to deal with propagation and mobility issues. Under high traffic network conditions, an efficiency enhancing module may be incorporated into the CAC schemes employed, renegotiating the resource allocation of ongoing calls. Through QoS re-negotiation and resource re-allocation, available resources can be retrieved and managed dynamically to serve a high priority SC call request.

CALL ADMISSION CONTROL IN MOBILE AND WIRELESS COMMUNICATION

Call Admission Control (Definition and Operating Principle)

During the last decades the wireless communication networks users have been rapidly increased along with their demand for new multimedia services. The need for high speed communications is in contrast to the scarce spectrum resources allocated for wireless systems in international organizations. Therefore, a proficient radio resource management (RRM) is vital, to allot the existing network resources among contenting users, taking into consideration their needs and respective priorities as to provide them with the required QoS. Moreindetail, RRM functionality intents to improve system performance by maximizing the overall system capacity in the wireless network preserving at the same time the QoS characteristics of mobile users.

A crucial RRM mechanism essential for QoS provision applied on wireless networks is CAC. The key idea of Admission Control (AC) is to ensure the QoS of individual connections by appropriately managing the network resources. The main characteristics that an efficient AC policy should provide are the following: a) establish a robust priority assigning mechanism for hand off calls and calls of different SCs, b) exhibit a low CBP, c) allocate resources fairly, d) achieve a high network throughput and e) avoid congestion. Moreover, a proficient CAC scheme should avoid congestion and system outages due to overloading. The admission of anew call, according to the CACscheme employed, should not violate the SLAsof ongoing calls. Admission decision is based on not only the available network resources but also the QoS requirements of the requesting and ongoing users. Hence, the decision should be taken considering multiple parameters such as the network characteristics, the service type, user mobility and the network conditions. In the case that the decision is positive, an appropriate quantityof networkresources should be reserved to maintain the QoS of the new user. Thus, CACis strictlyrelated to resource allocation, channel and base station assignment,power control and resource reservation.

CAC problem can be considered as a multi-objective optimization problem that is maximizing the efficiency, utility and revenue of the network while at the same time complying with the users QoS requirements. The latter are provided by the users SLAs agreements. The admission criteria employed in the decision making part of the CAC scheme could be the Signal-to Interference Ratio (SIR), the ratio of bit energy to interference density ratio (Eb/Io), the Bit Error Rate (BER),the Call Dropping Probability (CDP), the QoS at connection level as determined by the data rate and the delay bound. For instance, a CAC scheme may minimize the CBP by admitting a large number of call requests, provided that the BER violation probability does not exceed a satisfactory level £1 (Wu, 2005).

$$\Pr\{BER > BER_{thr}\} \leq \varepsilon_1 ,$$

where BER the denotes the BER threshold. In the case that CBP values are available the above constraint can be rewritten as

$$CBP \leq \varepsilon_2 .$$

Generally,CACschemes can be designed to provide different priority levels which correspond to the various SCs supported by the network.

Necessity for Call Admission ControlAnd Quality of Service Provision

CAC algorithms are employed to ensure that the admission of a new call into a resource constrained network does not violate the SLAs of ongoing users. To decide whether to admit a new call or not, many factors are taken into consideration, most of them contradictory such as optimizing the use of radio resources, maximizing revenue, providing fairness, etc. Thus, CAC constitutes a mechanism which is used to determine the number of call connections so that different priorities are given among users with different QoS characteristics, network utilization is increased and congestion is prevented. Thus, when a call request from a mobile user is initiated, it may be accepted or blocked. The blocking probability, defined as the probability that a new call request is denied service by the network is called

CBP and is subjected to the relevant decision made by the CAC schemeemployed. Efficient CACpolicies should achieve low CBPs.

Implementing practical CAC schemes is difficult; because traffic incommunication networks is inherently chaotic and busty, and traffic bursts are extremely difficultto be predicted. CAC schemes in wireless networks are complicated due to variable link quality and to users mobility. In particular, a call admitted in a certain cell may have to be handed off to a neighboring cell due to the users' mobility. The main consideration in handoff procedures is to preserve the continuity of the call while at the same time offering at least the minimum acceptable QoS.During a call,amobileusermaycr ossseveralcell boundaries, thus requiring a corresponding number of successful handoffs. With regard to the handoff process, the new cell may not have any available resources to serve a handoff call, resulting in handoff failure commonly knownas call dropping. In the literature, the probability that an ongoing call is terminated (dropped) is called CDP. It is widely accepted that users are more annoyed by call dropping than by call blocking; thus, efficient CAC schemes should keep CDPas low as possible. A simple wayimplemented in most CAC schemes, to achieve low CDP levels, is to assign higher priorities to handoff calls compared to new calls. Therefore, the admission criteria for new and handoff calls are different.

With regard to the number of active connections preserved, handoffschemes can be classified into hard handoff and soft handoff schemes. In the hard handoff schemes, a mobile terminal releases the channel from the original cell before its connection to the new Base Station (BS) is accomplished. Thus, a mobile terminal is connected to one BS at a time. In this case, the call is short-interrupted during the process of changing BS. In hard handoff schemes two waysleading to a handoff failure exist. The first is related to the waythe handoff is implemented since if the old radio link is released before the network completes the assignment of a new channel, the call is dropped. This demonstrates the susceptibility of hard handoff schemes to the linktransfer time. The second waymay be attributed to the resource allocation mechanism since, if there are no channels available in the new cell, then the handoff call is forced-terminated.

In soft handoff schemes, the handoff process is triggered at the boundaries between neighboring cells. Ascells in wirelesssystems overlapto assure complete coverage, the boundary areas may be served by more than one BS. Thus during the handoff, a mobile terminal may communicate with multiple BSs simultaneously, employing different radio links to achieve the communication with the network. When a channel from a BS is successfully assigned to a mobile terminal according to the specific handoff scheme QoS parameters, its originally occupied channels are released. In this case, the handoff procedure is insensitive to the duration of the handoff process, resulting in lower CDP compared to hard handoff schemes.

CAC schemes operate in real-time; hence, the algorithm used should be executed very fast. Moreover, the exact situation concerning the available resources at the BSs controller should be known as input data to the CAC algorithm. The design and implementation of a CAC scheme should be done very carefully aiming at minimizing false rejections and false admissions. A false rejection occurs when a call is rejected though the network has enough resources to serve it. In this case, optimization of network resources is not achieved, capacity is wasted and the operator's revenue is not maximized. On the other hand, a false admission occurs when a call request is accepted even if there are no available resources. In this case, the QoS level is not guaranteed and the CDP is increased, resulting in degradation of users satisfaction.

Challenges In Call Admission Control Design

The basic operation of CACschemes is to decide whether a call should be admitted by the network or not. This decision is based on several criteria which are related to the network parameters and to the specific QoS characteristics of the call request. Althoughthe QoS characteristics of the call are a priori determined, the network parameters are variable and adjustableintime.Thus,the CAC scheme employed should as sure that the QoS characteristics of ongoing calls willnot be violated throughout their whole duration. The factors employed in CAC schemes are presented below:

- Networkload/resources:The limited network resources constitute a criticalfactor in CACdesign. CACschemes based on this criterion must know the resources available in each cell before the decision is taken. In this case, the network load after the admission of a new call must be predicted; if the predicted network load remains below a certain threshold, the new is admitted; otherwise, it is blocked. Ashandoff calls are treated differentlyby most CAC schemes, a set of channels may be reserved at each cell for handoff calls. Therefore, the admission of a new call is more difficult,as the respective thresholdemployedinmost CAC schemes islower,than the relevantthresholdof handoff calls. These CACschemes are widely known as Guard Channel (GC) schemes.

- Connection/link quality: Link quality is an essential parameter that should be taken into account whendesigning CACin interference-limited wirelessnetworks.Linkquality refers to the radio linkbetween the user terminal and the BS. For its estimation,the signal strength received at a mobile terminal and the interference caused to this link by other mobile terminals in the area are used. Thus, CACschemes admit a new call if they can maintain the link quality of the admitted calls above a certain threshold. Otherwise, if the admission of a new call willresult in an unacceptable deterioration of the link quality, the call is rejected. CAC schemes based on link quality usuallyemploy the SIRor the Signal-to-Noise-plus-Interference Ratio (SNIR) as an admission criterion; hence, they are called SIR or SNIR-based schemes.
- QoS requirements/call context: Since users may request services characterized by different QoS requirement with regard to mean throughput, mean delay, BER and bandwidth demands, the call requests are classified into various SCs. For every SC call request different admission criteria can be employed taking into consideration the respective QoS constraints and the network resources available. Thus, CAC schemes can be classified with regard to the number of the SCs supported. CAC scheme for single SC constituted a simple and appropriate model for first and second generation (2G) wireless networks, as they were mainly destined for voice services. The growing need for new servicescombined withthe diffusion of new technologies, suchas the 2.5 and3G networks and also the Next Generation Networks (NGN), indicated the need to support multiple SCs with multimedia traffic and enhanced QoS characteristics. Thus, during the last decade, advanced CAC schemes supporting multiple SCs were introduced,

classifying stream flows and call requests into different SC types according to their QoS characteristics. CAC design for multipleSCs is more challenging since different CAC criteria are employed for the SCs supported often resulting in high complexity and difficulties considering their implementation in practice.

- Call priority/SC prioritization:This CAC criterion is solely related to SC prioritization. Assigning higher priority to some SCs over the rest is a common technique in CAC schemes for multiple SC networks.In particular,it is widely accepted that Real Time (RT) services have higher priority over Non-Real Time (NRT) ones, e.g. a voice call is considered of higher priority compared to internet browsing. Moreover, different priorities can be assigned even within the same SC reflecting the differentiation among different user classes, stemming from subscription fee policy. Also, higher priorities are assigned to handoff calls or to calls related to emergency services. Differentpriority levels reflect different CAC criteria, which are more strict for low priority SC calls and relaxed for high priority ones. Prioritization schemes can be implemented mainly through: channel borrowing, queuing and reservation schemes. In channel borrowing schemes, if a cell has all its channelsreserved, it can borrow channels from neighboring cells to serve high priority SC calls. In queuing schemes, if a cell has all its resources occupied, a high priority call request is set into a queue until resources, sufficient to accommodate the call request are released in the cell,. Queuing schemes can be applied either to high prioritycall requests or to all incoming call requests (regardless of their priority).In the latter case their position into the queue is adjusted according to the respective requests priority.On the other hand, the reservation schemes were first used to give priority to handoff calls by permanently reserving on a permanent basis a number of channels exclusivelyfor serving handoff requests. These schemes havebeen extended to supportmultipleSCsbyassigning different priority levels through reserving channels for high priority SC calls.
- User's mobility characteristics: Users mobility is a critical factor in wireless networks as users travel across multiple cells; thus, the traffic in the cells is variable and it cannot

be precisely predicted as an active terminal may move from one cell to a neighboring one, resulting in calls handoff. If a handoff call cannot be served by the BS of the new cell, it is droppedincreasingthecalldroppingrate. Sinceusersaremoresensitivetocall dropping than to call blocking, CAC schemes are employed to reduce the handoff failureprobability. Most schemes in the literature assign higher priorities to handoff calls resulting in less strict admission conditions for the admission of handoff calls. These schemes are the same with the prioritizationschemes mentioned above with the difference that they are destined to prioritize handoff calls.

- Transmissionrate: CAC schemes are employed to guarantee the minimumbandwidth requirements for ongoing calls. Moreover,everySC call may also have a maximum bandwidth requirement. Based on the available resources, a CAC scheme aims at providing the highest possible bandwidth between the minimumand maximum requirement to every call and, at the same time, reducing CBP. To this end, certain CAC schemes incorporate QoS renegotiation, a mechanism which is activated when the cell resources of network cell are not sufficient, to reduce the transmission rate of ongoing calls, as much as required for the admission of a new call. The reduced transmission rate may be increased when resources are released due to the termination of a call.
- Revenue optimization: By applying a proper network utilization policy, an efficient CAC scheme may provide a high revenue for the network operator. On the other hand, there are strict limitations imposed by the total bandwidth constraints and the QoS guarantee through the SLAs.Any admitted call contributes to the revenue increase but it may also cause a penalty if the QoS of ongoing calls is deteriorated. The reward may be represented by the number of users or the portion of occupied bandwidth whereas the various penalties may be defined via the probability of QoS deterioration. To determine in real time the optimum equilibriumbetween reward and penalties is a rather complicated problem. The relevant CAC schemes are named revenue optimization or economic CAC schemes.

- Fairness in resource assignment: The main drawback of CAC schemes basing their admission criterion on the call priority is that high priority calls often monopolize the network resources. This results in a severe blocking of low priority calls and, consequently, in high CBP levels for the low priority traffic flows. This is observed not only in networks supporting multiple SCs where different priority levels are assigned to each SC, but also among different users in the same SC with different SLAs and mobility characteristics. Specific CACschemes exist which take into consideration fairness criteria based on various network parameters, such as the network throughput or the CBP achieved, to ensure that no SC or user class dominates the network resources.

MOBILE & WIRELESS NETWORKS MODELING AND TRAFFIC ANALYSIS

Traffic Model and System Analysis

The majority of the studies concerning CACin wireless networks make certain standard assumptions to provide a tractable analysis. Most system models were obtained through common traffic theory and have been extended to cellular networks. These networks are not necessarily represented bythese traffic models, since users mobility and the emerging multimedia services necessitate new telegraphic assumptions and models that take into account the new aspects of wireless networks.

A fundamental assumption in modeling wireless networks with regard to CACis that the new call arrivals in a cell follow the Poisson distribution, that is, the new calls arrive in cell I according to a Poisson distribution with rate an,i. If the network is assumed homogeneous, the arrival rate is the same for every cell and the analysis may be limited to only a single cell the handoff call arrivalsin cell i are also assumed to follow the Poisson distribution with rate Ah,i. Such an assumption is not so obvious in the case of handoff calls as the handoff traffic is solely related to the user mobility characteristics. It has been proven (Chlebus & Ludwin, 1995) that this assumption is valid provided there is no blocking in the network. As this is an ideal case, in the same worka blocking scenario is assumed to examine how accurate is the assumption that handoff arrivals follow the Poisson distribution. The results indicate that through this approximation of the real situation the performance exhibited is satisfactory. Moreover, in the same workit is argued without providingthe proof that in blocking environment handoff traffic is a smooth process which means that the variance is less than the mean value. It must be noted that in Poisson distribution the variance is equal to the mean value. Apartfrom adopting the Poisson distribution for modeling the arrival rate, other traffic models have been proposed in the literature. In (Rajaratnam & Takawira, 2000) the authorssuggest that the callarrivalprocess inwirelessnetworksshouldbe modeled according to general distribution (Rajaratmam & Takawira,1999). Moreover, they have shown that the handoff traffic is a smooth process if the channel holding times follow the exponential distribution.

The channel holding time is defined as the time that a channel is assigned to a call in ab certain cell. The channel is released after the call is either terminated or handed off to a neighboring cell. Another important term in wireless networks is the call holding time (also referred to the literature as service time or Requested Call Connection Time, RCCT), defined as the total connection time originallyrequested by a call.The call holding time varies according to the type of the call, as calls belonging to different SCs may also have different durations. Howlong a call stays in a cell is another fundamental parameter in wireless networks and is widely called as Cell Residence Time (CRT) or cell dwell time. CRT is mainly dependent on users mobility characteristics and on the geometry of the cells.

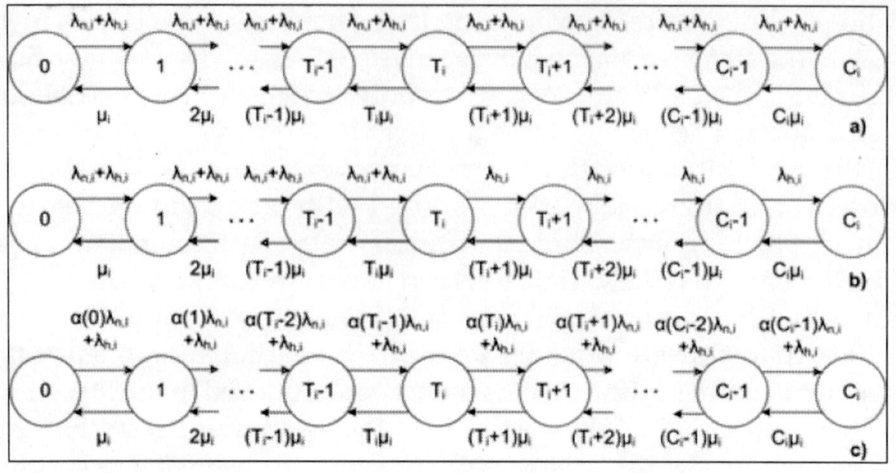

Figure 1. Transition diagrams considering network state. a) Complete resource sharing scheme, b) Guard Channel scheme and c) Fractional Guard Channel scheme

The majority of the analyses existing in the literature assume that the channel holding times follow the exponential distribution for both new and handoff calls. However,the channel holding time follow the exponential distribution, only under certain conditions investigated in (Fang, Chlamtac, & Lin,1998), where it is proven that channel holding time follows the exponential distribution if the CRTis also exponentially distributed. In all the other cases, the channel holding time cannot be modeled according to the exponential distribution whereas neither the handoff traffic nor the new incoming traffic flow follow the Poisson distribution. Some researchers adopt other distributions to model the channel holding time such as the lognormal (Jedrzycki& Leung, 1996) and general distribution (Rajaratmam & Takawira,1999). Although modeling the cell residence time and the channel holding time is not straightforward, most researchers model both these characteristics through the exponential since under this assumption the relevant analysisbecomes tractable yielding analytical formulas for the CBP. Amore rigorous approach is beyond the scope of this chapter; therefore, both new and handoff incoming traffic will be assumed as Poisson arrivals where as the channel holding time and cell dwell time in cell i will be modeled through the exponential distribution with mean $1/\mu_i$.

In a complete resource sharing scheme (Lai,Misic, & Chanson, 1998) a call is admitted as long as there are sufficient network resources to accommodate the call; otherwise it is rejected. The same policy is applied for new and handoff calls. By defining the state of a cell i at time t $\{c_i(t) \mid t \geq 0\}$ as the number of occupied channels in cell, the cell state can be modeled as a Continuous-Time Markov Chain (CTMC). If the respective number of channels is Ci, the system model is a typicalM/M/Ciqueue (Figure1a). Note that to adopt the M/M/Ci model an assumption should be made that when the network operates under congestion a new or handoff call arrival is blocked. This assumption reduces the analysis from M/M/Ci/K, where K is maximum number of calls waiting to be served, into M/M/Ci, where no buffer is used. The truncated state space of cell i is represented by Si, where

$$S_i=\{n_i;\ 0 \leq n_i \leq C_i\}.$$

Let rr(ni,ni')be the transition rate from state nito state ni', where ni, ni'ESi. Then,the transition probabilities for adjacent states are obtained from

$$\pi(n_i,n_i+1)=\lambda_{n,i}+\lambda_{h,i}$$

$$\pi(n_i,n_i-1)=n_i\mu_i.$$

Based on the transition diagram depicted in Figure 1a the following global balance equation is derived

$$(\lambda_{n,i}+\lambda_{h,i})\ p(n_i)=(n_i+1)\mu_i\ p(n_i+1),$$

Where $p(n_i)=\lim_{t\to\infty}\text{Prob}[c_i(t)=n_i]$ denotes the steady state probabilitythat the number of ongoing calls in cell iis ni, ni=0,1,.,Ci. From the global balance equation the steady state probabilities are obtained from

$$p(n_i) = p(0)\rho^{n_i}/n_i!, \quad 0 \le n_i \le C_i,$$

where $\rho=(\lambda_{n,i}+\lambda_{h,i})/\mu_i$ is the traffic intensity and p(0) is the normalization factor defined as

$$p(0) = \left[\sum_{n_i=0}^{C_i} \frac{\rho^{n_i}}{n_i}\right]^{-1}.$$

A new call destined for cell i is blocked if all its channels are occupied; hence, the new call blocking probability in cell i is given by

$$P_n^b(i) = p(C_i).$$

Since no prioritizationfor handoff callshas been assumed inthis general analysis,the handoff failure probability Phb(i) in cell i should be equal to Pnb(i). Therefore

$$P_h^b(i) = P_n^b(i) = p(C_i).$$

This analysis may be extended to multiple SCs and multiple cells but it proves very complicated (Li & Chao, 2007) as the transition diagram has multiple dimensions rendering the corresponding global balance equation difficultto solve. In most cases, different traffic flows, each of which corresponds to a specific SC, are considered to be independent; therefore, multiple one-dimensional transition diagrams are obtained, reducing the complexity of the problem. An interesting and mathematically robust analysis concerning this problem is provided in (Li & Chao, 2007) where expressions for CBPs, handoff rates and QoS (also called grade of service) are obtained in closed form.

As previously mentioned, in the case of multiple independent SCs, the previous analysis is carried out separately for every SC. Consider U SCs with arrival rates

$$\lambda_{u,i}(n_{u,i}) = \lambda_{nu,i}(n_{u,i}) + \lambda_{hu,i}(n_{u,i})$$

and death rates

$$\mu_{u,i}(n_{u,i})=\mu_{u,i}n_{u,i}\ ,$$

where u=l,U and λnu,i(nu,i), λhu, i(nu,i) are the respective call arrival rates for new andhandoff u SC calls in cell i and pu,i is the respective mean cell residence time. The steady stateprobability of having nu,i channels in cell i occupied by u SC calls is

$$p_u(n_{u,i})=\left(\frac{\lambda_{nu,i}+\lambda_{hu,i}}{\mu_{u,i}}\right)^{n_{u,i}}\frac{1}{n_{u,i}!}p_u(0),$$

where pu(0) is the normalization factor given by

$$p_u(0)=\left[\sum_{n_{u,i}=0}^{C_i}\left(\frac{\lambda_{nu,i}+\lambda_{hu,i}}{\mu_{u,i}}\right)^{n_{u,i}}\frac{1}{n_{u,i}!}\right]^{-1}.$$

Considering now the total number of SCs supported in cell i, the truncated state space is

$$S'_i=\{n_i=(n_{1,i},n_{2i},\ldots,n_{U,i});\ n_{1,i}+n_{2,i}+\ldots+n_{U,i}\leq C_i\}.$$

The steady state probability that the network is at state ni is given by

$$\mathbf{p}_{u,i}(n_i)=\mathbf{p}_{u,i}(0)\prod_{u=1}^{U}\left(\frac{\lambda_{nu,i}+\lambda_{hu,i}}{\mu_{u,i}}\right)^{n_{u,i}}\frac{1}{n_{u,i}!},$$

where pu,i(0) is the normalization factor given by

$$\mathbf{p}^{-1}_{u,i}(0)=\sum_{n_i\in S_i}\prod_{u=1}^{U}\left(\frac{\lambda_{nu,i}+\lambda_{hu,i}}{\mu_{u,i}}\right)^{n_{u,i}}\frac{1}{n_{u,i}!}.$$

For the complete resource sharing scheme, the CBP and CDP for u SC in cell i are equal to the probability that cell i is under congestion, e.g. all its channels are occupied. Thus, the corresponding probability is given by

$$\mathbf{P}_h{}^b(u,i)= \mathbf{P}_n{}^b(u,i)= \mathbf{p}(n_i{}^*),$$

$$\text{where } n_i^* = \left(n_{1,i}^*, n_{2,i}^*, \ldots, n_{U,i}^*\right); \; n_{1,i}^* + n_{2,i}^* + \ldots + n_{U,i}^* = C_i .$$

In literature, there are two approaches concerning the whole network problem where cells are supported, i=0,1,.,J. In the first case, the network may be assumed as homogeneous; then, it suffices to examine one cell only withits results representing the whole network behavior. Therefore, the CBP and CDP determined previouslyfor cell i apply for the whole network. In the second case, the network traffic is not uniformly distributed over all the cells supported; then, appropriate analysisshould be carried out to determine the admission failureprobabilities.Thisanalysisisanalyticallypresented in(Li& Chao,2007) where additional QoS network parameters are examined.

Service Classes Classification

Former generations of wireless networks used simple traffic shaping schemes where all traffic was shaped uniformly by rate. This model was realistic as only one service (voice calls) was offered. As modern wireless networks offer a variety of services, the incoming traffic should be classified into different traffic types. Each traffic type is called SC and the procedure followed to determine in which class a new call request falls into is called classification. Each SC has its own QoS characteristics with regard e.g. to bitrate, packet delay, duration etc. Therefore, each SC should be treated differently to differentiate the service destined for the user. Despite the increased complexity due to multiple SCs supported by the network, the control mechanisms are more flexible in resource allocation management and QoS provision. Apart from different QoS characteristics for each SC concerning physical and network layer, different priority levels are applied to different SCs supported employing certain policies. This SC prioritization is usually based on the QoS requirements, the pricing policy followed by the administrator and the users SLAs. This differentiation of the incoming calls can be utilized by a network operator to treat the various SC calls in different ways with regard to bandwidth allocation, call admission process, pricing policy, etc.

A usual classification is the differentiation of the incoming calls into two general SCs, real- time SCs and non-real-time SCs (Tsiropoulos, Stratogiannis, Kanellopoulos, & Cottis, 2008). This classification is primarily based on the latency characteristics of the various calls. In general, there is a deadline for a data packet to be delivered to its destination. If for a certain call this requirement is strict or lenient; the call is characterized as RT call or NRT, respectively. In modern wireless networks supporting multimedia traffic a broader call classification is required. Apart from taking into consideration the latency of each call, additional QoS requirements are considered such as the bandwidth required and the call duration. Therefore, calls are classified into multiple SCs (Tragos, Tsiropoulos, Karetsos, & Kyriazakos, 2008) such as voice, messaging, internet browsing and file transfer, teleconference etc.

Recent trends in traffic control classify the incoming calls into three SCs: Premium, Gold and Silver (Tragos, Tsiropoulos, Karetsos, & Kyriazakos, 2008) (Guo & Chaskar, 2002). Premium SC calls are assigned with the highest priority level and they are offered the negotiated bandwidth all the time, regardless of congestion, interference or degradation of channel quality. A lower priority level is assigned to Gold SC calls and the lowest one to Silver SC calls. The resources are allocated to calls according to the respective SC priority level. Thus, in case of congestion, Premium SC calls are still served under their initially requested QoS characteristics, whereas Gold and Silver SC calls are subject to QoS degradation in proportion to their priority levels so that congestion is mitigated. According to this classification of calls, each mobile user may associate each application with either of three SCs according to its QoS expectations and the pricing scheme applied (Guo & Chaskar, 2002). Thus, for a certain call, say a voice call, a user may associate it with the Premium SC, whereas other users may associate a voice call with the Gold SC. Regardless of the call classification scheme adopted, call classification simplifies the network analysis and enhances QoS provision, as calls are managed in groups and not independently

Efficiency and Performance Evaluation

CBP Estimation

The common criteria employed to evaluate the performance of all the CAC schemes proposed are CBP and CDP. When the assumptions made allow the application of Markov chain analysis, analytical formulas for CBP and CDP are derived (Li & Chao, 2007; Fang & Zhang, 2002; Tsiropoulos, Stratogiannis, Kanellopoulos, & Cottis, 2008). Therefore, the assessment of the CAC schemes employed can be based on these criteria. In measurement- based CAC schemes, CBP and CDP are estimated by measuring the calls blocked or dropped, respectively, during a predefined time window. The CAC scheme proposed in the literature aim at reducing as much as possible both these probabilities by adopting an appropriate decision making procedure. Moreover, the QoS requirements of the ongoing calls should be satisfied at the same time providing prioritization to handoff calls. Both CBP and CDP are mainly dependent on the input traffic load, the number of ongoing calls, the bandwidth requirements of each call and the policy applied for handoff calls (Tragos, Tsiropoulos, Karetsos, & Kyriazakos, 2008).

In single SC networks the assessment of CAC schemes with regard to their failure probabilities is focused on handoff prioritization (Fang & Zhang, 2002; Yavuz & Leung, 2006). The divergence between CBP and CDP becomes greater as the policy for handoff prioritization becomes stricter. In GC schemes this is realized by lowering the threshold level T whereas in fractional schemes the probability a(ni) becomes lower. To measure the prioritization achieved between new and handoff calls an appropriate priority index (PRIN) is defined as the fraction of CBP to CDP

$$\mathrm{PRIN} = \frac{\mathrm{CBP}}{\mathrm{CDP}}.$$

To achieve handoff prioritization, PRIN should be higher than unity, as the CBP should be greater than CDP.

A similar analysis is applied in multiple SC networks. Apart from prioritizing handoff calls, different SCs should also be assigned with different priority levels. Thus, considering that a SCs should have priority over SC u+1, (where u,u+1EU), then CBPu and CDPu should be lower than CBPu+1 and CDPu+1. Therefore, the divergence between failure probabilities among different SCs is more critical in multiple SC networks. The PRIN index can be modified to incorporate the prioritization level of different SCs. In particular,

$$PRIN(u, u') = \frac{CBP_u + CDP_u}{CBP_{u'} + CDP_{u'}},$$

measures the prioritization achieved among u and u′ SC, u,u′EU, where PRIN(u, u′) > l if u ′ u′ or PRIN(u, u′) ′ l if u > u′ .

CALL ADMISSION CONTROL DESIGN APPROACHES

Classification of Call Admission Control Schemes

CAC schemes can be classified into general categories based either on the criteria consider red in the decision part of the CAC scheme or on specific design characteristics. The admission criteria considered by CAC schemes are usually related to various QoS parameters and have been discussed earlier. Each design characteristics has its own advantages and disadvantages. The selection among different CAC approaches should be based upon the wireless technology used, the SCs supported and the geographical characteristics of the region where the network is installed.

With regard to the centralization level of CAC schemes, they are classified into centralized, distributed or collaborative. In centralized schemes, CAC is implemented at the Mobile Switching Center (MSC) which is responsible for handling the services supported by the network. The information from the BS of a cell must be aggregated at the MSC where the admission decision is taken; then, the BS is commanded to act accordingly. The main advantage of centralized

CAC schemes is their high efficiency, but the high level of complexity along with the increased redundancy due to the control data required, makes them unrealistic in practice. In distributed CAC schemes the decision making part is installed at the BS of each cell and completes the CAC procedure independently of the other cells. Therefore, they are more reliable and more easily implemented. However, they are less efficient as they lack global information about the network parameters, information available only in centralized CAC schemes. The collaborative schemes (O'Callaghan, Gawley, Barry, & McGrath, 2004), constitute a promising hybrid design option. In such schemes, information concerning resource allocation and admission control is exchanged between neighboring cells, though the decision is taken by the BS of each cell. Hence, the advantages of centralized and distributed CAC schemes are combined in effective powerful architecture offering high efficiency and increased reliability. The main disadvantage of collaborative schemes is the high overhead required.

CAC schemes can also be discriminated into traffic-descriptor-based - also called proactive - or measurement - based - also called reactive. In the former scheme, the admission decision is based on the traffic pattern which is available for the application of these schemes, which check whether the already reserved bandwidth increased by the bandwidth demand of the new call exceeds the cell capacity. In this case, the call is blocked otherwise it is admitted. The most common traffic-descriptor-based CAC scheme is the simple sum scheme (Tragos, Tsiropoulos, Karetsos, & Kyriazakos, 2008) (Jamin, Shenker, & Danzig, 1997) which simply ensures that the sum of the requested resources does not exceed the cell capacity. A new call with maximum bandwidth demand ra is admitted under the condition that the already occupied bandwidth demand increased by ra remains below the cell capacity p, that is if:

$$\nu + r_\alpha \leq \mu.$$

As multimedia traffic is busty in nature, traffic-descriptor-based CAC schemes overestimate the bandwidth demands since traffic descriptors specify the maximum bandwidth demand in each call which is rarely used. On the other hand, traffic-descriptor- based CAC schemes are very simple; ergo they are widely used by switch and router vendors.

In measurement-based CAC schemes the decision making module employs the actual network characteristics such as the actual traffic load, the packet error rate etc which are appropriately measured and, consequently, realistic. Some interesting measurement-based CAC schemes considered in (Tragos, Tsiropoulos, Karetsos, & Kyriazakos, 2008; Jamin, Shenker, & Danzig, 1997) are based on the actual traffic flow, the occupied bandwidth, the network load and packet loss accompanied with revenue award. The fundamental parameter in measurement-based CAC schemes is the measuring mechanism itself, in other words how the parameter employed in the CAC procedure is measured (Jamin, Shenker, & Danzig, 1997; Warfield, Chan, Konheim, & Guillaume, 1994; Dziong, Juda, & Mason, 1997; Casetti, Kurose, & Towsley, 1996). The measurement procedure is performed either by directly measuring the proper network parameter every sampling period following a time- window policy (Jamin, Danzig, Shenker, & Zhang, 1997), or by computing a relevant average value based on current and/or previous measurements (Jamin, Shenker, & Danzig 1997; Floyd, 1996). Most CAC schemes employed in CDMA systems are designed according the measurement-based technique (Stasiak, Wisniewski, & Zwierzykowski, 2005).

Another interesting classification of CAC schemes can be made based on the amount ofinformation available at the decision making module. This information may include the number of available or occupied cell channels, the total bandwidth allocated to ongoing users, the mean packet delay for each traffic flow etc. If this information can span over the whole network, the scheme is characterized as global. As expected, these schemes achieve high efficiency but exhibit exceptional complexity and require the exchange of a huge amount of information among the network cells. If the information exchange is done within a limited area including at least the neighboring cells of the cell under consideration, the CAC scheme is called semi-local. These schemes achieve also high efficiency and are less complex compared to global ones but they still require a lot of information exchange. Apart from information exchanging schemes, local CAC schemes exist which base their admission decision only on the information concerning a specific cell. Local schemes are simple to implement; however, they are less efficient compared to global or semi-local schemes since they do not take into account that, due to users mobility the load of a cell is influenced by the load of the neighboring cells

Many CAC schemes are available in literature proven to achieve the optimal solution to the CAC problem, according to the inputs for the admission decision process. However, optimal CAC schemes often require a high computational power for their implementation, due to the large number of states associated with the Markov Decision Problem (MDP). The large scale of the problem and the multiple interdependent network parameters employed in optimal CAC schemes result in high complexity and increased processing time. Thus, theoretically optimal CAC schemes are not applicable in practice, as the admission decision must be taken instantaneously upon a call request. As an alternative approach to optimal CAC schemes, suboptimal CAC schemes have been proposed which operate online with significantly lower complexity. Suboptimal CAC schemes obtain a near-optimal solution to the CAC problem, usually by employing intellectual techniques (heuristic functions, alternative approaches, etc) to reduce the complexity of the original problem.

CAC schemes can be also classified based on information granularity (Jain & Knightly, 1999) which depends on the traffic model adopted, the spatial distribution of network users and the way network information is obtained. CAC schemes may adopt a specific users mobility pattern, otherwise a simple resource policy for mobile users will be used. In the first case, the exact knowledge of the users mobility characteristics, such as direction and velocity, helps to predict the handoff traffic load destined to each cell. The spatial users distribution may be uniform or non-uniform; consequently, the wireless network is considered as homogeneous or non-homogeneous respectively. Information can be obtained at each cell for either each call or each SC stream flow. As the information about the network increases, the complexity of the CAC scheme increases along with its efficiency.

An additional classification of CAC schemes can be done based on the differentiation of the data rates between the uplink and the downlink. Unlike traditional voice services, the demand for bandwidth between uplink and downlink is asymmetric in many multimedia applications. In relevant systems, if the CAC scheme employed allocates equal bandwidth to both uplink and downlink traffic, system capacity might be limited by the downlink traffic (Yang, Feng, & Kheong, 2006); then resources are used inefficiently, bandwidth is wasted and efficiency performance of the CAC scheme is low. Some CAC schemes adopt a joint admission policy, by accepting a new call provided that enough resources can be allocated to both uplink and downlink according to the QoS characteristics of the new call.

Call Admission Control based on Signal Quality

In modern wireless access technologies, interference poses critical constraints concerning mainly the signal quality. This situation has an impact not only on network conditions but also on systems capacity. Particularly, in CDMA wireless networks interference is the dominant factor affecting their performance in terms of capacity and QoS provision to end users. Thus, the SINR is an adequate metric of the signal quality. CDMA-based air interfaces are mainly influenced by interference caused by other users from the same network instead of Gaussian noise, so the noise effect is usually neglected focusing mainly on SIR.

Therefore, CAC schemes implemented for interference - limited networks employ as admission criterion either the interference levels caused by a new incoming call or the signal quality levels achieved. Hence, interference based CAC schemes admit new calls only if the SNR/SIR values can maintain a minimum signal quality level. The SNR/SIR levels correspond to predefined QoS levels for new and ongoing users. This simple approach offers a tool to reduce interference in wireless networks, while on the other hand is constitutes an efficient admission criterion.

Two simple SIR-based solutions were first proposed by (Liu & Zarki, 1994) for controlling the signal quality. This is achieved by checking the achievable SIR value by the new call. The call is admitted provided that this value is higher than the minimum SIR value. Both implemented schemes are based on the residual capacity of the cell formulating each time an appropriate admission criterion. In the first scheme the residual capacity of the network is defined as

$$R_k = \left[\frac{1}{SIR_{th}} - \frac{1}{SIR_k} \right],$$

Where SIR k is the uplink SIR value in a cell k and SIRth is the threshold value that imposes whether a call is admitted or not. The residual capacity of the cell is calculated when a new user arrives and if is greater than zero the incoming call is admitted otherwise the call is rejected. The second proposed algorithm follows the same rationale taking also into account the impact of admitting one call on cell k itself and its adjacent cells C(k) as well. This is done by encompassing an interference coupling parameter β in the above definition of the residual capacity leading to

$$R_{k,j} = \left[\frac{1}{\beta} \left(\frac{1}{SIR_{th}} - \frac{1}{SIR_j} \right) \right], \quad j \in C(k).$$

These simple algorithms were evolved taking into account inter-cell interference. In residual capacity estimation, the parameter Lm(j, k) is used, representing the predicted additional inter cell interference. The use of this parameter results into service enhancement in terms of reduced CBPs. QoS guarantees are also provided by using certain bounds for threshold, maintaining specified levels for blocking rate (Kim, Shin, & Lee, 2000). The residual capacity is estimated by

$$R_{k,j} = \left[\frac{1}{SIR_{th}} - \frac{1}{SIR_j} - \frac{1}{L_m(j,k)} \right] j \in C(k).$$

The SINR is a sufficient metric for the signal quality providing also supplementary information. In particular, through SINR measurement BER can be estimated given the coding and modulation techniques applied. Additionally, from SNR/SIR values Eb/N0 and energy per bit to interference density ratio (Eb/I0) can be calculated respectively. CAC schemes control the signal quality employing as a decision criterion the equivalent constraints applied on Eb/N0. Such

SIR based schemes were developed for multicode CDMA systems (Ayyagari & Ephremides, 1998). The proposed scheme orders users based on the Eb/N0 required. Before admitting a user, the CAC scheme checks whether the user can be assigned a minimum number of codes (corresponding to the minimum transmission rate) beginning from the user with the lowest Eb/N0. If the minimum number of codes can be assigned without violating the constraints on Eb/N0, the user is admitted. In the next step, additional codes are attempted to be assigned to the user to increase the transmission rate up to the maximum designated rate. Then, the system proceeds to the next user until all users are checked. Therefore, every user is either admitted and allocated multiple codes or rejected due to system infeasibility.

The SIR-based CAC schemes offer a reliable platform for dynamic adaptive admission control facing the problems of non-stationary and non-uniform traffic. This is realized through either the adoption of a local adaptive scheme employing the traffic parameters and the channel characteristics or a global scheme collecting information from all the neighbouring cells. Dziong & Jia (1996) proposed a relative framework that estimates the mean and variance of the interference level measuring them via a Kalman filter and predicts mean and variance of the interference concerning the new call The total interference is assessed as the sum of the estimated interference of all calls, the predicted interference emerged by the admission new call and the reservation threshold (a reservation for the estimated interference variance and errors). Then, the admission decision is taken comparing the total interference to the maximum tolerable interference threshold Imax.

Apart from interference - limited CDMA networks CAC schemes based on signal quality control were developed for TDMA systems. This kind of system suffers from signal quality constraints especially when a tight frequency reuse plan is employed to increase the number of available channels. Thus, in TDMA networks SIR based CAC schemes are utilized to guarantee SIRmin since cochannel interferers are in close distance one each other, causing significant problems in signal quality. The CAC scheme checks all available time slots in the cell and admits the user if at least one time slot has SIR > SIRmin. If SIR remains below SIRmin throughout the call duration, the call is reassigned to a different time slot that satisfies the SIR requirements offering the desired QoS (Haleem, Avidor, & Valenzuela, 1998). Moreover, CAC schemes remain a prevailing solution for hybrid T/CDMA systems combining multi code techniques with SIR based CAC (Casoni, Immovilli, & Merani, 2002).

SIR based CAC schemes performance can be improved employing optimization techniques. In such schemes a constrained optimization problem is formulated employing an objective function including the signal quality constraints. Through the optimization of the objective function, the system capacity is maximized avoiding high failure probabilities. An optimum CAC policy for multiservice networks is proposed by (Singh, Krishnamurthy, & Poor, 2002), accomplishing to minimize blocking probability for one class, while using as constraints blocking rates for the supported SCs and the SIR conditions. The problem of optimization is solved by means of linear programming. Applying these techniques the efficiency of the CAC scheme is increased leading to an advanced resource management

Handoff and Service Class Prioritization Schemes

Complete resource sharing schemes cannot guarantee a certain QoS level for handoff calls, especially during network congestion, as the total numbers of channels are allocated to new and handoff calls with no discriminations. Therefore, GC schemes, also called reservation schemes, have been first proposed by Hong and Rappaport (1986) in the mid 80s to prioritize handoff calls over new ones. The basic concept behind this scheme is to reserve a certain number of channels only for serving handoff calls. The rest of the channels are available for both new and handoff calls. Thus, assuming that the total number of channels in cell i is Ci and that the number of channels available for common use are Ti (Ti<Ci), the number of channels dedicated to handoff calls only is Ci-Ti. Therefore, Ti operates as a threshold, implying that a new call is admitted provided that at least Ci-Ti+1 channels are available, whereas the admission of a handoff call requires only one available channel. Under the same network assumptions as with the single SC complete resource sharing scheme the transition diagram for the CTMC is shown in Figure 1b, represented by the same truncated state space Si. The transition probabilities to adjacent states in GC schemes are given by

$$\pi(n_i,n_{i+1})=\lambda_{n,i}+\lambda_{h,i} \quad \text{for } 0\le n_i\le T\text{-}1$$

$$\pi(n_i,n_{i+1})=\lambda_{h,i} \quad \text{for } T\le n_i\le C\text{-}1$$

$$\pi(n_i,n_{i-1})=n_i\mu_i.$$

Based on the global balance equations provided by the CTMC depicted in Figure 1b, the following expression is derived for the state space probability p(ni), that is

$$p(n_i)=p(0)\left(\frac{\lambda_{n,i}+\lambda_{h,i}}{\mu_i}\right)^{n_i}\frac{1}{n_i!}$$

$$p(n_i)=p(0)\left(\frac{\lambda_{n,i}+\lambda_{h,i}}{\mu_i}\right)^{T_i}\left(\frac{\lambda_{h,i}}{\mu_i}\right)^{n_i-T_i}\frac{1}{n_i!}$$

where p(0) is the normalization factor defined as

$$p(0)=\left[\sum_{n_i=0}^{T_i-1}\left(\frac{\lambda_{n,i}+\lambda_{h,i}}{\mu_i}\right)^{n_i}\frac{1}{n_i!}+\sum_{n_i=T_i}^{C_i}\left(\frac{\lambda_{n,i}+\lambda_{h,i}}{\mu_i}\right)^{T_i}\left(\frac{\lambda_{h,i}}{\mu_i}\right)^{n_i-T_i}\frac{1}{n_i!}\right]^{-1}.$$

According to the CG CAC scheme, a new call is blocked if the total occupied channels in cell i exceeds Ti-1; hence, the CBP is given by

$$P_n^b(i)=p(T_i)+p(T_{i+1})+\ldots+p(C_i).$$

As GC schemes provide prioritization to handoff calls, a handoff call is dropped if all channels of cell i are occupied; consequently CDP is given by

$$P_h^b(i)=p(C_i).$$

If T is equal to C, the CG scheme reduces to a complete resource sharing scheme. The main issue in GC schemes is the evaluation of the threshold value T that minimizes CBP under the constraint set for CDP (Ramjee, Towsley, & Nagarajan, 1997) (Harine, Marie,

Puigjaner, & Trivedi, 2001). The stricter the constraint for handoff calls, the better is the QoS provided by the network. On the other hand, lower values of CDP result in higher values for CBP. Hence, there is a tradeoff between CBP and CDP, which is reflected in the evaluation of the threshold level.

As modern wireless networks support multiples SCs with different QoS characteristics,sophisticated CAC schemes should be employed to guarantee the various QoS levels. Thus, GC schemes, which were originally destined to prioritize handoff calls over new ones, may be modified by adopting different thresholds for each SC calls (new and handoff) in the relevant decision process. These schemes are commonly known in the literature as multi- threshold bandwidth reservation schemes (Haung & Ho, 2002) (Chen, Yilmaz, & Yen, 2006). In such schemes, two kinds of prioritization can be applied, SC priority and call type priority. The former characterizes the type of the service and addresses the problem of prioritizing different SC calls by employing different thresholds for the calls of each SC. The analysis is similar to the one presented above for the complete resource sharing scheme supporting multiple SCs.

The different SCs supported are usually RT and NRT SCs. In other cases, the SCs supported may be more than two (Tragos, Tsiropoulos, Karetsos, & Kyriazakos, 2008) each with its own QoS requirements. The main problem of multiple threshold schemes is the exact evaluation of the threshold values. Several algorithms exist in the literature for the evaluation of thresholds mainly based on revenue optimization, but most of them are computationally expensive and difficult to solve (Chen, Yilmaz, & Yen, 2006). The evaluation of the proper threshold is a multi-constrained problem, where multiple network limitations should be taken into account.

The fixed number of channels reserved for handoff calls or high priority SC calls by GC or multi-threshold schemes, respectively, is determined mainly based on a priori knowledge of the traffic patterns. As they are static in nature, they lack adaptability thereby being unable to adapt to the network variations. In realistic situations, the call arrival rates are not static and cannot be efficiently described through traffic patterns. Hence, a network with time-varying traffic requires dynamic CAC schemes which usually achieve a better performance. Dynamic (also called adaptive) GC schemes are based either on mobility prediction employing the users mobility, the direction and the location of the mobile terminal, or on measurements of certain network parameters such as CBP, CDP or the available resources. Their main objective is to adapt the thresholds employed by the CAC scheme to optimize a given objective function formulated through a penalty - revenue approach concerning the admission or rejection of incoming calls, a network utilization optimization policy, etc. Both the prediction of mobility and the measurement-based dynamic CAC schemes are strongly dependent on the efficiency of the mobility estimation algorithm or the measurement technique employed, respectively. The extensive results presented in the literature indicate that dynamic GC schemes outperform static GC schemes (Yu & Leung, 1997) (Bartolini & Chlamtac, 2001). On the other hand, dynamic GC schemes are more complex compared to static schemes, resulting in increased exchange of information between the BSs and large processing load.

Another variation of the GC schemes presented above is the Fractional Guard Channel (FGC) schemes. The FGC scheme was first proposed by Ramjee (1996) and was proven to be more general than the GC schemes. The basic idea of the FGC scheme lies in the admission of an arriving new call in cell i under a certain probability a(ni), 0::a(ni)::1, where the parameter ni=0,1,.,Ci, depends on the number of busy channels in cell i. In general, this probability varies with the network status. If a(0)>=a(1)>=a(Ci), the stream of new call becomes thinner as the number of occupied channels increases. Handoff calls are unhinderly admitted unless no channels are available. CBP and CDP vary significantly as the number of occupied channels varies. On the other hand, in FGC schemes the application of admission probabilities eliminates the use of threshold in admission decision providing a smoother variation of CBP and CDP.

Consider the operation a FGC scheme under the same network assumptions as in the CG schemes previous referred to. The network states, represented by the same truncated state space Si, can be modeled according the CTMC depicted in Figure 1c. As observed in Figure 1c, the transition probabilities for adjacent states in FGC schemes are obtained from

$$\Pi(n_i, n_{i+1}) = \alpha(n_i)\lambda_{n,i} + \lambda_{h,i}$$
$$\Pi(n_i, n_{i-1}) = n_i\mu_i.$$

Consequently, the global balance equation is obtained applying the fundamental rule of the birth-death process in Figure 1c "rate up equals' rate down" (Cooper, 1981) as follows

$$p(n_i) = \frac{\prod_{k=0}^{n_i} \alpha(k)\lambda_{n,i} + \lambda_{h,i}}{\mu_i^{n_i} n_i!} p(0) \quad \text{for } 0 \le n_i \le C_i,$$

Where

$$p(0) = \left[\sum_{n_i=0}^{C_i} \frac{\prod_{k=0}^{n_i} \alpha(k)\lambda_{n,i} + \lambda_{h,i}}{\mu_i^{n_i} n_i!} \right]^{-1}.$$

CBP and CDP may be obtained from

$$P_n^b(i) = \sum_{n_i=0}^{C_i} (1 - \alpha(n_i)) p(n_i)$$

and

$$P_h^b(i) = p(C_i),$$

respectively.

When a(0)=a(1)=.=a(Ti)=1 and a(0)=a(Ti+1)=.=a(Ci)=0, the FGC scheme reduces to the simple GC scheme with Ti acting as threshold for new calls. Also, setting all fractional probabilities equal to unity, e.g. a(0)=a(1)=.=a(Ci)=1, the complete resource sharing scheme is obtained. Thus, the FGC schemes are proven more general with the GC and the resource sharing schemes being special cases. Due to the incorporation of the fractional probability a(ni), the FGC schemes may be extended to comply with network administrator specifications and SCs QoS requirements in multimedia wireless networks.

The FGC schemes are further employed to prioritize high priority SCs in multimedia wireless networks. These schemes are also known as thinning or probabilistic CAC schemes (Wang, Fan, & Pan, 2008) (Tsiropoulos, Stratogiannis, Kanellopoulos, & Cottis, 2008). Each SC call is assigned with its own probability. SCs of higher priority are assigned with higher probabilities. In this case, the previous analysis of FGC schemes can be generalized according to the analysis employed for multi-SCs in complete resource sharing and GC schemes (Wang, Fan, & Pan, 2008).

Bandwidth Adaptation and Quality of Service Renegotiation

Wireless networks support a variety of services which can be classified into rate-adaptive applications and constant bitrate (CBR) services. In such services, e.g. voice calls, a bandwidth increase beyond the standard requirement will not improve the respective QoS. On the other hand, in rate adaptive services users specify, at their connection request, the minimum and maximum bandwidth required. Apart from specifying the bandwidth range required by every SC, rate variations may originate from the dynamic nature of the wireless environment along with the mobility of user terminals. Thus, in modern wireless networks bandwidth adaptation algorithms are employed to improve network utilization and guarantee the QoS of ongoing calls, assigning the minimum bandwidth required. When the network conditions are favorable and enough resources are available, they may be assigned to ongoing rate-adaptive users according to two general strategies based on SCs priorities (Li & Chao, 2007). According to the first strategy, the available resources are fairly assigned to all ongoing users without taking into account any priorities. According to the second, resources are first assigned to SC calls of high priority; until the resources are exhausted or all high priority SC calls have taken the maximum bandwidth required. If resources are still available, the scheme assigns them to SC calls of the next high priority. The procedure continues until all resources are exhausted or all calls are served with their maximum bandwidth demand. Apart from taking into account priorities, resource assignment in rate- adaptive services may be performed through more complicated schemes. In (Sen, Jawanda, Basu, & Das, 1998), an optimal resource assignment strategy is proposed for maximizing the total revenue obtained, while in (Sherif, Habib, Nagshineh, & Kermani, 2000), an adaptive resource allocation scheme is proposed to maximize bandwidth utilization and attempt to provide fairness with a generic algorithm.

In general, when a call arrives in a certain cell, the network may either have enough resources to provide bandwidth between the minimum and the maximum demand or be congested, that is, it cannot provide the minimum bandwidth requested by the new call. In the first case the call is admitted, whereas in the second, bandwidth adaptation CAC algorithms, also known as rate-adaptive schemes, are applied to determine an optimal resource allocation aiming at serving as many users as possible while reducing the admission failure probability. This is accomplished by reducing the rate of some users when possible as much as required to accommodate the new call. In some bandwidth adaptation CAC schemes, this procedure is followed only for handoff or for call requests of high priority SCs (Tragos, Tsiropoulos, Karetsos, & Kyriazakos, 2008; Lindemann, Lohmann, & Thiimmler, 2004). However, it should be mentioned that user rates cannot be reduced below the minimum rate values required to assure QoS; thus, when all users operate at their lowest bandwidth requirement, a new call request will be rejected. Rate degradation may be enforced according to a prioritization or to a non-prioritization scheme. In the former, the rate degradation policy is first applied to the SC calls of the lowest priority. If the resources released are still not sufficient for the admission of a new call, the calls of the next priority level are examined. In the non-prioritization schemes, all calls served with higher rates than their minimum bandwidth demand reduce their rate to admit the call request. A useful metric in QoS renegotiation CAC schemes is the degradation ratio which is defined as the ratio of the number of degraded calls to the number of ongoing calls (Kwon, Choi, Bisdikian, & Naghshineh, 1999). Moreover, the degradation probability can be determined though network measurements. Higher or lower degradation probabilities correspond to how aggressive a CAC design approach is.

The reverse procedure is followed when enough available resources exist to offer higher rates to ongoing calls. This rate upgrade policy can be applied in two ways. According to the first one, a rate adaptive resource allocation scheme is employed to exploit the available resources (Li & Chao, 2007). According to the second one, the calls having had their rate decreased more recently are the first calls to have their rate restored (Tragos, Tsiropoulos, Karetsos, & Kyriazakos, 2008). If enough available resources still exist, a resource allocation scheme is employed to assign them to ongoing users.

QoS renegotiation, especially rate degradation must be used carefully and should be the last step of a CAC scheme in an effort to acquire the resources necessary for the admission of a new call. There are many applications, such as voice calls or video streaming, with rates that cannot be reduced (QoS degradation) at not noticeable levels by the user. A drawback of rate adaptive CAC schemes comes up when a network operates near congestion. Then, a certain number of calls may undergo multiple rate degradations followed by respective rate restorations, as call requests arrive and ongoing calls are terminated, respectively. As usersn are sensitive to rate fluctuations, it is preferable to employ appropriate thresholds in the rate upgrade procedure which implies that a rate upgrade is done only if the available resources remaining after the upgrade are above the threshold (Tragos, Tsiropoulos, Karetsos, & Kyriazakos, 2008).

REFERENCES

1. Ahmed, M. H. (2005). Call Admission Control in Wireless Networks: A Comprehensive Survey. IEEE Communication Surveys & Tutorials 7 (1), 50-66.
2. Ahn, C.W., & Ramakrishna, R. S. (2004). QoS provisioning dynamic connection-admission control for multimedia wireless networks using a Hopfield neural network. IEEE Transactions on Vehicular Technology, 53 (1), 106-117.
3. Ayyagari, D. & Ephremides, A(1998). Admission Control with Priorities: Approaches for Multi-rate Wireless Systems. IEEE International Conference on Universal Personal Communications 1998 (ICUPC'98) 1, pp. 301-305. Florence: IEEE.

4. Bartolini, N., & Chlamtac, I. (2001) Improving call admission control procedures by using hand-off rate information. Wireless Communications and Mobile Computing, 1 (3), 257-268.
5. Casetti, C. Kurose, J. F., & Towsley, D. F. (1996) A new algorithm for measurement-based admission control in integrated services packet networks. Fifth International Workshop on Protocols for High-Speed Networks (PfHSN '96) 73, pp. 13 - 28. Sophia Antipolis: Chapman & Hall, Ltd.
6. Casoni, M., Immovilli, G., & Merani, M. L. (2002) Admission control in T/CDMA systems supporting voice and dataapplications. IEEE Transactions on Wireless Communications, 1 (3), 540-548.
7. Chen, I. R., Yilmaz, O., & Yen, I. L. (2006) Admission Control Algorithms for Revenue Optimization With QoS Guarantees in Mobile Wireless Networks. Wireless Personal Communications An International ournal, 38 (3), 357-376.
8. Chlebus, E., & Ludwin, W. (1995) Is Handoff Traffic Really Poissonian? Fourth IEEE International Conference on Universal Personal Communications (pp. 348-353). Tokyo: IEEE.
9. Cocchi, R. Shenker, S., Estrin, D. & Zhang L. (1993) Pricing in computer networks: motivation formulation, and example. IEEE/ ACM Transactions on Networking, 1 (6), 614-627.
10. Cooper, R. B. (1981). Introduction to Queueing Theory New York: Elsevier North Holland Inc.
11. Dziong, Z., & Jia, M. (1996) Adaptive traffic admission for integrated services in CDMAwireless-access networks IEEE ournal on Selected Areas in Communications, 14 (9) 1737-1747.
12. Dziong, Z., Juda, M., & Mason, L. G. (1997) A framework for bandwidth management in ATM networks-aggregate equivalent bandwidth estimation approach. IEEE/ACM Transactions on Networking, 5 (1), 134-147.
13. Evci, C., & Fino, B. (2001) Spectrum management, pricing, and efficiency control in broadbandwireless communications. Proceedings of the IEEE, 89 (1), 105-115.
14. Fang, Y., & Zhang, Y. (2002) Call admission control schemes and performance analysis in wirelessmobile networks. IEEE Transactions on Vehicular Technology, 51 (2), 371-382.
15. Fang, Y., Chlamtac, I. & Lin, Y. B. (1998) Channel Occupancy Times and Handoff Rate for Mobile Computing and PCS Networks. IEEE Transactions on Computers, 47 (6) 679-692.

Chapter 7

MECHANISM AND INSTANCE: A RESEARCH ON QOS BASED ON NEGOTIATION AND INTERVENTION OF WIRELESS SENSOR NETWORKS

Nan Hua[1] and Yi Guo[2]

[1]Institute of Telecommunication Engineering, Air Force Engineering University China [2]East China University of Science and Technology China

INTRODUCTION

The definition of QoS (Quality of Service) varies with the concerned network techniques wired networks, wireless access networks, wireless Ad hoc networks or wireless sensor networks, etc) and the viewpoint of observation (application level or network level) (Chen & Varshney, 2004; Crawley et al.,1998). The concerned topics of QoS in traditional networks are all end-to-end, and the bandwidth utilization is a core issue of QoS mechanism due to the requirements of multimedia applications. Although there are differences among the specific realization techniques, the research models of QoS are similar and the metrics for evaluating and describing QoS are roughly the same (Chen & Varshney, 2004).

Today, the research on the QoS of traditional networks is mature considerably in theory and practice. In wireless sensor networks (WSN), due to the features such as the limited resource (including energy, bandwidth, cache ability, storage capacity, processing capacity, transmission power, etc), high data redundancy, dynamic topology of network and specific application, the QoS problems are different from that of the traditional networks in the design and implementation. For example, in IP networks, a primary intention of QoS is to ensure that the traffic streams which have different grades or types can get corresponding and predictable transmission services. The grade of service can be classified into best-effort service, differentiated service and guaranteed service. In WSN, because of the unpredictable behavior of edge-to-edge, it is not realistic to provide predictable and reliable transmission service for traffic stream. Hence the QoS of WSN is based on unreliable and best-effort data transmission, but it does not exclude the expression method of traffic (task) stream based priority level. Moreover, WSN reduces the requirements for the packet loss rate to a certain degree; the main concerned issues are no longer the efficient utilization of bandwidth, and the QoS is not always end-to-end.

The researches on QoS mainly involve two aspects: mechanisms and metrics. The classical QoS research results of WSN were summarized by Chen and Shearifi. (Chen & Varshney, 2004; Sharifi et al., 2006). In addition, the issues about QoS of WSN are involved or taken into account in many papers in recent years, while conducting the research on the routing and clustering (topology control) protocol, MAC protocol, as well as application issues, etc (Fapojuwo & Cano-Tinoco, 2009; Hoon & Sung-Gi, 2009; Zytoune et al., 2009; Peng et al., 2008; Chen and Nasser, 2008; Yao et al., 2008; Gelenbe & Ngai, 2008; Navrati et al., 2008; Youn et al., 2007; Zhang et al., 2007; Zhang & Xiong, 2007). The QoS issues involved mainly focus on the instantaneity, fault tolerance capacity and energy consumption of networks, and are studied with the respective research fields of these papers conjointly. All these researches on QoS mentioned above belong to the research field of metrics, these researches neither focus on the QoS mechanism nor discuss the QoS issues of WSN specially and systematically from the basis and architecture. To the best of our knowledge, in the research field of QoS mechanisms of WSN, few distinctive researches are conducted at the present time. In these researches, some QoS schemes based on cross-layer QoS optimization (Cai and Yang, 2007), adaptable mobile agents (Spadoni et al., 2009), cloud model (Liang et al., 2009) and limited service polling discipline analytical model (Aalsalem et al., 2008), and so on, were presented, but are not very mature yet.

In this chapter, we focus our research domain on the mechanisms, the concrete QoS metrics is beyond our discussion scope. In this chapter, we bring forward an Active QoS Mechanism (AQM), the core of it is the negotiation between applications and network and the active intervention for them. On this basis, we conduct a further research, present and realize a common QoS infrastructure as an instance of AQM, named QISM (QoS Infrastructure base on Service and Middleware). The application, state and role oriented QoS optimization scheme, the middleware and service based architecture, the Topic and functional domain based expression method are important characteristics of QISM. Proved by simulation of a typical scenario, QISM has good QoS control ability and flexibility, can support complex applications, and is independent of network architectures.

The rest of chapter is organized as follows. In section 2, we present two QoS levels of WSN and analyze the relationship between the essential problems and QoS. In section 3, we bring forward the concept of AQM, and the working processes, the fundamental of state evaluation and strategy generation are discussed. In section 4, the design philosophy and important characteristics of QISM are studied. In section 5, the infrastructure and realization of QISM are presented and analyzed from four aspects in detail. Then, the simulation results are illustrated in section 6. Finally, we conclude this chapter in section 7.

ESSENTIAL PROBLEMS AND QOS OF WSN

Three Essential Problems of WSN

We present three essential research problems which should be considered seriously in the applications of WSN through a representative application scenario: In order to deploy WSN nodes in hostile battlefield or terrible conditions, we normally use airdrop to execute this task. After the nodes bestrewn, it is possible that quite part of them cannot work properly, which leads to heterogeneous distribution of the nodes. Furthermore, it is impossible to supply power when the node energy is exhausted. So, when the network is established, we should face three essential problems as follows:

- *Network Organization*: When old nodes invalidated or new nodes joined, the network will be reorganized. Reorganization of network involves many complex processes, such as route rebuilding (the route optimization), topology reconstruction (the selection between the plane architecture and the hierarchical architecture of network, and the transformation from one to another) and task transference (new joined nodes or other working nodes resume the tasks of the disabled nodes), etc.
- *Lifetime of Network and Nodes*: To prolong the lifetime of whole network, nodes should work in an energy-efficient way, which includes node dormancy and exchanges of node roles (for example, cluster head, cluster member and router node are three different roles of the nodes, which node acts as which role can be decided through elections and the role of node should alternate periodically). Through these methods, it is mostly possible to average energy consumption of the nodes and ensure the lifetime of key nodes.
- *Quality of Service*: We must get tradeoff between lifetime and QoS demand of the network. For example, for the nodes in a lower-density region or executing key tasks, we should find a way to get the necessary tradeoff between application quality and node energy consumption, ensure the achievement of application and the maximum lifetime of network.

Two QoS Levels of WSN

WSN is a fully distributed network, the QoS of it can be divided into two correlative levels as follows:

- *Network (Application) QoS Level*: This level focuses on the whole network, and considers quality of service with a global view of network. The concerned issues involve network organization, network lifetime, and so on. Since Application is a concept correlative with Network, the issue about the analyses of application quality and network state should also be considered in this level.

- *Node (Task) QoS Level*: This level focuses on the network nodes, regulates nodes based on the analyses of metrics and data of concrete nodes under the direction of network (application) QoS level, and feeds back data to it for the problem solving of network (application) QoS level. Since Task is a concept correlative with Node, the issue about the analyses of task quality and node state should also be considered in this level.

These two levels of QoS are correlative. For example, the node energy consumption (an issue in node (task) QoS level) is closely related to the network lifetime (an issue in network (application) QoS level), while the energy saving strategy of network (an issue in network (application) QoS level) would affect the lifetime of single node (an issue in node (task) QoS level). The problems in network (application) QoS level have no way to be solved just through the data of some isolated nodes, but the acquisition and analyses of global network situation. The problems in node (task) QoS level generally are the basis of the problems solving of network (application) QoS level, but it is also independent to a certain extent.

Relationship between Essential Problems and QoS of WSN

Each essential problem of WSN described in 2.1 is not isolated, but is correlative and interact as both cause and effect. Each problem can be divided vertically into two levels: network and node, which is also correlative and affect each other. Hence, we can consider and design a mechanism that could synthetically consider the problems of network organization, lifetime and quality of service of WSN. Above all, this mechanism should associate the regulation in network level with the adjustment in node level and make them become an organic whole, which will guarantee the achievement of applications and prolong the lifetime of network furthest, meanwhile the requirement of application for network behavior is satisfied as far as possible. As discussed in 2.2, the QoS of WSN is composed of two correlative levels: network and node, so we have reason to believe that a specially designed QoS mechanism is a good way to solve the problems mentioned above.

ACTIVE QOS MECHANISM

Generally speaking, the core of QoS mechanism in traditional networks (for example IP networks) is that how to satisfy the requirements of applications for network capability through given methods and mechanisms. The basic process of it can be described that network try its best to satisfy the requirement proposed by application; if the requirement cannot be satisfied, the network will degrade the quality of service and feeds back it to the user. We call this traditional QoS mechanism.

However, the traditional QoS mechanism will bring some problems in WSN. For example, under the circumstance of battlefield supervision application, traditional QoS mechanism will terminate the application and return errors when the object node executing key tasks or the cluster head is disabled. But actually, the application can be achieved if we reorganize network in right time and transfer the tasks in disable nodes to other normal nodes properly.

Theory of AQM

The key to solving problems mentioned above is that a feedback and negotiation mechanism must be established between the applications and network when the support of network to applications or / and the applications demand to network is / are changed. This mechanism regulates the network and applications under certain strategies dynamically, makes the applications adapt to network and network support applications furthest, and improves the support ability of WSN to applications and adaptability of applications to WSN. This feedback and negotiation mechanism between network and applications is named Active QoS Mechanism (AQM) by us.

The key of AQM is the process of active intervention for applications and network. This process is built on the analysis and evaluation for the states of applications and network, which involves two aspects: the regulation of applications to network and the reaction of network to applications. Collecting information from applications and network, and analyzing / evaluating the states of them with the information collected is the foundation of AQM. This mechanism is not necessary in traditional networks, but it is directly related to the lifetime of applications and network in WSN. The fundamental reason of this lies in the unreliable network elements, the instability and resource-constrained nature of WSN.

Working Process

The working process of AQM involves four phases: initialization phase, surveillance phase, negotiation phase and regulation phase. The relationship of these phases is illustrated in Fig. 1. Besides, the relationship of application, network, AQM and main output in each phase are presented in Fig. 2.

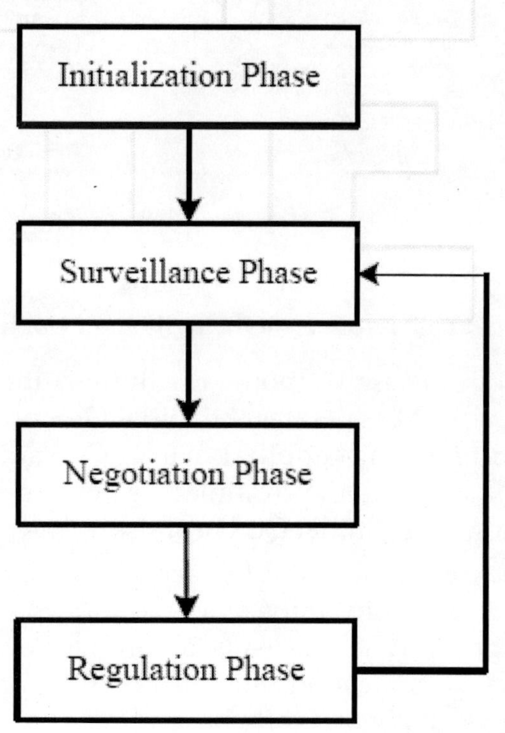

Fig. 1. Four phases in working processes of AQM

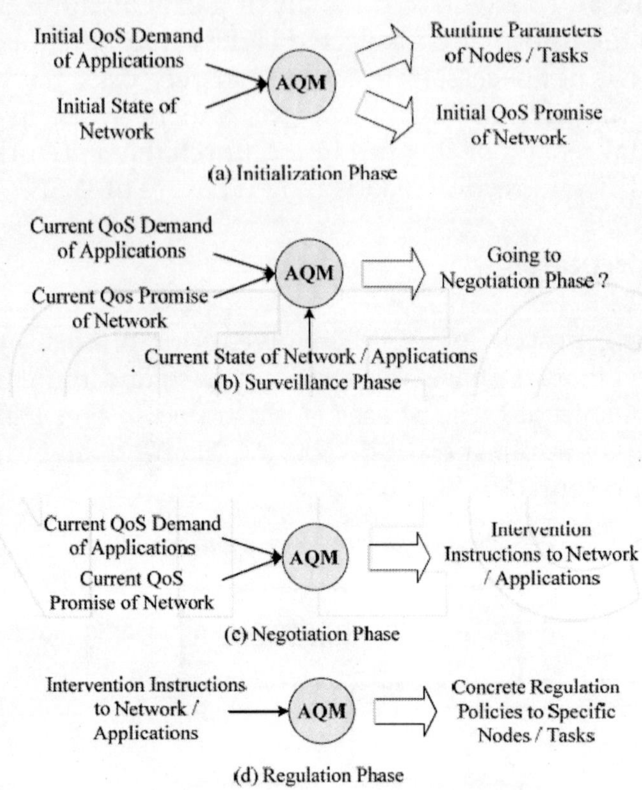

Fig. 2. Main input and output of AQM in different working processes

- *Initialization Phase*: Combined with the initialization process of network, AQM generates the initial QoS promise according to the requirements of applications for QoS and the initial state of network, and sets the runtime parameters of nodes and tasks according to the initial QoS promise.
- *Surveillance Phase*: AQM traces the state of applications and network constantly, and monitors the QoS demand of applications. When there is a conflict between current QoS demand of applications and current QoS promise of network, AQM goes to negotiation phase.
- *Negotiation Phase*: Through AQM, a negotiation and tradeoff is achieved according to the QoS demand of applications and the QoS promise of network, and then the intervention instructions to the network and / or applications are generated. AQM goes

to regulation phase.

- *Regulation Phase*: According to the intervention instructions to the network and / or applications, the concrete regulation policies to specific nodes and / or tasks are generated and the runtime parameters of specific nodes and / or tasks are modified by AQM, AQM goes to surveillance phase.

State Evaluation and Strategy Generation

AQM produces the evaluation to the state of applications and network, generates regulation strategy to applications (network) and tasks (nodes). This is a process of analyzing and optimizing applications and network according to the states of them combining with the requirement of applications, this process is application, state and role oriented. We can regard state evaluation and strategy generation function of AQM as a black box, which owns a predefined method set. The input of this black box is correlative with the application demand to network, current application state, current and previous network state and current QoS promise of network. The output of it involves the intervention instructions to network and / or applications, the concrete regulation policies to specific nodes and / or tasks (in the form of runtime parameters), as shown in Fig. 3.

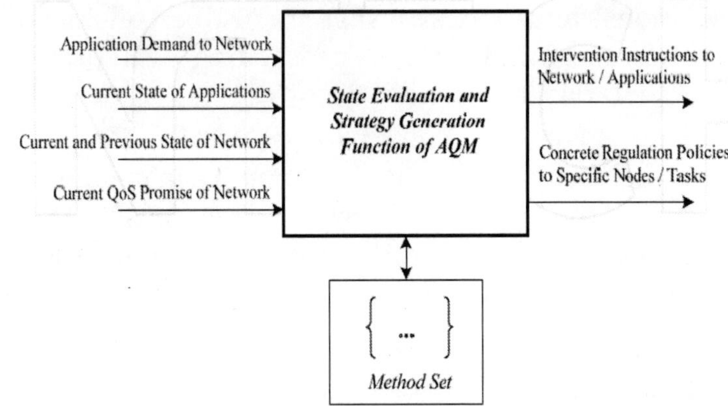

Fig. 3. Fundamental of state evaluation and strategy generation of AQM

QISM: AN INSTANCE OF AQM

From this section, we design and realize a common QoS infrastructure as an instance of AQM, named QISM (QoS Infrastructure base on Service and Middleware) by us. The design philosophy of QISM is as follows:

Application, State and Role oriented QoS Optimization Scheme

The core of AQM is negotiation and intervention, which is based on the analyses of previous accomplishment quality of applications, current requirements of applications for the quality of service, the current and previous states of network, as well as the current service promise of network. These analyses are based on applications, states and roles. Since the application, state and role are time variant in WSN, these analyses are dynamic too.

- *Application-oriented*: The main idea is to distinguish task streams, and different kind of task stream should acquire the support of different QoS in different time. This assignment of QoS should consider the previous and current states of network. Not only the distribution according to need but also the possible carrying capacity of network should be considered.
- State-oriented: The previous and current states of network (applications) and nodes (tasks) should be considered when negotiation and intervention is proceeding; even previous data packets should be analyzed if necessary.
- *Role-oriented*: The Regulations to network and nodes should consider the status and functions of nodes in current network. For example, the nodes that carry out a key sensing task should avoid becoming cluster head or router node in order to save energy and prolong its lifetime.

Middleware and Service based Architecture

Currently, there are close coupling between software and hardware, as well as applications and operating system of WSN, which has brought inconvenience for the task transference as well as the development and adjustment of hardware and software. Middleware is a software layer, which can provide services for various applications and enable different application processes to communicate via network under the circumstances of shielding difference among platforms. Through the middleware, it is convenient to provide standard system services, support and coordinate multiple runtime environments, and efficiently utilize the resource of network. The architecture of QISM based on middleware is shown in Fig.4

When an application is being performed, the application is decomposed into relatively independent tasks firstly, and then the services are abstracted from tasks. The system requests and subscribes the services, gets the required data and completes the requested functionality. Service is a concept about "set", it is a logical abstraction of homogeneous tasks from the viewpoint of network. Service indicates "what to do" and implies the functional domains related with service. Task is concept about "individual", including not only "what to do" but also "how to do". For instance, for the service such as "temperature", many nodes possibly support the task of temperature acquisition. But how to acquire, i.e. "how to do", such as the thresholds and sampling frequency setting, is related with the tasks and nodes. Different nodes probably have different parameter values, which are decided by their runtime parameters. The relationship between services and tasks is shown in Fig. 5.

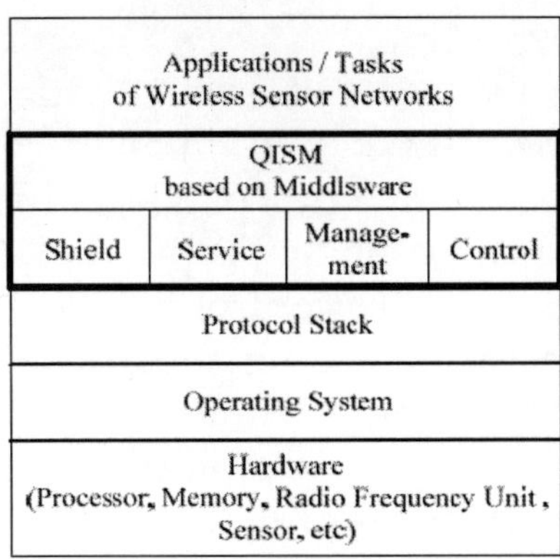

Fig. 4. Architecture of QISM based on middleware

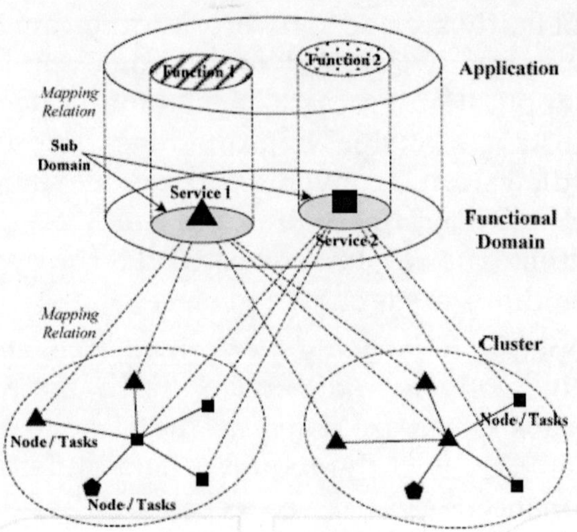

Fig. 5. Relationships among application, services, tasks and functional domain

Topic and Functional Domain based Expression Method

Topic is always associated with the concept application, an application can have more than one Topic, and a Topic can be associated with multiple applications. The syntax of Topic is defined as follows:

Topic < AppName > [< AppName > [...]] < TpStyle > < TpDesp > [< TpDesp > [...]]

where AppName is the name of an application and unique in the network, which is the distinction from other Topics of applications. The style of Topic is identified by TpStyle and TpDesp is the specific description of the content of the Topic. TpDesp can be Interests and Events of WSN, or other control information related with the application, such as various commands or messages. The control information is denoted as SysCtrlInfo. Different from Interest and Event, Topic is based on the application (network) level while Interest and Event is in the task (node) level.

Functional domain is a node set that involves all nodes which provide all kinds of services requested by a specific application, no matter whether the tasks of the nodes are working or not. The node subset that provides different services is a sub domain of the functional domain of the specific application. Functional domain is related with specific application and associated with specific Interest and Event. For example, for the application of fire monitoring, if we wants to acquire the data of temperature and smoke fume, the functional domain related with fire alarm application is the node set that involves temperature and smoke sensor nodes, the sub domain of it are the node subset that involves temperature sensor nodes and the node subset that involves smoke sensor nodes only, respectively associated with the Interest and Event of temperature and with that of smoke. Functional domain is presented from the viewpoint of application and is unrelated with the architecture models that the network uses. In the hierarchical architecture model of network, such as cluster, a functional domain or its sub domains can cover several clusters. The relationships among application, services, tasks, and functional domain are shown in Fig. 5

INFRASTRUCTURE AND REALIZATION OF QISM

Architecture and Function

According to the discussion in 4.2, QISM is base on middleware and is a software layer that located between the protocol stack and applications, communicating with application / task and protocol stack through standard API. QISM is composed of six modules: application analysis, application / task regulation and control, strategy generation / analysis, state analysis, service management, Topic generation / resolving. The hierarchical relationship of the above-mentioned modules is shown in Fig. 6. Each module lies in sink and (or) sensor node, as shown in Table 1.

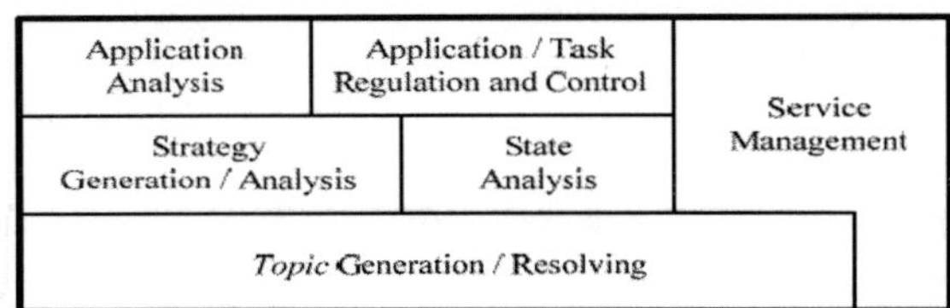

Fig. 6. Hierarchical architecture of QISM

Table 1. Main modules and functions of QISM

Module Name		Location	Function
Application Analysis		Sink	Decomposing application into tasks according to the description of application, and determining whether the tasks are supported by existing available services through Service Management Module. If necessary, indexing and subscribing related services through Service Management Module.
Application / Task Regulation and Control	Application Regulation and Control	Sink	Analyzing implementation status depending on functional domain states and services states, evaluating whether or not the network supports application, and completing application regulation and control.
	Task Regulation and Control	Sensor Node	Completing task regulation and control through setting runtime parameters of task.
Strategy Generation / Analysis	Strategy Generation	Sink	Generating runtime parameters of tasks according to application requirements as well as current application and node state in the states library.
	Strategy Analysis	Sensor Node	Resolving runtime parameters, determining whether current node is in specific functional domain.
State Analysis		Sink	Analyzing task implementation status, determining functional domain and service state, evaluating network state, maintaining the states library.
Service Management		Sink, Sensor Node	Realizing service publication and subscription mechanism, and functions of service discovery, indexing and maintenance.
Topic Generation / Resolving		Sink, Sensor Node	Packing and unpacking *Topic*.

Service Management

The functions of service management of QISM, which consist of publication, subscription, inquiry, index and maintenance of services, are implemented through Service Management Module. The service publication and subscription mechanism is the basis of QISM and the main usage mode of service, where the task side (sensor node) publishing services initiatively and the application side (sink) subscribing and using them. Furthermore, the service inquiry and index mechanism provides the methods that can acquire the state of service, and the methods of requesting and activating service from the application side. The function of service maintenance is used in recording and maintaining the services which are published in the network already, and the function is realized in sink and sensor nodes locally. In sink, table TASvc and TOSvc have the records of current available services and subscribed services respectively; in sensor node, the subscribers of node services are recorded in table TSvcOd. Subscription, inquiry and index function are implemented in the sink, publication function is done in sensor nodes, maintenance function both in the sink and sensor nodes.

The processes of service publishing, subscribing, inquiring and indexing in QISM are illustrated as Fig. 7.

- *Publication and subscription of service*

Publication and subscription of service involve two kinds of messages: MsgSvc and

MsgSvcOd, their syntaxes are defined as follows:

MsgSvc < SvcName > < SvcPrvdID > [< SvcDesp >]

MsgSvcOd <AppName> < SinkID > < SvcName > [< SvcPrvdID > < SvcDesp >]

where SvcName is the name of service; SvcPrvdID and SinkID are the IDs of the service provider and the sink respectively, which can be addresses, domains or coordinates and so on; SvcDesp is the description of the service.

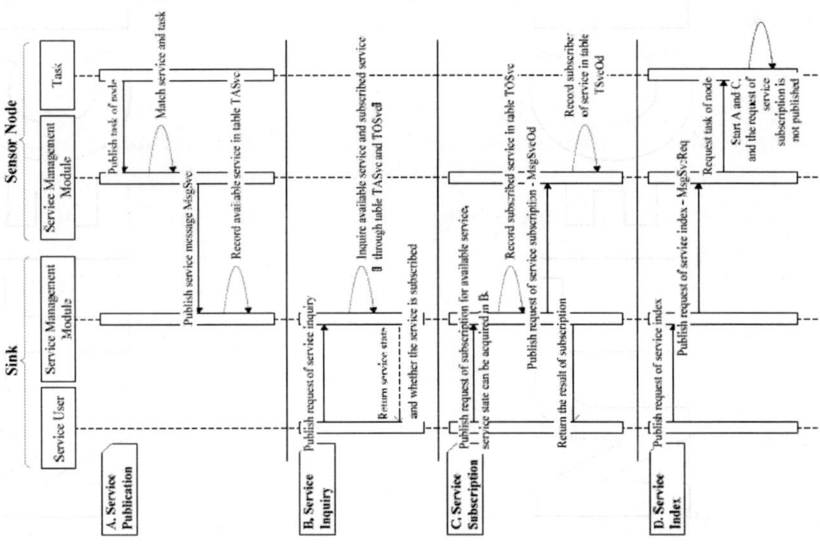

Fig. 7. Processes of service publishing, subscribing, inquiring and indexing in QISM

After the network deployed, sensor node will publish and broadcast the tasks (which can be performed by it) through MsgSvc in the form of service; after received by sink, the services are saved in TASvc and determined whether to be subscribed according to the requirements of application. If the service is useful, the sink sends message MsgSvcOd to SvcPrvdID to subscribe it, and records the subscribed service in TOSvc. After the sensor node receives MsgSvOd which is sent to it, it records the subscriber in TSvcOd. Based on the consideration of resource saving and network survivability, sensor node dose not record MsgSvcs that are sent by other nodes.

If SvcPrvdId is specified in MsgSvcOd, which means the sink subscribes the service that is provided by specific sensor node; otherwise, which means the sink subscribes all the same services that are provided by all nodes in the network. When sending service data, sensor node will specify the data receiver. In the case of multiple sinks, the sink that did not subscribe the service, will discard service data directly after the service data is received.

Inquiry and index of service

The state of service is either Available or Unavailable; the state of specific service can be acquired through inquiring TASvc in sink. If a service is available, it can be used through subscribing. Otherwise, it means that the service has not been published by any nodes yet. In this case, if we want to use the service, we should start the service index mechanism in sink. The sink sends message MsgSvcReq to the network firstly, then the sensor nodes that are capable of providing the service publish the service, finally the sink subscribes the service and uses it. The syntax of MsgSvcReq is defined as follows, where SvcReg stands for the region where the service is located.

MsgSvcReq < SvcName > < SinkID > [< SvcReg > < SvcDesp >]

Maintenance of service

The service maintenance functions of QISM mainly include the table maintenance and update of TASvc, TOSvc and TSvcOd, as well as service cancelling and unsubscribing. When sensor node is unable to provide services, such as under the circumstances that sensor is damaged, MsgSvcFail is broadcasted and TSvcOd is cleared by the sensor node. After the sink receives MsgSvcFail, TASvc and TOSvc (if the service is subscribed already) are updated in order to cancel the service. The syntax of MsgSvcFail is defined as follows:

MsgSvcFail < SvcName > < SvcPrvdID > [< SvcDesp >]

When the application no longer needs a specific service, the sink sends message MsgSvcCancel, and deletes the corresponding service from TOSvc. The sensor node that provides the service maintains a user counter, and when it receives MsgSvcCancel, the corresponding counter of the service is decreased by one and TSvcOd is updated at the same time. When the counter is reduced to 0, the sensor node broadcasts MsgSvcFail. The syntax of MsgSvcCancel is defined as follows:

MsgSvcCancel < SvcName > < SinkID > [< SvcPrvdID > < SvcDesp >]

It should be noted that the service publication only means that sensor node has the ability of carrying out a task, but when to start or to terminate the task, as well as how to implement the task depends on the runtime parameters. More specifically, under the control of the application, task-performing is achieved through the built-in mechanism of QISM by correlative modules generating, sending and implementing the runtime parameters, and it is unrelated with service management module. Moreover, the runtime parameters of tasks are not saved in service management module. Besides, the above-mentioned messages related with service, are sent directly through network protocol stack by service management module.

Basic Working Process

From the viewpoint of the operator of QISM, QISM includes two basic working processes: dynamic adjustment of application and active regulation of task, as shown in Fig. 8. Both are associated closely and reciprocal causation, as a unified organic whole.

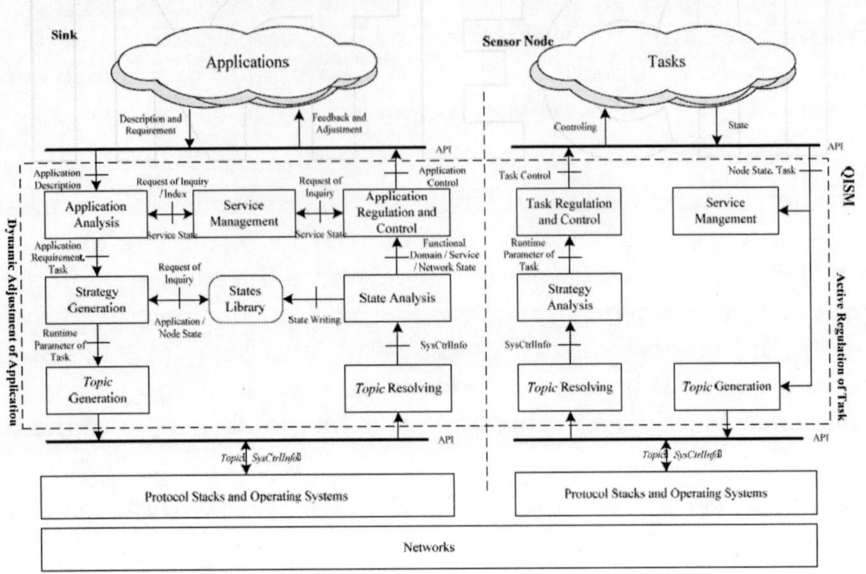

Fig. 8. Data stream of QISM

QISM first completes the service subscription process according to the description and requirement of the application, and then generates the runtime parameters. Afterwards, QISM publishes the runtime parameters of the tasks, and starts the processes of regulations of application (network) and task (node). In sensor node side, QISM intervenes the execution of tasks by setting runtime parameters of tasks, and feeds back the states of nodes and tasks to sink; QISM regulates the application after state analysis process, and then generates the new requirements and (or) descriptions of the application. Such a repetition will form a closed loop until the ends of tasks.

It should be noted that, we do not reflect the processing methods and flow direction of the Interest and Event in Fig. 8 and in the following discussion. In fact, since Interest and Event is a kind of organization and representation method of data, the requirements and descriptions of application may contain the content of Interest, and the states that fed back to QISM from tasks may include a part of data of Event. Transmission of Interest and Event can be implemented by Topic mechanism or other methods. A detailed discussion of Interest and Event is beyond the scope of this chapter.

1)*Dynamic adjustment of application*

Dynamic adjustment of application, whose operator is sink, consists of two processes: application publication and application adjustment, as shown in Fig. 9(a) and (b).

Application publication (the downlink process from application to network)

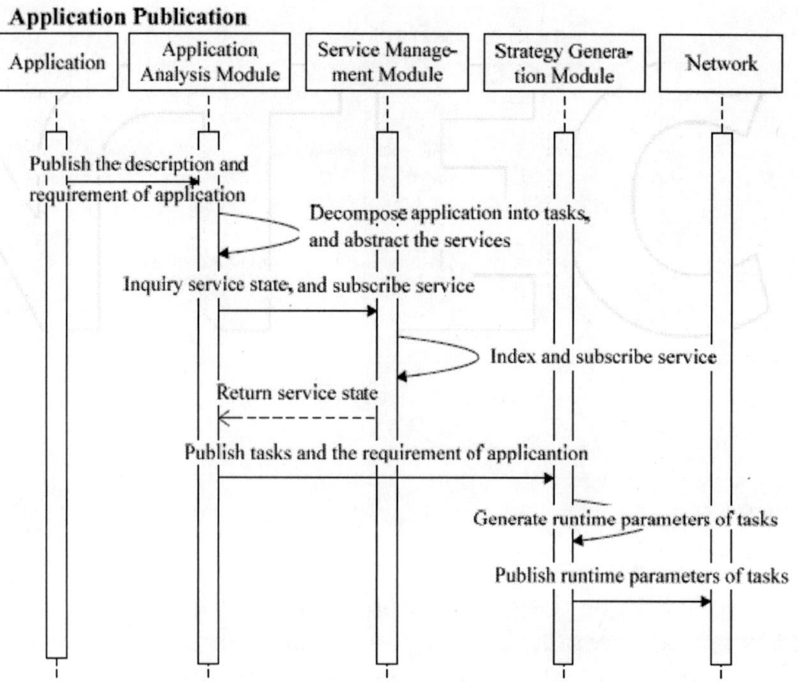

(a) Application publication

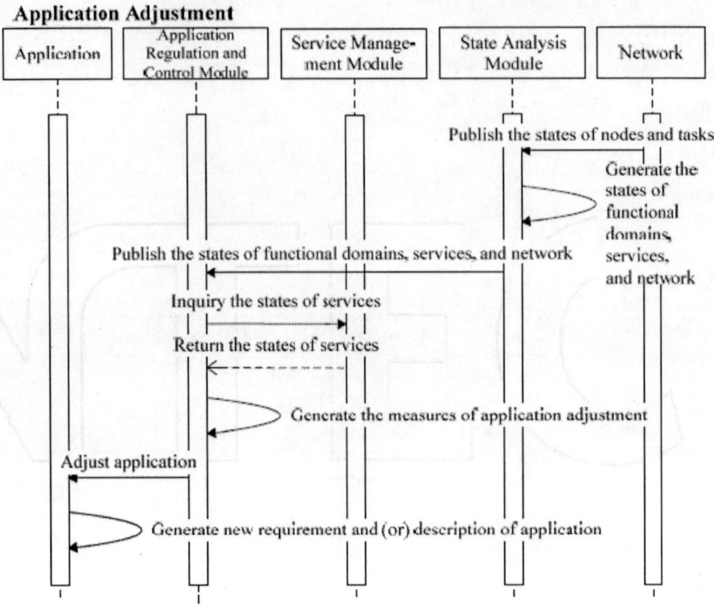

(b) Application adjustment

Fig. 9. Basic working process of QISM - Dynamic adjustment of application

Firstly, QISM decomposes application into several independent tasks according to the description of the application, and abstracts the service corresponding to the tasks. For example, for the fire monitoring application, temperature monitoring and smoke monitoring are two tasks that need to be accomplished; in the node level, the services that are provided by the nodes with the ability of sensing temperature and sensing smoke are temperature sensor service and smoke sensor service respectively. The division, abstraction and correspondence of task and service, is based on the pre-defined rules, which are fixed when the network is deployed.

Secondly, QISM subscribes services. If the services are available, they can be used after subscription; if not available, they can be activated by service index mechanism and then be subscribed. Eventually, all the services required by the application should be available; otherwise, QISM will terminate the application and cancel all the tasks.

Thirdly, QISM generates the runtime parameters of the tasks according to the request of application. The runtime parameters, including functional domain, sampling frequency, thresholds and so on, have great influence on the service quality and execution manner of tasks. In addition, energy strategy is also an essential parameter. The death of some important nodes whose functions are irreplaceable, such as the cluster headers in hierarchical structure, the key routing nodes in multi-hop routing, the key sensor nodes, and so on, may cause the failure of the application or the collapse of the network. So the energy strategy should be established in order to prolong the lifetime of nodes.

Finally, QISM publishes the runtime parameters of tasks to the network in terms of Topic (SysCtrlInfo), for sensor node receiving and performing.

Application adjustment (the uplink process from network to application)

The Topic (SysCtrlInfo) received by sink from network includes the current state information of tasks and nodes; its specific content is determined by the pre-defined rules and is different with different tasks. The above-mentioned state information is the basis of application adjustment.

Firstly, QISM confirms that SysCtrlInfo is for this application (sink) through resolving the domain of Topic AppName, for there are multiple applications (multiple sinks) in the network probably.

Secondly, the state information of a single node is transformed into measurable QoS metrics, and on this basis, the state of functional domains and that of services are generated and the network state is evaluated. The related QoS metrics consist of network delay, packet loss rate, data reliability of node, node lifetime, node energy consumption per bit, packet transmission delay of node, invalid packet rate of node and node remnant energy, etc.

Finally, QISM generates adjustment measures (i.e. intervention instructions to network / applications) for application and informs application to perform, based on the state analysis results, current states of functional domain / service / network and current requirements of application. Application adjustment is faced to functional domain, network and service, not single node and its tasks, though its basis is the information collection and analysis of single node and its tasks. The measures of application adjustment include resuming application, pausing application, resuming application after adjustment, ceasing application, etc.

Active regulation of task

Active regulation of task, whose operator are sensor nodes, consists of two processes: task regulation and state publication, as shown in Fig. 10(a) and (b)

Task regulation (the uplink process from network to task)

In sensor node side, Topic (SysCtrlInfo) received from network consists of the requirements of application for task in the form of runtime parameters of task (i.e. regulation policies to specific nodes / tasks) sent from sink. First of all, QISM confirms that SysCtrlInfo is for the functional domain where current node is located through resolving the domain of Topic AppName. And then, QISM completes task regulation by setting runtime parameters of the task.

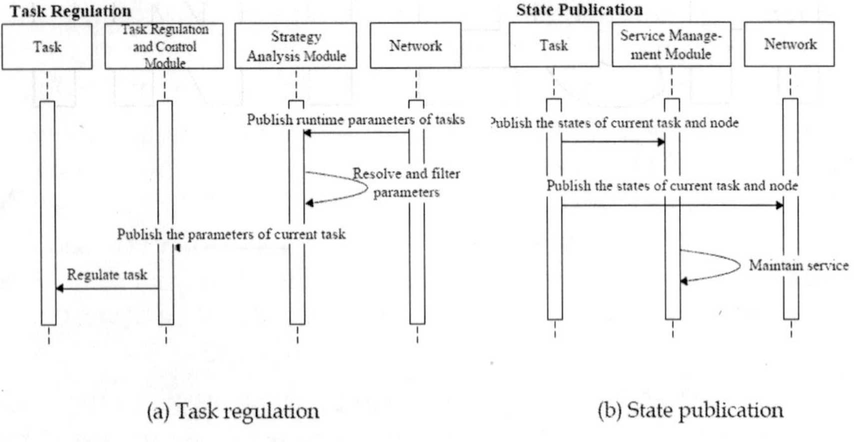

(a) Task regulation (b) State publication

Fig. 10. Basic working process of QISM - Active regulation of task

State publication (the downlink process from task to network)

During the implementation of task, sensor node needs to inform QISM of the current task state (such as whether the task is completed or not, the implementation progress of task) and node state (such as working state of sensor, remnant energy of node). On the one hand, QISM adjusts current services of node according to this, e.g. service is canceled when sensor node is disabled; on the other hand, QISM sends the states to related sink through network for the preparation of state evaluation

Task (Node) Refactoring

Through the generation of concrete regulation policies to specific nodes and tasks based on the intervention instructions to applications and network, QISM realizes the task and node refactoring by means of resetting the runtime parameters of specific tasks and nodes. The so-called refactoring means that the functions and performance of tasks and nodes are modified through the reset of runtime parameters of them, which leads to the change of the support ability of network to applications and the QoS demand of applications to network.

The more ideal methods for the implementation of task (node) refactoring involve three schemes as follows, but the concrete implementation method in QISM should be studied more deeply in our further research:

- *Self-adaptive Adjustment of Protocol Architecture*: The protocol stack involves several components (protocol elements) which are served for different purposes or applications and have different performances and functional characteristics. When external conditions are changed, the QISM selects and applies proper the protocol element automatically.
- *Software Component Technology*: Component is a kind of reusable software element which can be used to construct other software. Software component technology is an object-oriented technical system, which builds applications through the combination of different components and involves a series of correlative operations and services. The core of it is the concept of PnP

(Plug and Play) soft component that can work immediately after it is embedded.

- *Downloading and Updating of Protocol and Application*: QISM downloads new protocols and updating programs dynamically and on demand from the base station (for example the sink). This method is more flexible but need the coordination with the base station or service center.

SIMULATION AND ANALYSIS

QISM has a complex active regulation process for application and task, and its specific logics, including application analysis, application / task regulation and control, strategy generation / analysis, state analysis and service management, etc, depend on specific application and specific realization of system. So we only prove the feasibility of QISM through the simulation for fire monitoring application below.

In fire monitoring application, the network consists of temperature sensor nodes and smoke sensor nodes, crossly deployed in the adjacent regions A and B, as shown in Fig. 11. After the network is deployed, system performs the tasks of temperature and smoke sensing on the support of QISM.

We used ns2 v2.27 to simulate the above scenarios with Linux Red Hat 9. Thirty-six static nodes deployed uniformly in a grid-like plane scene, the temperature sensor nodes and smoke sensor nodes were crossly deployed.

The clustering algorithm was DSCO (Hua & Shi, 2007) and cluster head did not alternate. The protocol of MAC layer was 802.11b, Interface Queue (IFQ) length was 50, and Two-ray Ground Reflection was as wireless transmission model. To be brief and without loss of generality, the single-hop communication was adopted between the cluster head and sink.

After cluster organization is completed, the simulation uses the following logic to control and regulate the application and network:

Logic 1: Service publication. Node publishes temperature and smoke service to sink through cluster head.

Logic 2: Application publication, service decomposition and service subscription. Application (sink) subscribes the temperature service Svc_Tmp and smoke service Svc_Fg of nodes in region A through QISM.

Logic 3: Task runtime parameters generation and task control. The nodes in region A are activated by QISM through dispatching the task runtime parameters (such as sampling frequency fs) to them, as shown in Fig. 11(a).

Logic 4: Node state and service state publication. Nodes in region A report current node states (such as remnant energy Er) to QISM meanwhile they feed back the sensing data (such as temperature and smoke concentration) to application through sink.

Logic 5: State analysis of task and node, application active regulation, task regulation and control. QISM ceases the data acquisition task in region A according to pre-defined logics when the energy of 50% nodes decrease to Er/3, and subscribes services Svc_Tmp and Svc_Fg of region B. The nodes in region B are activated and replace the work of nodes in region A, as shown in Fig. 11(b). Then logic 1-4 are repeated, where nodes in region A is replaced by nodes in region B.

An important reason for designing logic 5 is to prove that active regulation of QISM for application and service can effectively prolong the lifetime of network and application. The results of simulation shows, in the above simple working model based on energy, the lifetime of cluster members are longer than that of members which do not use QISM (all deployed nodes working synchronously) by 30%. The longer lifetime of node is, the longer lifetime of network and application is.

It should be noted that in the above-mentioned simulation, we have not considered the lifetime of cluster head. Energy consumption of cluster heads can be averaged to prolong its lifetime through dynamic alternating cluster head in cluster organization algorithm (Hua & Shi, 2007). The study on dynamic cluster organization is beyond the scope of this chapter.

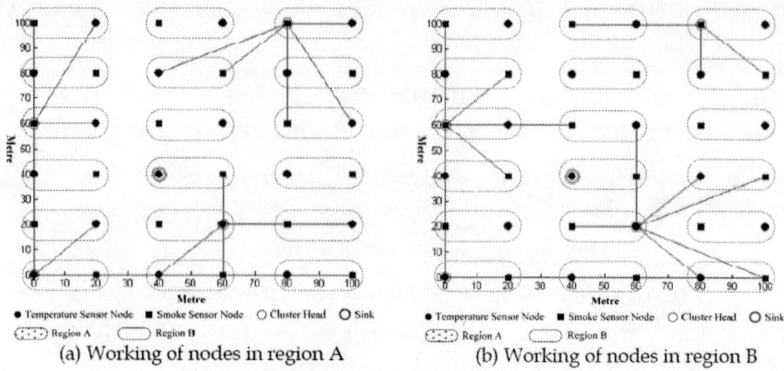

(a) Working of nodes in region A
(b) Working of nodes in region B

Fig. 11. Simulation results of QISM

We can get the following conclusions through above simulation:

- Simulation process covers the main work processes of QISM, and the mechanism of QISM is feasible.
- The illustration of main functions of QISM in the simulation, including switch of node working state of region A and region B, node working parameters (runtime parameters) setting, feedback and analysis of node state, modifying application logic, etc, have proved that the flexibility and ability of QISM in QoS control aspect. Complex application can be supported by more complex control logic.
- In the simulation, the nodes were organized as cluster, and the nodes in the same region (region A or region B) spread in different clusters, which proved QISM is unrelated with network architecture and two kinds of network architecture plane and hierarchy are all supported.
- The lifetime of network and application can be prolonged through reasonable dynamic regulation for the application and tasks, for example, nodes in region A and those in region B alternated working under specific energy strategy.

CONCLUSIONS

Although the research on the QoS of traditional networks (such as IP networks) is mature considerably, but due to the features of

WSN such as the limited resource, high data redundancy, dynamic topology of network and specific application, and so on, the research on QoS of it is different from the traditional networks in design and implementation. In this chapter, we focus our research on the QoS mechanism of WSN, and bring forward an Active QoS Mechanism (AQM), the core of which is the negotiation between applications and network and the active intervention for them. On this basis, we conduct a further research, present and realize a common QoS infrastructure as an instance of AQM, named QISM (QoS Infrastructure base on Service and Middleware). The application, state and role oriented QoS optimization scheme, the middleware and service based architecture, the Topic and functional domain based expression method are important characteristics of it. Proved by simulation of a typical scenario, QISM has good QoS control ability and flexibility, can support complex applications, and is independent of network architectures.

In further research, we will focus on the "full" realiazation of the mechanism proposed by us, but many theoretical and technical difficulties should be solved firstly. For example, the negotiation between applications / network, and the active intervention for them is the core of AQM, the concept of "cognition" can be very helpful for them. But how to achieve "cognition" is a more challenging work.

REFERENCES

1. Aalsalem, M. Y.; Iftikhar, M.; Taheri, J. & Zomaya, A. Y. (2008). On the provisioning of guaranteed QoS in wireless sensor networks through limited service polling models, Proceedings of the 5th IFIP International Conference on Wireless and Optical Communications Networks 2008 (WOCN '08), pp. 1-7, 5-7 May 2008.
2. Cai, Wen-Yu & Yang, Hai-Bo. Cross-layer QoS optimization design for wireless sensor networks, Proceedings of IET Conference on Wireless, Mobile and Sensor Networks 2007 (CCWMSN07), pp.249-252, 12-14 Dec. 2007.
3. Chen, D. & Varshney, P. K. (2004). QoS support in wireless sensor networks: a survey, Proceedings of International Conference on Wireless Networks (ICWN), 2004, Las Vegas.
4. Chen, Yunfeng & Nasser, N. (2008). Enabling QoS multipath routing protocol for wireless sensor networks, Proceedings of IEEE

International Conference on Communications 2008 (ICC '08), pp. 2421-2425, 19-23 May, 2008.

5. Crawley, E. et al. (1998). A framework for QoS-based routing in the internet, RFC 2386, http://www.ietf.org/rfc/rfc.2386.txt.
6. Fapojuwo, A. O. & Cano-Tinoco, A. (2009). Energy consumption and message delay analysis of QoS enhanced base station controlled dynamic clustering protocol for wireless sensor networks, IEEE Transactions on Wireless Communications, Vol. 8, No. 10, pp. 5366-5374.
7. Gelenbe, E. & Ngai, E. C.-H. (2008). Adaptive QoS routing for significant events in wireless sensor networks, Proceedings of the 5th IEEE International Conference on Mobile Ad Hoc and Sensor Systems 2008 (MASS 2008), pp. 410-415, Sept. 29 - Oct. 2 2008.
8. Hoon, Kim & Sung-Gi, Min (2009). Priority-based QoS MAC protocol for wireless sensor networks, Proceedings of IEEE International Symposium on Parallel and Distributed Processing 2009 (IPDPS 2009), pp. 1-8, 23-29 May, 2009.
9. Hua, Nan & Shi, HaoShan (2007). DSCO: a simple distributed cluster organization algorithm of wireless sensor networks, Chinese Journal of Sensors and Actuators, vol. 20, No. 6, June, 2007, pp. 1397-1403.
10. Liang, Jun-bin; Chen, Ning-jiang & Yu, Min-min (2009). A cloud model based multidimension QoS evaluation mechanism for wireless sensor networks, Proceedings of the 4th International Conference on Computer Science & Education 2009 (ICCSE '09), pp. 348-352, 25-28 July 2009.
11. Navrati, Saxena; Abhishek, Roy & Jitae, Shin (2008). Dynamic duty cycle and adaptive contention window based QoS-MAC protocol for wireless multimedia sensor networks. Computer Networks, Vol. 52, No. 13, 17 September 2008, pp. 2532-2542.
12. Peng, Shanghong; Yang, S. X.; Gregori, S. & Tian, Fengchun (2008). An adaptive QoS and energy-aware routing algorithm for wireless sensor networks, Proceedings of International Conference on Information and Automation 2008 (ICIA 2008), pp. 578-583, 20-23 June, 2008.
13. Sharifi, M.; Taleghan, M. A. & Taherkordi, A. (2006). A middleware layer mechanism for QoS support in wireless sensor networks, Proceedings of International Conference on Networking, International Conference on Systems and International Conference on Mobile Communications and Learning Technologies, pp. 118-118, 2006.
14. Spadoni, I. M. B.; Araujo, R. B. & Marcondes, C. (2009). Improving QoS in wireless sensor networks through adaptable mobile agents,

Proceedings of IEEE INFOCOM Workshops 2009, pp. 1-2, 19-25 April 2009.

15. Yao, Lan; Wen, Wenjing & Gao, Fuxiang (2008). A real-time and energy aware QoS routing protocol for multimedia wireless sensor networks, Proceedings of the 7th World Congress on Intelligent Control and Automation 2008 (WCICA 2008), pp. 3321-3326, 25- 27 June, 2008.
16. Youn, MyungJune; Oh, Young-Yul; Lee, Jaiyong & Kim, Yeonsoo (2007). IEEE 802.15.4 based QoS support slotted CSMA/CA MAC for wireless sensor networks, Proceedings of International Conference on Sensor Technologies and Applications 2007 (SensorComm 2007), pp. 113-117 ,14-20 Oct. 2007.
17. Zhang, Xuemin & Xiong, Zenggang (2007). Research on pertinence of QoS metrics based on IEEE 802.15.4 in wireless sensor networks, Proceedings of the third International Conference on Intelligent Information Hiding and Multimedia Signal Processing 2007 (IIHMSP 2007), pp. 663-666, Vol. 2, 26-28 Nov. 2007.
18. Zhang, Ye; Chen, He & Jiang, Lingge (2007). Energy and QoS trade-off analysis of S-MAC protocol in wireless sensor networks, Proceedings of IET Conference on Wireless, Mobile and Sensor Networks 2007 (CCWMSN07), pp. 76-79, 12-14 Dec. 2007.
19. Zytoune, O.; Fakhri, Y. & Aboutajdine, D. (2009). An energy aware QoS routing protocol for wireless sensors network, Proceedings of International Conference on Multimedia Computing and Systems 2009 (ICMCS '09), pp. 245-248, 2-4 April, 2009.

Chapter 8

DISTRIBUTED NETWORK, WIRELESS AND CLOUD COMPUTING ENABLED 3-D ULTRASOUND; A NEW MEDICAL TECHNOLOGY PARADIGM

Arie Meir[1*], Boris Rubinsky[1,2]

[1]Center for Bioengineering in the Service of Humanity and Society, School of Computer Science and Engineering, Hebrew University of Jerusalem, Jerusalem, Israel,

[2]Graduate Program in Biophysics, Department of Mechanical Engineering, University of California, Berkeley, California, United States of America

ABSTRACT

Medical technologies are indispensable to modern medicine. However, they have become exceedingly expensive and complex and are not available to the economically disadvantaged majority of the world population in underdeveloped as well as developed parts of the world. For example, according to the World Health Organization about two thirds of the world population does not have access to medical imaging. In this paper we introduce a new medical technology paradigm centered on wireless technology and cloud computing that was designed to overcome the problems of increasing health technology costs. We demonstrate the value of the concept with an example; the design of a wireless, distributed network and central (cloud) computing enabled three-dimensional (3-D) ultrasound system. Specifically, we demonstrate the feasibility of producing a 3-D *high end* ultrasound scan at a central computing facility using the raw data acquired at the remote patient site with an inexpensive *low end* ultrasound transducer designed for 2-D, through a mobile device and wireless connection link between them. Producing high-end 3D ultrasound images with simple low-end transducers reduces the cost of imaging by orders of magnitude. It also removes the requirement of having a highly trained imaging expert at the patient site, since the need for hand-eye coordination and the ability to reconstruct a 3-D mental image from 2-D scans, which is a necessity for high quality ultrasound imaging, is eliminated. This could enable relatively untrained medical workers in developing nations to administer imaging and a more accurate diagnosis, effectively saving the lives of people.

INTRODUCTION

During the last century, major advances in medical technology have led to substantial improvements in health care. This has come at a cost; the health care technology has become complex and expensive which, in turn, has led to a very wide disparity in health care delivery between those who have the financial resources to benefit from the advanced medical technology and those that do not. The ultimate outcome of this situation is that the majority of the world population does not have access to advanced medical technology and advanced health care. For instance, according to WHO reports, "Around 95% of medical technology in developing countries is imported, much of which does not meet the needs of national health care systems. Over 50% of equipment is not being used, either because of a lack of maintenance or spare parts, because it is too sophisticated or in disrepair, or simply because the health personnel do not know how to use it." [1]. This situation is particularly acute in the field of medical imaging, which is required for correct diagnostic in about 20% to 30% of cases worldwide and which is not available to over 60% of the world population [2]. The challenges in diagnostic imaging in developing countries include: a severe lack of safe and appropriate diagnostic imaging services because of the cost and complexity of the devices as well as a severe lack of technical skills and trained radiographers/technologists leading to a large number of images being misread or of poor quality and therefore of no diagnostic use [3].

For over a decade, our group has been working on trying to find solutions to the medical technology delivery disparity between those who have the financial resources to purchase and use these technologies and those who do not. We have identified that one major factor affecting the cost and the complexity of advanced medical technologies, such as medical imaging, is the hardware and software for data processing. Currently, medical devices are mostly stand-alone units, with redundant and practically limited computational parts, both software and hardware. The computational part becomes increasingly complex and expensive with an increase in the sophistication of the technology. In the recent years, advances in computer science, telecommunication and the Internet made information technology available at low cost to even remote villages everywhere in the world. Inspired by this fact, we conceived of a similar concept for delivering advanced medical care and medical technology. The key concept is that the computational part (hardware and software) is at a central facility, now called "cloud" which does the data processing and provides the most advanced computational service, at any time, to an unlimited number of users, connected through telecommunication to the central processing facility.

The devices at the user site have limited or no data processing facility and are used primarily to transfer the raw data to the central processing facility and to display the processed data. To focus ideas, the remote devices become a dumb terminal for a central computational facility. This removes the cost and limitations of the computation, manipulation and interpretation of data from the vicinity of the patient and uses instead a central and effectively unlimited computational facility. In the vicinity of the patient only the components that directly interact with the patient and which acquire or use the raw data are needed. It should be emphasized that this is different from conventional telemedicine in which the data processing is still done in the vicinity of the patient and the processed images, for example, are sent on. In our concept the majority of the processing is done at the central facility that can be at a completely different geographical location than the patient. The central facility serves a large number of remote users and the telecommunication is used to transfer the raw or minimally processed data to this central processing.

We have demonstrated the feasibility of the concept described above using the Internet and land telecommunication for imaging with electrical impedance tomography (EIT) and for EIT monitored minimally invasive surgery [4], [5]. We have also shown that this concept can be used with cellular phone based wireless technology for remote medical imaging with EIT and that it is valuable to other computationally expensive procedures, such as developing classifiers and data bases for medical data analysis [6], [7], [8]. A review of some of the aspects of our cellular phone based work can be found in a recent Nature news feature [9].

The goal of this study is to elaborate on the fundamental paradigm we developed earlier and to illustrate the value of this paradigm with a new implementation, which could be immediately useful for medical imaging in economically disadvantaged parts of the world. We believe that in addition to EIT, ultrasound is one of the imaging modalities with the best potential to become widely used with this paradigm, due to its relatively small physical dimensions and relatively low-cost. Conventional ultrasound produces a two dimensional image. Successful use of ultrasound relies heavily on understanding the significance of the image displayed and optimal placement of the transducer through hand-eye coordination. The highly trained and experienced users of ultrasound have had to develop hand-eye coordination skills which enable them to create the mental 3D picture of the human body while watching 2D images acquired by the ultrasound system in real-time. They know exactly how to position the ultrasound (US) probe, at what angle to scan and how fast to move it along the patient's body to get a good image. Since medical personnel with such skill-sets are scarce in economically disadvantaged parts of the world, medical imaging is usually not done. In cases when medical imaging is performed the patients may be subject to wrong diagnosis and ultimately wrong treatment or no treatment at all. Three dimensional ultrasound image reconstructions, which is a relative recent addition to ultrasound, removes the need for high quality radiological expertise by allowing the physician to perform the scan without getting into the minute details of the data acquisition process such as the precise probe angle and position [10]. The challenge with industrial 3D ultrasound systems is their prohibitive cost which precludes them from being used in the developing nations, the place they are needed the most. Even in developed countries, small clinics that lack highly trained specialists, which could benefit from owning a 3D-US system, cannot afford purchasing it due to the high market price.

In this work we took the concept of processing at a central facility a step forward by implementing a fully functional 3D ultrasound system in which the 2-D intended raw data acquired at the patient site by a medical untrained person is transferred through telecommunication to a central processing facility, where it can be processed into a 3-D image or, in fact, for any conceivable use. The 3-D processed data can then be made available through communication to the data acquisition site or to an expert at any other location. The idea of coupling an ultrasound device with a communication device such as Wi-Fi adapter or a cellular phone is not new. In [11] Martini et al. have focused on the possibility of utilizing 3 g/WiFi networks for the purpose of video-streaming the acquired and processed ultrasound imaging data to the remote expert station. In [12] Dickson has evaluated several wireless communication options for ultrasound systems focusing on video-streaming capabilities in his analysis. However, to the best of our knowledge no other work has evaluated the feasibility of using telecommunication and wireless technology to transmit *raw ultrasound* data for processing on the central processing station that serves a large number of users and generates 3D image from the *raw data*.

We believe that the work presented in this study illustrates the value of our paradigm in a meaningful way. The powerful central processing facility, which can serve unlimited numbers of remote users, allows a remote unskilled user to employ an inexpensive technology and nevertheless obtain a state of the art product in terms of a 3-D ultrasound image, at a fraction of the cost and without the need for complex data processing facilities and software at the user site.

RESULTS

The system architecture aligned with the proposed general paradigm is shown to contain two major components: Mobile Console and Remote Expert System (Fig. 1a). The mobile console with its sensors acts as the data acquisition device which collects the raw data from the patient, and sends it to the remote server for processing. The processing server is capable of transforming the large amount of otherwise meaningless measurements into a human understandable form such as an image or diagnosis.

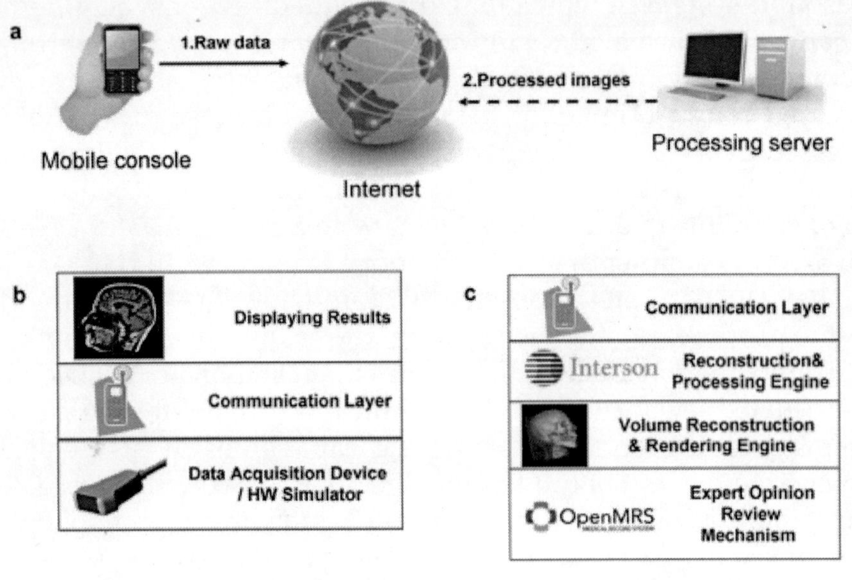

Figure 1. System Architecture.

(a) Overall system architecture includes the mobile console component and the remote processing server (Expert System) which performs the computation-extensive work. (b) Mobile Console Architecture. The console has one or more data acquisition devices, a communication module and a display capability. (c) Server Architecture. Contains a communication module, a processing engine, a visualization engine and an expert assessment mechanism.

doi:10.1371/journal.pone.0007974.g001

The mobile console (Fig. 1b) contains a hardware data acquisition device, a display and a communication component able to send raw data and receive results. The Processing Server (Fig. 1c) contains a communication component to receive the raw data, a processing (reconstruction) component to process the data into a useful form and a visualization (rendering) engine which shapes the data in a visually meaningful way. Optionally the server side can contain a human-assessment mechanism, which enables an expert doctor to review the results before sending them back to the mobile console.

The implementation of the general paradigm of Fig. 1 for 3-D ultrasound is given in detail in the Materials and Methods section. Specifically, we have used Lenovo R61 1.5GHz, 2GB RAM Windows XP as our server test bed running the server-side of the application software including the processing engine and Open MRS server. For the purpose of this study we've focused primarily on a data flow in a typical obstetrics US scan, performed in B-Mode, with spatial resolution of 256×256, maintaining a contrast resolution of 8 bits (256 shades of gray). In such a study, the raw data required for the reconstruction is acquired by driving the transducer in a rectilinear, uniform direction with constant speed [13], [14]. The number of slices acquired depends on the specific application. We've used 80 slices in our study. We've used a standard, very inexpensive 3.5 MHz abdominal ultrasound probe manufactured by Interson Corporation for 2-D ultrasound (http://www.interson.com).

Our system is based on Google's Android platform which we chose because it is fully open source and capable of utilizing all the modern features provided by cellular operators. We have tested the system in two configurations: a) running on HTC G1 mobile phone and b) running in an emulator environment on Asus EEE 1000HE netbook computer.

Since USB host mode is not enabled on the conventional HTC G1 phone, it was not possible to connect the USB ultrasound probe to the mobile phone. For this reason we have designed a frame-grabber software module, which is responsible for capturing the raw data from the ultrasound probe and sending it to the G1 phone over short-range wireless network. We've used the same frame-grabber interface when we tested the system in an Android emulation environment running on Asus netbook. Android-powered netbooks are expected to appear in the nearest future and we envision our system running natively on those computers, getting the ultrasound data directly from the available USB port.

Although they have made great progress in the recent years, the cellular data channels available today are still limited when compared to broad-band Wi-Fi alternatives. Even HSDPA, commonly referred to as 3.5G, provides 14.0 Mbps downlink under optimal conditions and HSUPA, which is the uplink component of 3.5G, provides an uplink of up to 5.76 Mbps. This is especially true in developing nations where available cellular services tend to lag behind the cutting edge technologies available in the developed world. This is important because medical imaging devices are often known for generating large quantities of data.

For this reason it is important that the mobile console provides a buffering zone between the actual sensor and the processing station. Even if the connection channel is low-speed and/or unreliable, given enough storage space, the mobile console will eventually succeed to send the data to the processing station once the connection becomes stable.

An alternative scenario might involve a local health worker acquiring large amounts of data from multiple patients and later, when he is back to the local clinic where wi-fi is available, uploading all the accumulated data to the remote station for processing.

Fortunately, the costs of memory have dropped dramatically in the recent years (a 16 gb micro-sd supported by the G1 costs less than $45) so the buffering problem can be efficiently solved; the mobile device (netbook/cellular phone) would accumulate the data on it's internal memory card until connection for uploading this data is available. The raw data flows from the acquisition device, an US probe in our case, to the mobile device which is a mobile phone acting as a storage device, and then transferred to the processing server when the connection is available (Fig. 2).

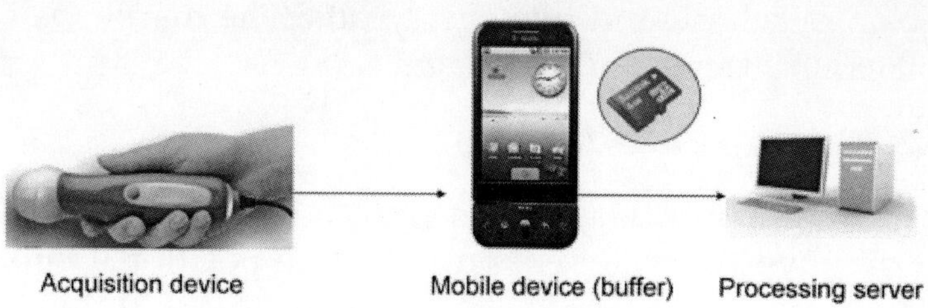

Figure 2. Data Storage Mechanism.

The raw data flowing from the mobile device which acts as a storage device. Once a connection is available, the data is being transferred to the server for processing.

doi:10.1371/journal.pone.0007974.g002

To demonstrate a typical scan, we have followed an example from [15] and created an agar based box-shaped phantom, sized 3.5"x2.75"x2". During the solidifying process, we've embedded a marble ball, a peach pit and two cherry pits inside the phantom to be able to trace those objects in the resulting ultrasound scan (Fig. 3)

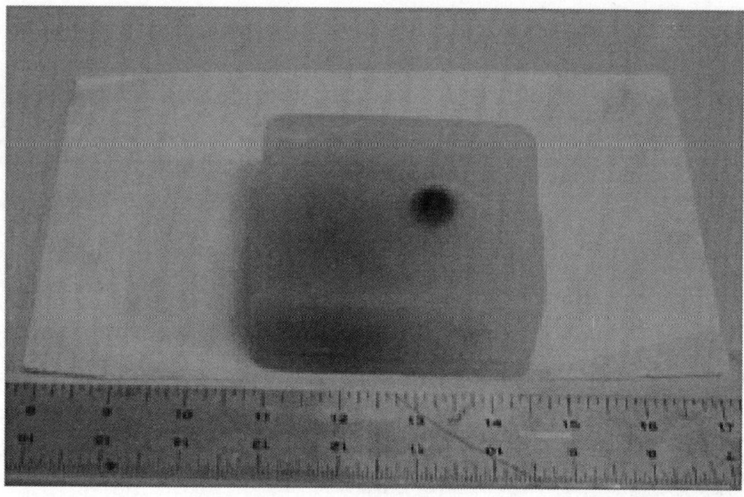

Figure 3. Ultrasound Phantom.

Agar based 3.5"x2.75"x2" box shaped phantom with embedded marble ball, peach pit and two cherry pits. The marble ball and the peach pit can be seen from the image.

doi:10.1371/journal.pone.0007974.g003

Since our purpose was to generate 3-dimensional images, we needed some type of system to provide with positional information. We used a hand held steadily moved probe to avoid the need for a more complex positioning system. It has not escaped our attention that for a truly freehand 3D-US a positioning system is preferable, otherwise the image resolution is extremely low and the image is unusable for clinical purposes.

Nevertheless we have intentionally chosen to work around the position information problem since the focus of our work is the feasibility of the overall data acquisition and 3-D processing framework. We provide a brief review of possible alternatives for position and orientation estimation later in this paper.

For performance evaluation, relevant measurements are summarized in Table 1.

Table 1. Performances measurements.

doi:10.1371/journal.pone.0007974.t001

Table 1. Performances measurements.

Raw data size for a single B-Mode raw image	512 kB
Average raw data transfer for a single B-Mode raw image data (Wi-Fi)	3.9 sec
Volume rendering of 80 slices	28 sec
Snapshot generation for angular resolution of 10 degrees, yielding 36 projections per rotation axis	115 sec
36 Angular snapshot images transfer back to the mobile console (Wi-Fi)	31 sec

As can be seen from the time measurements, we transfer substantial amounts of raw data over the wireless connection, thus the round-trip time is not real-time. Although it is possible to make our system more efficient by using various data compression and channel quality adaptive algorithms, we'd like to emphasize an important point: *due to the nature of the 3D ultrasound, the need for real-time feedback is removed because no hand-eye coordination is required anymore. The relatively unskilled health worker can acquire the data in a freehand manner and after the remote processing is done, have the complete 3D volume data available for review and diagnostic purposes.*

A snapshot of the 3D reconstructed phantom is presented in multiple projection views (Fig. 4a and 4b). The ROI (region of interest) is shown in higher zoom level (Fig. 4c and 4d) where the marble ball can be seen on the top, the peach pit on the right and two cherry pits on the left part of the scan (Fig. 4c)

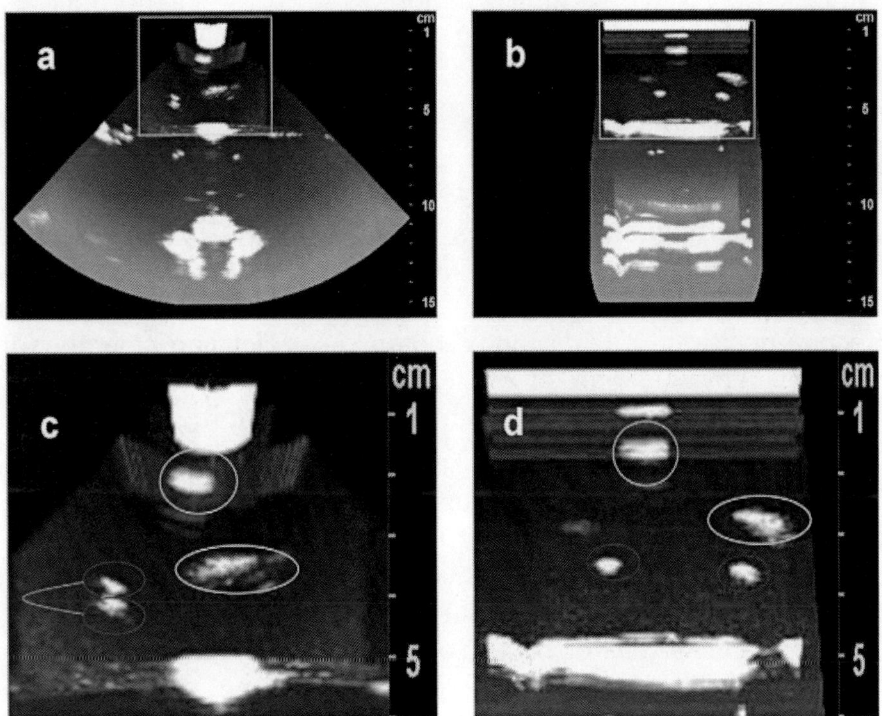

Figure 4. Resulting 3D Volume Visualized.

(a) Front projection, axial angle 0°, depth of 15 cm (b) Side projection, axial angle 90°, depth of 15 cm (c) Zoom on ROI from (a): the cherry pits, the peach pit and the marble ball are clearly seen. (d) Zoom on ROI from (b) the cherry pits, the peach pit and the marble ball are clearly seen.

doi:10.1371/journal.pone.0007974.g004

Discussion

We've shown in this work the feasibility of performing a 3D ultrasound scan using an inexpensive ultrasound transducer designed for 2-D, a mobile device, a remote processing station and a wireless connection link between them. Acquiring 3D ultrasound data removes the requirement of having a highly trained expert since hand-eye coordination process becomes obsolete. This enables medical workers in developing nations to administer a more accurate diagnosis, effectively saving the lives of people who would have otherwise been misdiagnosed.

It has to be noted that although our system did not incorporate any position information, due to the relatively steady motion of a US transducer by an untrained US user, we managed to get reasonable 3D results, without any positioning device or hand-eye coordination. To provide the health worker with even higher degree of freedom and flexibility during data acquisition we intend to research cost-effective position information mechanisms which can be embedded in our system as a part of our effort to design an affordable and effective medical imaging mechanism for developing nations.

Although our case study focused on US, the implementation of any another medical technology would be identical in its conceptual essence. We chose US since, due to it's mobility and wide availability, it seems like the natural choice of medical diagnostic modality for the developing world. In addition, ultrasound utilizes the available cellular connection as opposed to EIT described in [7] which sends very little data. We expect medical imaging solutions following the paradigm we've demonstrated in this work to appear in the foreseeable future. Constantly lowering mobile devices costs and communication technology advancements will contribute to this process.

An alternative and conceptually similar solution, might include integrating a data acquisition device such as the ultrasound probe used in our case-study with a cellular-phone chip such as, for example Gobi or Snapdragon technologies by Qualcomm (http://www.qctconnect.com/products/snapdragon.html,http://gobianywhere.com/). This solution would include a small display which is capable of displaying the diagnostic information after the remote server has finished processing the raw data. This architecture can be utilized in a consumer device. The possible drawback of such architecture is binding the medical device to a specific cellular technology such as CDMA or GSM. A solution to this problem might include a Bluetooth transmitter in the end device which will send the raw data to any standard cellular phone; most modern phones include Bluetooth capabilities in them. This would expand the possible reach of the technology, since now we can leverage any existing cellular infrastructure.

One such possible device could be used to perform the scan by a health worker or even a home user. The raw data acquired by the Data Acquisition Device would be sent to remote station for processing and a diagnostic result in the form of a text message would be displayed on the LCD line: *"Healthy"* or *"Thorough test is required"* (Fig. 5).

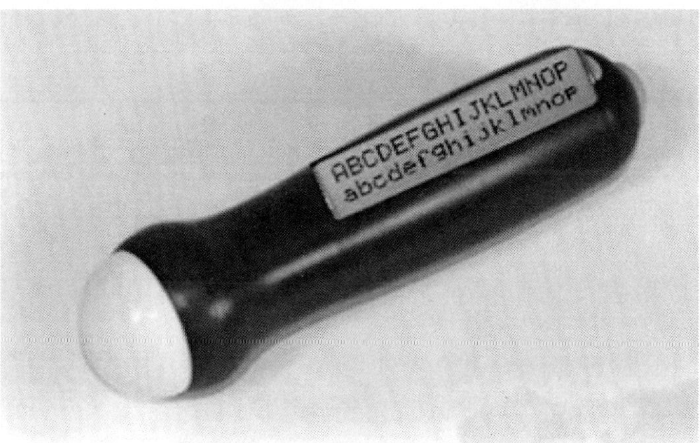

Figure 5. Integrated breast cancer self-examination device for home use.

doi:10.1371/journal.pone.0007974.g005

A class of such devices for self-diagnosis is the natural extension of our work and having such a device would enable early detection of diseases, such as cancers or internal bleeding, thus potentially saving the lives of many.

MATERIALS AND METHODS

We will describe here the details of the 3-D ultrasound system implemented in this study using the general raw data transfer and data processing algorithm described in Fig. 1. Ultrasound imaging utilizes acoustic waves for the mapping of internal organs and tissues from changes in acoustic impedance between the tissues. Ultrasound works by sending acoustic pulse waves towards the mapped organ and then reconstructing the echoes of those waves into a visual image used for medical diagnosis. Due to the relatively compact size and low power consumption, ultrasound provides an important alternative to other medical imaging modalities such as CT and MRI.

In classic 2D ultrasound, the trained radiologist views the monitor while constructing a mental 3D image of the patient's body. The quality of the diagnostic is heavily biased in the favor of a well-trained radiologist with excellent hand eye coordination and ability to integrate a sequence the 2-D images into a 3-D mental understanding of the image. In 3D ultrasound systems, computer algorithms reconstruct a 3D image from the acquired 2-dimensional images, and therefore simplify the diagnostics. Since the reconstruction engine needs to position the 2D image in the 3D volume, in addition to the image data itself, the exact position and orientation of the US probe are required for each 2D image taken. Several approaches to estimating position and orientation are described at the end of the materials and methods section.

On a highly abstract level, any typical Ultrasound Imaging System includes 4 primary components: a) Transducer – a unit which emits and receives the acoustic waves and records the correlation between them, b) Control unit – used to control the operation of the transducer, c) Processing unit – which converts the raw data acquired by the transducer into a human usable form, usually a visual image, and d) Imaging – the final stage of the ultrasound scan chain where the visual image is being displayed on the monitor for diagnostic purposes.

The detailed step-by-step implementation of our wireless 3-D ultrasound algorithm as illustrated (Fig. 6):

- The raw data arrives from the ultrasound probe.

- The data arrives to the mobile device which stores the information on its internal memory card until a reliable connection channel becomes available.
- Every once in a while (frequency can be configured trading-off responsiveness vs. battery life) the mobile device tests the available connection in order to detect the right moment to send the data. Once a connection has been established, the data transfer begins to the processing server. The communication protocol between the mobile device and the processing server is based on XML-RPC (http://www.xmlrpc.com/) which in turn is based on the standard HTTP protocol for transport. The data is packaged in a way that supports operating in slow, unreliable connection channels.
- Once all the raw data arrives to the server, the processing stage can begin. The data is grouped by the slice number it belongs to.
- In this stage a stack of parallel slices is being turned into a volume data-set for later manipulation. This can be achieved using the "DICOM Volume Render" open source software module by Mark Wyszomierski which is based on the popular graphics engine VTK. **D**igital **I**maging and **Co**mmunications in **M**edicine (**DICOM**) is a standard for handling, storing, printing, and transmitting information in medical imaging. In addition to the raw image data, DICOM format enables incorporation of various meta-parameters for example, in our case slice sickness, slice number e.t.c. To design and build a quick prototype, we have decided to skip the direct generation of DICOM files, a process which might easily become mundane. Instead we have downloaded an existing 3D Ultrasound and simply replaced the raw image data with our data, in addition to modifying the relevant parameters. Once this process of generating the DICOM files is complete, the renderer can process the stack of 2d images in DICOM format and create a volumetric data-set which is later snapshot to generate multiple view projects for 3d visualization.
- Once the volumetric data-set has been created, it is projected in multiple directions to create the effect of 3D viewing on the mobile device. Given a high enough angular resolution,

the effect is close to a full 3D manipulation in the commonly used axial, sagittal and coronal planes. It's worth noting that recent technological advances in mobile devices, specifically in CPU power and graphic processing abilities, already allow many cellular phones to perform 3D rendering on the mobile unit itself, as demonstrated by [16]. The trade-off decision of battery life vs. visualization power will have to be taken into account by any application designer in the mobile medical imaging field. We've decided to benefit from both worlds by enabling limited 3D visualization by pre-computed projections. Once the projections have been generated they are saved as jpeg formatted images which are sent back to the mobile device, again using the XML-RPC over HTTP protocol. By using jpeg images as opposed to sending the volumetric data and rendering the data on the mobile device, we engage only the image-displaying capability of the mobile device as opposed to it's power-hungry 3D engine, thus saving precious battery life. One minute, yet important aspect of communication has to be noted: due to the nature of a mobile device, its IP address is highly unstable. The cellular network might decide at a certain point that the IP address of a certain mobile device has to be changed to a different one. This makes it difficult for the server to contact the mobile console to notify it that the processing was completed and results are pending. Even if the mobile console sends its ID to the server, in the time period between the raw-data transmission to the termination of the processing phase, the IP address might have been changed. For this reason we've implemented a console-driven polling mechanism. Once the raw data has been sent, every once in a while, the mobile console polls the server if the results are ready. If they are, the console makes a request for them. The frequency of the polling procedure is a system parameter which can be configured to trade off responsiveness vs. battery life. We've found that the value of T_{period} = 30 seconds provides reasonable results.

- Global Expert Opinion: to provide an optional expert opinion to the remote health worker, we have integrated our system with OpenMRS® (http://www.openmrs.org), a popular open source medical records system. Once the raw data has been reconstructed and 3D images are available, the processed images are being displayed in a "pending" queue in OpenMRS. After a medical expert reviews the data and adds his comments, the result is sent to the mobile console for display. Because we adapted the concept of distributing the components of the imaging system, the expert reviewing the diagnostic images can be at any geographic location, unrelated to the location of the health worker or the processing station. What this means is that a local health worker in rural Uganda can perform a scan that is being processed in data servers in India and an expert radiologist from the U.S. provides a diagnostic opinion which is sent with the results back to the local health worker effectively in real-time.

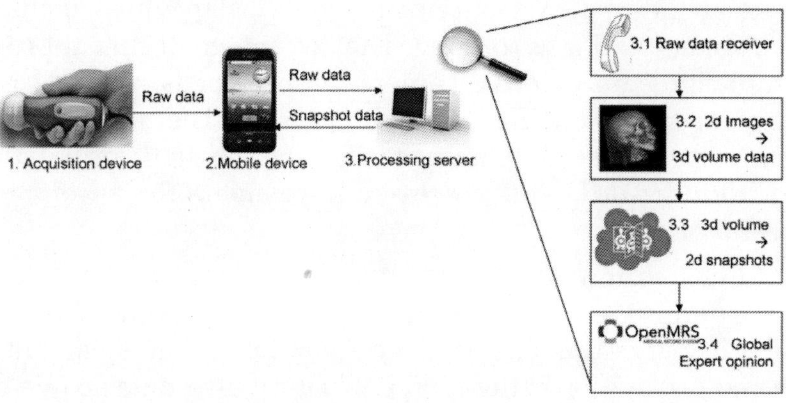

Figure 6. Data flow.

The raw data flows from the hardware acquisition device to the mobile console which acts as a storage and communication conduit. Once the data is processed on the server, the results are transferred back to the console for review and diagnosis.
doi:10.1371/journal.pone.0007974.g006

An important aspect of any 3D ultrasound system concerns position and orientation information. During the process of 3-dimensional image reconstruction, every surface element (pixel) from the 2-dimensional images is mapped to a volume element (voxel) in the 3D reconstructed volume. To perform such a mapping accurately, the reconstruction algorithm needs to know the precise position and orientation of the ultrasound probe at the moment of the 2D image acquisition. There are several techniques to this end. Mercier et al. review common technologies for medical instruments tracking [17]. Electro-magnetic and optical technologies for ultrasound probe tracking are the most popular. While those approaches provide good accuracy, they are also relatively bulky and expensive. Since we are working with the needs of developing countries in mind, we want to emphasize more mobile, cost-effective solutions.

Abdul Rahni et al. have studied the possible usage of Micro Electro-Mechanical Systems (MEMS) based approach to estimate position and orientation in 3D [18]. In their study, the authors have used an Internal Measurement Unit (IMU) which included an accelerometer and a gyroscope. The advantage of this approach is its simplicity - no external camera or receiver is needed, as in the electromagnetic/optical technology case. The raw physical measurements (acceleration, angular velocity and static orientation) are read from the IMU and processed to calculate the absolute 3D position and orientation.

By adding redundant sensors, it is possible to compensate for some of the numeric errors inherent to the process. Another work that has caught our attention has used a conventional digital camera for position and orientation estimation [19]. During the data acquisition process, in addition to the US data, a video clip focusing on the ultrasound probe is captured. After the acquisition process is over, the position and orientation information are extracted by applying machine vision algorithms to the acquired video stream. By using a conventional digital camera, which often comes as an integral part of any modern cell-phone, it is possible to build a low-cost, ultra-mobile 3D position mechanism.

We believe that the approaches presented in [18], [19] can be used as a basis for a cost-effective, mobile position and orientation estimation mechanism which are required by a 3D reconstruction algorithm and we intend to explore those research directions. Since the primary focus of our current work was to illustrate the concept of the overall data acquisition and 3-D processing framework, we've decided to relax the freehand requirement and work around the 3D positioning issue by steadily moving the US probe in a straight line during the data acquisition stage. By sticking to the straight line trajectory, we were able to use a more straightforward reconstruction algorithm since it could simply stack the 2D images one next to each other and still get a 3D images of reasonable quality. In the future we intend to develop relevant variants of the techniques described in [18], [19].

Acknowledgments

We would like to thank Mr. Eric Stein and Google Corporation for donating an HTC G1 mobile phone which made our work possible.

Author Contributions

Conceived and designed the experiments: BR. Performed the experiments: AM. Analyzed the data: AM. Wrote the paper: AM BR.

REFERENCES

1. WHO report (2003) Essential Health Technologies Strategy 2004–2007. World Health Organization. http://www.who.int/eht/en/EHT_strategy_2004-2007.pdf.
2. WHO report, Essential Diagnostic Imaging. World Health Organization,http://www.who.int/eht/en/DiagnosticImaging.pdf.
3. WHO report, About Diagnostic imaging. World Health Organization,http://www.who.int/diagnostic_imaging/en/.
4. Rubinsky B, Otten D (2004) Method and apparatus for remote imaging of biological tissue by electrical impedance tomography through a communication network. US Patent #6725087.
5. Otten D, Onik G, Rubinsky B (2004) Distributed Network Imaging and Electrical Impedance Tomography of Minimally Invasive Surgery. Technology in Cancer Research and Treatment Vol. 3, No. 2: 1–10.
6. Granot T, Ivorra A, Rubinsky B (2008) A New Concept for Medical Imaging Centered on Cellular Phone Technology. PloS ONE 3(4): e2075.
7. Laufer S, Rubinsky B (2009) "Tissue characterization with a

multimodality classifier: electrical spectroscopy and medical imaging" IEEE Trans Biomed Eng Feb;56(2): 525–8.

8. Laufer S, Rubinsky B (2009) Cellular Phone Enabled Non-Invasive Tissue Classifier. PLoS ONE 4(4): e5178. doi:10.1371/journal.pone.0005178.
9. Kwok R (2009) Personal technology: Phoning in data. Nature 458: 959–961.
10. Gee A, Prager R, Treece G, Berman L (2003) Engineering a freehand 3-D ultrasound system. Pattern Recognit Lett vol. 24, no. 4–5: 757–777.
11. Martini MG, Istepanian RSH, Mazzotti M, Philip N (2007) A Cross-Layer Approach for Wireless Medical Video Streaming in Robotic Teleultrasonography. Conf Proc IEEE Eng Med Biol Soc 3082–5.
12. Dickson BW (2008) Wireless Communication Options for a Mobile Ultrasound System, MSc. Thesis, Worcester Polytechnic Institute,http://www.wpi.edu/Pubs/ETD/Available/etd-090208-162440/.
13. Goes CE, Schiabel H, Nunes FLS, Berezowski AT (2006) "Volume Rendering for Ultrasound Computer Phantoms Images by Using Multiplatform Software" IFMBE Proceedings World Congress on Medical Physics and Biomedical Engineering. 2456–2459.
14. Kelly M, Gardener JE, Brett AD, Richards R, Lees WR (1994) Three-dimensional US of the fetus —work in progress. Radiology 192: 253–259.
15. Bude RO, Adler RS (1995) An easily made, low-cost, tissue-like ultrasound phantom material. J Clin Ultrasound 23: 271–273.
16. Moser M, Weiskopf D (2008) : Interactive volume rendering on mobile devices. In Vision, Modeling, and Visualization '08 Conference Proceedings 217–226.
17. Mercier L, Langø T, Lindseth F, Collins LD (2005) A review of calibration techniques for freehand 3-D ultrasound systems. Ultrasound in Medicine & Biology Volume 31, Issue 4: 587.
18. Abdul Rahni AA, Yahya I, Mustaza SM (2008) "2D Translation from a 6-DOF MEMS IMU's Orientation for Freehand 3D Ultrasound Scanning", Proceedings of 4th Kuala Lumpur International Conference on Biomedical Engineering.
19. Ali A, Logeswaran R (2007) " A visual probe localization and calibration system for cost-effective computer-aided 3D ultrasound", Computers in Biology and Medicine 37: 1141–1147.

Chapter 9

AVAILABLE BANDWIDTH ESTIMATION AND PREDICTION IN AD HOC NETWORKS

Haitao Zhao, Jibo Wei, Shan Wang and Yong Xi

National University of Defense Technology China

INTRODUCTION

Wireless ad hoc networks provide quick and easy networking in circumstances that require temporary network services or when cabling is difficult. With the widespread use of multimedia applications that require Quality of Service (QoS) guarantees, research in providing QoS support in wireless ad hoc networks has received much attention recently (Nafaa, 2007). The term QoS gathers several concepts. Some efforts, like admission control, intend to offer guarantees to the applications on the transmission characteristics, for instance bandwidth, delay, delay jitter, or packet loss. Other solutions, like QoS routing, only select the best path among all possible choices regarding the same criteria. In both cases, an accurate evaluation of the amount of resources available (i.e., available bandwidth) on a given path is necessary. Therefore, obtaining accurate information of available bandwidth is a crucial basis for QoS-aware controls in wireless ad hoc networks. In the followed analysis, the term available bandwidth will be denoted by "AB" for brevity. Since the IEEE 802.11 Distributed Coordination Function (DCF), based on Carrier Sense Multiple Access with Collision Avoidance (CSMA/CA), is the most popular MAC protocol used in ad hoc networks, the AB estimation problem in 802.11-based ad hoc networks has been a focus of recent research. Some approaches that used to be applied in wired networks have been adopted in wireless scenario, e.g., (Hu & Steenkiste, 2003; Jain & Dovrolis, 2003; Melander, Bjorkman et al., 2000; Ribeiro, Riedi et al., 2003; Strauss, Katabi et al., 2003). Meanwhile, some new proposed approaches that specialize for wireless networks have been proposed, e.g., (de Renesse, Friderikos et al., 2007; Sarr, Chaudet et al., 2008; Wu, Wang et al., 2005). So far, however, there is neither consensus on how to precisely measure the AB in ad hoc networks nor a practical approach that has been widely adopted, which makes all these approaches on the stage of experiment or simulation and no standard is agreed yet. So it's time to rethink the AB estimation in ad hoc networks, and find out the challenges that make it so difficult to arrive at an agreement. In this chapter we'll review the existing approaches for AB estimation, presenting the efforts and challenges to AB estimation in 802.11 or 802.11-alike ad hoc networks, and we will also give some proposals to tackle these challenges. Analyzing these problems will help to not only develop an accurate AB estimation approach but also design QoS support schemes in ad hoc networks. This chapter is based on our work that previously, in parts, have been published in (Zhao, Garcia-Palacios et al., 2009; Zhao, Wang et al., 2009; Zhao, Wang et al., 2010). And the rest of this chapter is organized as follows. In Section 2, we first give a review of the state-of-the-art of AB estimation in ad hoc networks. Then in Section 3, we present the challenges of sensing-based approaches for AB estimation in 802.11 or 802.11-alike ad hoc networks and also give some solutions to them via analysis and simulation experiments. And in Section 4, we present the model-based approaches for AB prediction. In the end, we conclude this chapter in Section 5.

STATE OF THE ART

In ad hoc networks, AB is defined in the context of end-to-end network path. Specifically, the path is a sequence of nodes, i.e., N1, N2, N3 and Nn+1 (n is the hop count), that communicate using identical, half-duplex wireless radio based on 802.11 DCF mode. The data packets are relayed from N1 till Nn+1. The link (or hop) between Ni and Ni+1 is referred to as Link i. See the illustration in Fig. 1.

$N_1 \xrightarrow{\text{Link 1}} N_2 \xrightarrow{\text{Link 2}} N_3 \cdots N_i \xrightarrow{\text{Link } i} N_{i+1} \cdots N_{n+1}$

Figure. 1. n-hop path to calculate the end-to-end AB

The state of Link i at time t is

$$S_i(t) = \begin{cases} 0, & \text{when Link } i \text{ is idle} \\ 1, & \text{when Link } i \text{ is busy} \end{cases} \tag{1}$$

Note that the node being busy can be caused by its transmitting, receiving or the neighboring interference. In the time period of [t, t+τ], the utilization of Link i is]

$$U_i(t) = \frac{1}{\tau}\int_t^{t+\tau} S_i(t)\, dt \tag{2}$$

The AB is defined as the unused bandwidth over the time interval τ, here □ is usually referred to as the estimation period (namely the time needed for estimating AB once). It is not a constant value and can be changed in different estimation tools, or even in a tool according to the network scenario. Then the AB of Link i in the time period of [t, t+τ] can be expressed as

$$AB_i(t) = C_i(1 - U_i(t)) \tag{3}$$

where Ci is the channel capacity of Link i. And the end-to-end AB of a path is mainly determined by the link with minimum AB along the path. AB estimation has generated several contributions in the wired and wireless networking communities. Several classifications of these solutions may be imagined. We chose to classify the approaches that could be adopted to estimate AB in 802.11 ad hoc networks into three categories: probe-based approaches, sensing-based approaches and model-based approaches.

Probe-Based Approaches

Probe-based approaches estimate the AB along a path via sending end-to-end probe packets. All these approaches are principally based on Probe Gap Model (PGM) or Probe Rate Models (PRM) (Strauss, Katabi et al., 2003). In PGM, the AB is obtained by first building the mathematical formula of AB regarding the sending gaps and receiving gaps between probe packets, and then measuring the sending gaps and receiving gaps between probe packets to obtain AB. While PRM adopts a more straightforward principle as follows: if the probe packets sending rate is faster than AB, the probe packets will queue at some routers so that end-to-end delay increase gradually; On the other hand, if the probe packets sending rate is slower than AB, the probe packets will experience little delay. Therefore, the AB can be obtained while observing the delay variation and deciding the time when congestion begins. Furthermore, PGM can be cooperated with PRM, for instance in IGI (Initial Gap Increasing) method that proposed in (Hu & Steenkiste, 2003). In the past decade, many probe-based AB estimation tools have been developed, such as Spruce (Strauss, Katabi et al., 2003), TOPP (Melander, Bjorkman et al., 2000), Pathchirp (Ribeiro, Riedi et al., 2003), IGI (Hu & Steenkiste, 2003), Capprobe (Kapoor, Chen et al., 2004) and Pathload (Jain and Dovrolis, 2003) to name a few. The developing course of these approaches is to build a more accurate relationship between AB and metrics in probe packets and thus increase the AB estimation accuracy. And a survey of them can be found in (Zhou, Wang et al., 2006). This type of approaches is most proposed originally for wired networks, and with the requirement of estimating AB in wireless ad hoc networks they are also adopted in wireless scenario. However, the difference between wired networks and wireless networks, especially that wireless ad hoc networks cannot bare the heavy overhead brought by the probe packets, impulses approaches specifically for wireless ad hoc network to be proposed. These approaches are trying to reduce the amount of probe packets and thus decrease the estimation overhead, among which the representative work are SenProbe (Sun, Chen et al., 2005) and the approach in (Hoang, Shao et al., 2006). SenProbe uses a return-way technique to estimate the unidirectional path capacity in wireless sensor networks, and thus simplify the path capacity estimation process. To further decrease the, estimation overhead, authors in (Hoang, Shao et al., 2006) use a one-way probe (The destination node sends the probe to the source node and the source node estimates the AB). In theory, (Hoang, Shao et al., 2006) can reduce half of the overhead comparing to SenProbe. Whereas, reducing the probe packets will inevitably decrease the estimation accuracy. Though the research on probe-based approaches is still moving on to find a balance between accuracy and overhead, some practical drawbacks of this type of approaches make it difficult to break through in its application in wireless ad hoc networks. First, the accuracy of probe-based approaches is not satisfactory. C. Dovrolis etc. (Dovrolis, Ramanathan et al., 2004) proved that PGM model actually estimates the Asymptotic Dispersion Rate (ADR) instead of the AB (The ADR is asymptotic dispersion rate between AB and channel capacity, and is an upper bound of the AB). At the same time, authors in (Lakshminarayanan, Padmanabhan et al., 2004) showed that in a CSMA- based wireless networks, a new probe packet enqueued at one of the stations might in fact be transmitted sooner than the older cross-traffic packets waiting at other stations. So the probe packet may not experience a delay commensurate with the total volume of cross-traffic, leading to over-estimation of the AB. On the other hand, (Lao, Dovrolis et al., 2006) arrived to a conclusion that contrary to the former two research: in general cases PGM can significantly under-estimate the AB of an end-to-end path. Maybe this can explain why Lakshminarayanan etc. (Lakshminarayanan, Padmanabhan et al., 2004) had arrived to the conclusion, via experiments, that most of probe-based approaches can only used in wired networks, and if they are used in 802.11, wireless networks, the measurement result will have big error without obvious disciplinarian. Second, there are some practical problems when deploying existing probe based bandwidth measurement approaches in ad hoc networks. It was observed(Johnsson, Melander et al., 2005), for instance, that the measured link capacity show dependence on the probe packet size and a smaller probe packet size will result in a lower bandwidth estimation. Besides, the source node is supposed to have the ability to send probe packets at a higher rate than AB via using PGM model. And the most but not the last drawback is that when every node in an ad hoc network needs to perform such an estimation for several destinations, the number of probe packets introduced in the network can be important and interact on the traffic as well as on other probes.

Sensing-Based Approaches

With the effort to avoid the presented problems in probe-based approaches, recent research contributes to estimate the AB on a given wireless link via sensing-based approaches. These approaches need not to send probe packets, but sense nodes' channel utilizations and eventually exchange this information via local broadcasts to calculate the AB. Usually these local broadcasts are performed using Hello packets that are used in many routing protocols to discover local topology. If these exchanges are not too frequent, this technique can be reasonably considered as non intrusive (Sarr, Chaudet et al., 2008). And thus sensing-based approaches are very suitable for wireless networks. In (Zhai, Chen et al., 2006), the authors proposed the index CBR (channel busyness ratio) for AB estimation, which is easy to obtain and can timely represent channel utilization. Though this algorithm is proposed for single-hop WLAN, it is straightforward to get the idea that the AB of the multi-hop path as illustrated in Fig. 1 can be got by calculating $\min\{1 - CBR_i, i = 1,2,...n+1\}$, where CBRi is the channel busy ratio that sensed by node Ni. K. Xu, etc. (Xu, Tang et al., 2003) adopted this idea and added a smoothing factor to mask transient effects. But they only considered the AB estimation at each node within the path and did not consider any possible distant interfering nodes. To fix this problem, QoS-AODV proposed in (de Renesse, Ghassemian et al., 2004) also performs such per-node AB estimation, but the bandwidth available to a node is computed as the minimum of the AB over its single-hop neighborhood. However, with 802.11 protocol, two nodes within carrier sense range share the medium and thus the bandwidth, even if they cannot directly communicate. To consider carrier sense range interfering, most existing literatures such as FAT (Wu, Wang et al., 2005) and CACP (Yang & Kravets, 2005), approximate the carrier sense area by the two-hop neighborhood. The basic ideas of them are alike: each node provides information about the total bandwidth it uses to route flows and about its one-hop neighbors as well as their usage of the bandwidth, by periodically broadcasting a Hello message containing this information. Then, each node can compute the bandwidth usage and then derive the AB in its two-hop neighborhood. Since the interference ranges of nodes within the same multi-hop path overlap, this phenomenon prevents a node from forwarding transmissions while any path members within its interference range are sending. Thus multiple links on the path of a flow contend for bandwidth, which is known as the intra-flow contention problem and was first studied in (Sanzgiri, Chakeres et al., 2004). Because of intra-flow contention, the actual AB for a flow should be further divided by the contention count (CC), namely the number of nodes that contend for bandwidth. The CC at node Ni can be represented as

$$CC_i = | CSN_i \cap NoP | + 1 \tag{4}$$

where CSNi is the set of nodes that within Ni's carrier sense range, NoP is the set of the nodes in the path. This problem is nontrivial because of the difficulty to find out the nodes within one node's carrier sense range. In literature, four methods were proposed to calculate CC: (1) based on the assumption that the interference range is the two-hop range, CC equals the hop count if the hop count is not more than 4, or 4 otherwise. This is the most popular approach in literature, e.g., (Chen & Heinzelman, 2005; Sarr, Chaudet et al., 2008); (2) increase the transmit power so that the packet can be successfully received by all the nodes in carrier sense range, e.g., CACP (Yang & Kravets, 2005); (3) sense the duration of the packet to determine the nodes in its carrier sense range, e.g., (Sanzgiri, Chakeres et al., 2004);

or (4) use localization information with the help of Global Position System (GPS)(Gupta, Musacchio et al., 2007). In the end, besides considering the carrier sense range media usage, the recent study ABE (Available Bandwidth Estimation) (Sarr, Chaudet et al., 2008) further considered the overlap probability of two adjacent nodes' idle time (Po), packet collision probability (Pc) and the proportion of bandwidth (K) consumed by the waiting process of 802.11 to improve the accuracy of AB estimation. Then the end-to-end AB of the path {N1, N2, N3 Nn+1} at time t is

$$AB(t) = min\left\{P_o \cdot (1-P_c) \cdot (1-K) \cdot \frac{AB_i(t)}{CC_i}, i = 1,2,...,n\right\} \quad (5)$$

Sensing-based approaches were first proposed for single-hop wireless networks and then extended to multi-hop wireless scenarios. In this research, improving the estimation accuracy acts as the main driver. And so far, there is still work to do. For instance, AAC (Adaptive Admission Control) protocol (de Renesse, Friderikos et al., 2007) and ABE scheme (Sarr, Chaudet et al., 2008) are recently proposed schemes for AB estimation in 802.11-based ad hoc networks, but both of them need further improving in the consideration of the overlap probability of two adjacent nodes' idle time, i.e., Po. In AAC, the transmitter and receiver are assumed to obtain perfectly synchronization, i.e., Po = 1. But, in fact, there is possibility that when the transmitter is sensing idle the receiver is busy and thus cannot receive the packets from the transmitter, and vice versa. Under this case, AAC will overestimate AB on the link between this transmitter-receiver pair. To resolve this problem, ABE use probability analysis to calculate Po under the assumption that each node's surrounding medium occupancy is a uniform random distribution and independent to each other. This assumption, however, ignores the factual dependence of the interfering around the sender and the receiver, and thus will also result in inaccurate estimation of AB. This observation inspired our work in (Zhao, Garcia-Palacios et al., 2009) to calculate the overlap probability for two adjacent nodes' idle periods while taking into consideration the factual dependence of the interfering around them. And consequently improve the accuracy of AB estimation in IEEE 802.11-based ad hoc networks.

Model-Based Approaches

The AB estimation approaches that utilize currently sensed information are often insufficient because they lack predictive power and scalability, just considering that the entrance of a new flow will result in the change of network parameters (i.e. collision probability) and further the real AB. We need an approach that with predictive power and has the ability and scalability to find the quantitive consequences of the entrance of new flows, and to achieve this goal, a proper model is necessary. In the seminal work of Bianchi (Bianchi, 2000), the authors provided an analysis model for the behavior of 802.11 DCF protocol assuming a two dimensional Markov model at the MAC layer. The main assumptions in this work are (i) every node is saturated (i.e. always has a packet waiting to be transmitted), (ii) transmission error is a result of packets collision and is not caused by channel errors and (iii) the network is homogeneous (i.e. each node acts the same). Provided that these assumptions are satisfied, the resulting model is remarkably accurate. However, these assumptions are not necessarily true in practical networks. First, the saturation assumption is unlikely to be valid in real multi-hop wireless networks. And even in WLANs, it is proved that the optimal work point1 of a network lies before it entering saturation (Zhai, Chen et al., 2005). Thus more recent studies have shifted the focus onto 802.11 networks operating in non-saturated conditions, such as (Malone, Duffy et al., 2007) and (Kun, Fan et al., 2007), where the authors extended the underlying model in order to consider unsaturated traffic conditions by introducing a new idle state that accounts for the case in which the node buffer is empty, after a successful packet transmission. To relax the dependence on the second assumption in (Bianchi, 2000), authors in (Chatzimisios, Boucouvalas et al., 2003) deal with the extension of Bianchi's Markov model in order to account for channel errors. And in (Qiao, Choi et al., 2002), the authors look at the impact of channel errors and the received SNR (Signal-to-Noise Ratio) on the achievable throughput in a system with rate adaptation, where the transmission rate of the terminal is adapted based on the link quality. (Daneshgaran,

Laddomada et al., 2008) extends the previous works on this subject by looking at a more realistic channel condition for unsaturated traffic, and their assumptions are essentially similar to those of Bianchi's with the exception that they do assume the presence of both channel errors and capture effects due to the transmission over a Rayleigh fading channel. To relax the dependence on the third assumption in (Bianchi, 2000), authors in (Ergen and Varaiya, 2005) propose a novel Markov model for the 802.11 DCF in a scenario with various nodes contending for the channel and transmitting with different transmission rates. An admission control mechanism is also proposed for maximizing the throughput while guaranteeing fairness to the involved transmitting nodes. And (Qiu, Zhang et al., 2007) develops a more general model to estimate the throughput, based on SNR or RSSI (Received Signal Strength Index) measurements from the underlying network itself and thus is more accurate than abstract propagation models based on distance. Their model also takes into account the general case of heterogeneous nodes with different traffic demands and different radio characteristics. While management decisions can be based on SNR or RSSI measurements from the PHY layer, it is known that these may be only weakly correlated with the actual channel behavior perceived at the MAC layer (Aguayo, Bicket et al., 2004). Model-based approaches are very useful for network performance analysis, but the challenge is that to build an accurate analysis model for multi-hop wireless networks is not an easy job.

1 The optimal work point is the turning point that the network should work around. Before that point, as the input traffic increases, the throughput keeps increasing, the delay and delay variation does not change much. After that point, the throughput drops quickly and the delay and delay variation increase dramatically.

SENSING-BASED APPROACHES FOR AB ESTIMATION

We already mentioned that the probe-based approaches presented above do not yield accurate results in a wireless ad hoc context because of their practical drawbacks. In this section, we will mainly focus on sensing-based approaches, considering the challenges for accurate AB estimation and then presenting some solutions to them.

Identification of the Nodes in the Carrier Sense Range

Under the DCF mode, a transmission within one node's carrier sense range will interfere its receiving, which means while estimating one node's busy time (which is the first step to obtain the AB) we have to consider the interference in the carrier sense range. Thus identifying the nodes in one node's carrier sense range, which is represented by CSN in (4), is important to accurately estimate end-to-end AB.

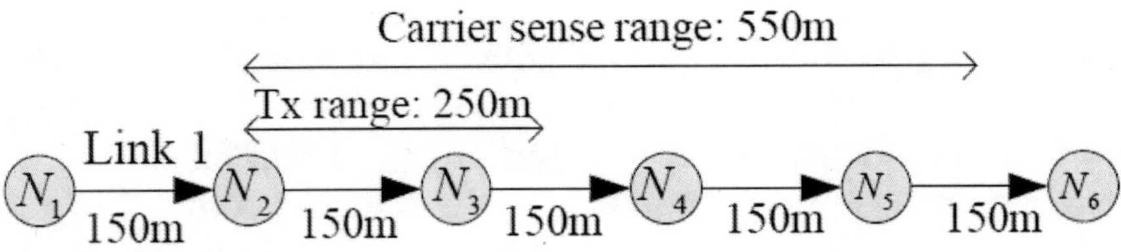

Figure. 2. Example scenario

In the majority approaches to identify the CSN, the node's carrier sense range is commonly expressed in terms of number of hops, k. And then use hello messages broadcast over the khop range to identify CSN. The most popular value of k is 2, e.g., (Chen & Heinzelman, 2005; Sarr, Chaudet et al., 2008; Wu, Wang et al., 2005) and the CACP-multihop in (Yang & Kravets, 2005) . However, this is not necessary true in real wireless scenarios. Take the case shown in Fig. 2 as an example. Node N5 is within the carrier sense range of N2, but 3 hops away from it. When N5 is transmitting to N6, the transmission will reduce the AB on Link 1 (N2 will sense the transmission from N5 and thus shut itself down according to 802.11 protocol, which prevents Link 1 being on). But this effect is not counted by the aforementioned approach which assumes the carrier sense range is two-hop range. To resolve this problem, in AAC (de Renesse, Friderikos et al., 2007), the value of k switches between 2 and 3 with respect to the roughness of the path. And it is claimed that the roughness of the path is very likely to depend on the network node density. A high node density involves more paths existing between two mobile hosts. If nodes are uniformly distributed, there is a high possibility that the shortest path will be the smoothest. However, this theory holds only when assuming all nodes have an identical circular propagation region. In (Yang & Kravets, 2005), Yang and Kravets also proposed two other different approaches, CACP-power and CACP-CS, to identify CSN. CACP-power assumes that the transmission power is variable. This approach consists of increasing the transmission power for bandwidth query messages such that all carrier sense nodes are able to decode it, which implies high power consumption and potential interferences as drawbacks. CACP-CS analyzes channel activity at a power threshold called Neighbor-carrier- sensing Threshold, which is set much lower than the carrier sensing threshold. Thus, each node is able to derive the bandwidth consumption of all its CSN. This technique minimizes overhead but could include isolated nodes that do not belong to any carrier sensing range. In real scenarios where noise interferes with almost any signal, such a low power threshold detection system might wrongly interpret channel activity. Without increasing the transmission power or decreasing the analysis power threshold, K. Sanzgiri, etc. (Sanzgiri, Chakeres et al., 2004) propose two methods, Pre-Reply Probe (PRP) and Route Request Tail(RRT), to obtain the number of CSN along a multi-hop path, i.e., CC in (4). The highlight of the proposed solutions is that carrier-sensing metrics such as the ,duration of sensed transmissions, is used to deduce the information of neighbors within carrier sense range, and no high power transmissions are necessary. But they either requires an additional message (PRPM) to be transmitted during route discovery (in PRP) or a tail is attached to RREQ packets (in RRT), which will increase the network overhead. Furthermore, counting sensed packets of a particular duration can enhance computing complexity and thus increases the route acquisition latency.

Estimation of the Collision Probability Under Unsaturated Ad Hoc Networks

Collision is one important characteristic of wireless networks (Bianchi, 2000; Zhai, Chen et al., 2005). There are two main reasons to bring collision: (1) after each node's backoff, two nodes start to transmit packet to a same node at the same time; (2) the collision brought by the problem of hidden node. After collision, a node has to back off and waits to retransmit. So the airtime taken by collision and back off can not be used to transmit data, thus should be eliminated from the AB, see (5). And to do that we have to first estimate the collision probability. The overwhelming majority of the analysis on collision probability is based on saturated scenario, i.e., Bianchi's landmark Markov model (Bianchi, 2000) and some research following it (Kuan & Dimyati, 2006). Unfortunately, as aforementioned that a very important task of network control is to avoid the network from saturation and keep it work at an unsaturated "optimal work point" (Zhai, Chen et al., 2005). It means the controlled network will work under unsaturated scenario. Thus recent research is focus on the analysis or estimation of the collision probability under the unsaturated scenario. The first inspiration is that we can rely on the models for non-saturated networks. In (Malone, Duffy et al., 2007), (Ahn, Campbell et al., 2002) and (Ergen & Varaiya, to appear), modifications of (Bianchi, 2000) are considered where a probability of not transmitting is introduced that represents a node which has transmitted a packet, but has none waiting. With these models, we can derive the collision probability in non-saturated networks. However, it is important to note that the Markov chain's evolution is not real-time, and so the estimation of collision probability and throughput requires an estimate of the average state duration. Furthermore, as aforementioned that accurate analysis models for multi-hop networks are difficult to build up and maintain in distributed networks. Without relying on analysis model for network behavior, ABE (Sarr, Chaudet et al., 2008) mconsidered the real-time estimation of collision probability via calculating the collision rate of Hello packets. The idea is that since every node knows how many Hello packets should be received from one neighbor during a specific period (usually defined by the routing protocol) thus it can measure the collision rate of Hello packets, p Hello, via keeping an account on the number of Hello packets it actually received. And then obtain the collision probability of data packets, pc, by multiplying a Lagrange interpolate polynomial to compensate the different packet size between data packets and Hello packets as follows,

$$p_c = f(m) \cdot p_{Hello} \tag{6}$$

$$f(m) = am^3 + bm^2 + cm + d \tag{7}$$

where m is the size of data packets; a, b, c and d are polynomial parameters, which are obtained after different simulations varying data packet sizes and network load in (Sarr, Chaudet et al., 2008). However, there are two main shortcomings when using this approach. The first issue is that Hello packets are sent at a much lower rate than that of data packets. For instance, when considering AODV routing protocol (Perkins, Royer et al., 2001), Hello packets are usually sent at the frequency of 1 packet per second. Only to recognize that at a rate of 2 Mbps and assuming packet sizes of 1K bytes around 250 data packets are sent for just 1 Hello packet. In theory we could adopt a wider measurement period (e.g., 10 seconds), however the ratio to data packets is still as high and the measurement period can be too long for fast changing topology scenarios that are likely to emerge in Ad hoc networks. Therefore, although collisions on Hello packets can give some idea on collisions rates of Data packets, it is impossible to get an accurate estimate. A second issue is that experiments have to be run in advance in order to get a relative accurate expression of the Lagrange interpolating polynomial (f(m)) for a given scenario, and this expression will change when varying the scenario (e.g. number of stations, topology and packet size profile).

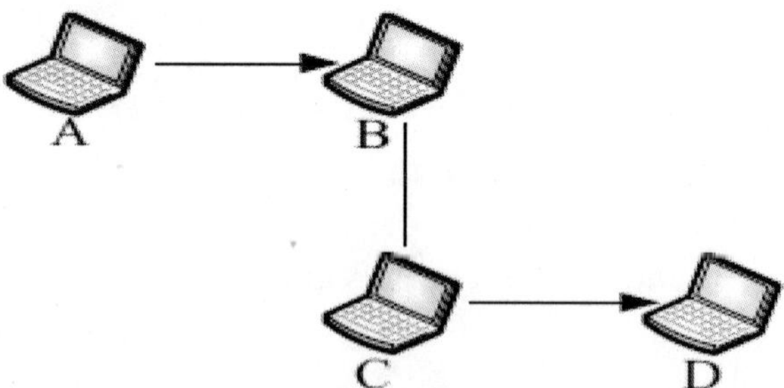

Figure. 3. A typical collision scenario

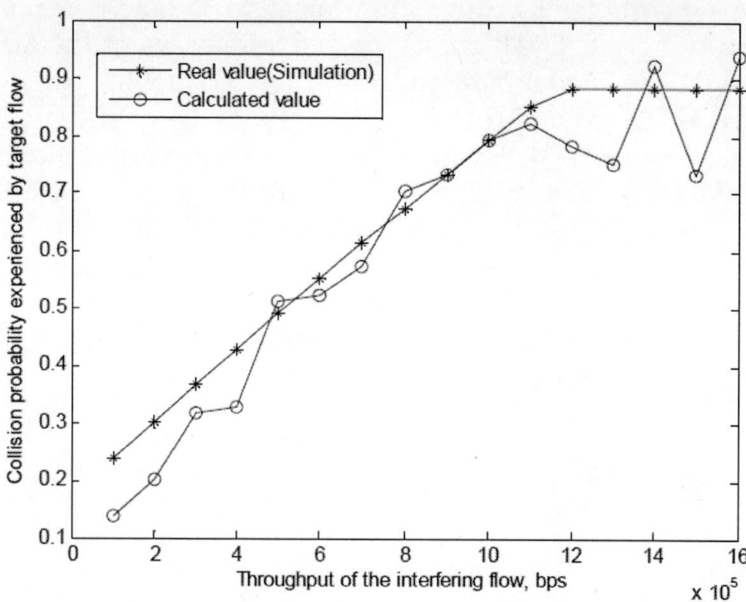

Figure. 4. Evaluation results

Let's consider the same typical collision scenario as in (Sarr, Chaudet et al., 2008), shown in Fig. 3, where C is a hidden node to A. Our aim is to use the aforementioned approach to estimate the collision probability over the target link A-B, which caused by the interfering flow C-D. As the throughput in the interfering flow changes, the collision probability over our target link changes. The simulated medium capacity is set 2 Mbps with a packet size of 1K bytes. And the results are plotted in Fig. 4, which shows the instability and the inaccuracy of estimating p by using Hello packets as in (Sarr, Chaudet et al., 2008).

Airtime Synchronization

For the communication to happen, the medium has to be free on the sender's side so that the sender gains access the medium. On the receiver's side, the medium has to be free during the time required to transmit the whole data frame to avoid colliding. In other words, the medium availability on the sender and receiver sides has to somehow synchronize for the communication to take place. Fig. 5 (Sarr, Chaudet et al., 2008) shows two extreme case of the airtime availability at the sender side and the receiver side: (a) when they are never overlapped and (b) when they are totally overlapped. We can see that though in both cases, the idle airtime values measured at each node are the same but in case (a), the periods of airtime availability of both peers never overlap and the AB on the link is null. In the opposite case, the scenario depicted in (b) offers several communication opportunities on the link, when both sides are idle. So we have to consider this synchronization problem of the airtime at the sender and receiver side when estimate the AB.

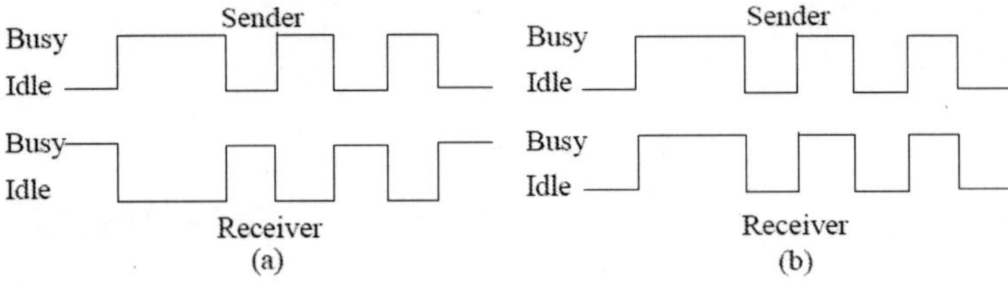

when they are never overlap; (b) when they are totally overlap

Figure. 5. Airtime at the sender side and the receiver side

Many existing publications, e.g., AAC (de Renesse, Friderikos et al., 2007) and (Wu, Wang et al., 2005), calculating the idle time ratio on Link i, enoted as Ri , as

$$R_i = \min\{r_i, r_{i+1}\} \tag{8}$$

where ri and ri+1 are the idle time ratio sensed by Ni and Ni+1. These works actually assume that the airtime is totally overlapped. In order to obtain a more accurate consideration of the airtime synchronization, ABE (Sarr, Chaudet et al., 2008) assumes that the each node's surrounding medium occupancy is a uniform random distribution and the idle time ratio on Link i is represented by

$$R_i = r_i \cdot r_{i+1} \quad (9)$$

But for adjacent nodes, neither their airtime could be synchronized naturally nor are they independent to each other. In our recent research (Zhao, Garcia-Palacios et al., 2009), we have evaluated the approaches proposed in AAC and ABE to reveal the insufficiency of them. And we further proposed an AB estimation approach IAB (Improved Available Bandwidth estimation) which achieves more accurate estimation in [25]. The main contribution of IAB is that it considered the natural dependence between the medium state that sensed by two adjacent nodes. And this consideration is realized as follows. We first differentiate the channel busy state caused by Transmitting/Receiving and the channel Sensing state. And this differentiation results in a more accurate estimation of the overlap probability of the idle times between two adjacent nodes and consequently a more accurate estimation of the AB between these nodes.

Intra-Flow Contention

Intra-flow contention prevents a node from forwarding transmissions while any path members within its interference range are sending, thus reduce the end-to-end AB of a multi-hop path. Therefore, we have to take this phenomenon into consideration when estimate the end-to-end AB in multi-hop ad hoc networks. As described in Section 2.2, the overwhelming approaches to consider the intra-flow contention is to divide the AB further by the contention count, i.e., CC, and in literature there are three methods to calculate the CC. These methods are not satisfactory in that they either too simplified to reflect the real scenario (Chen & Heinzelman, 2005; Sarr, Chaudet et al., 2008), or increase the power consumption (Yang & Kravets, 2005) or complexity (de Renesse, Friderikos et al., 2007; Sanzgiri, Chakeres et al., 2004) of the network control. And what makes the problem worse is that even if we can accurately get the value of CC, dividing the bottleneck link's AB by CC (this method is referred to as the average-based method for brevity) cannot provide the accurate information of the end-to-end AB. The reason lies in that there is a throughput deviation of each link which leads to overlapping of simultaneously transmitting packets and collisions. Recently, authors in (Jae-Yong & JongWon, 2007) use the central limit theorem to model the throughput deviation, assuming the summation of uniformly distributed backoff times, which is referred to as the deviationbased method. Unfortunately, the proposed throughput deviation model can only consider the collisions due to two simultaneous transmissions along a path.

This is invalid when there are more than 4 hops, in which case more collision scenarios exist. For clarity, let's consider an n-hop path, as illustrated in Fig. 1. The distance between two adjacent nodes is kept 200m in order to ensure that a flow generated in N1 will go through each intermediate node and reaches the destination while we set transmitting range and carrier sense range respectively as 250m and 550m. In Fig. 6, we vary the number of hops, i.e., n, and plot the calculated end-to-end AB using average-based method, deviation-based method as well as the real value via simulation (The simulated medium capacity is also set 2 Mbps with a packet size of 1K bytes as in Fig. 4). Fig. 6 clearly shows that the average-based method does not reflect the real value when the hop count is 4 or more because it neglects the collision due to throughput deviation of each link. Note that there is no collision for 3 or less hops, in which case the throughput average method matches the real value. Deviation-based method still accurately estimates the AB when the hop count is 4. However, it disagrees with the real AB after the path exceeds 4 hops, which keeps on decreasing.

This estimation error can be explained by that more collisions appear when the hop count exceeds 4 which will further decrease the AB. (The average collision probability is also showed in Fig. 6.) The results demonstrate that the model in (Jae-Yong & JongWon, 2007) which only considers the collisions due to two simultaneous transmissions will produce an inaccurate AB calculation when the hop count is more than 4. To solve this problem, our recent study (Zhao, Wang et al., 2010) proposes and validates a model to analyze the intra-flow contention of a given path in multi-hop wireless networks. The basic idea is twofold: (i) We consider the intra-flow contention problem with an analysis model that account for the contenting links' behavior, instead of just calculating the contention count. (ii) The model envelops important factors for intra-flow contention, i.e., neighboring interference, hidden-node collision and possible multi-rate scenario, which make it approach reality and obtain accurate results. (The results obtained by our proposed model under the aforementioned scenario are also shown in Fig. 6, with the legend of Modelbased AB estimation.)

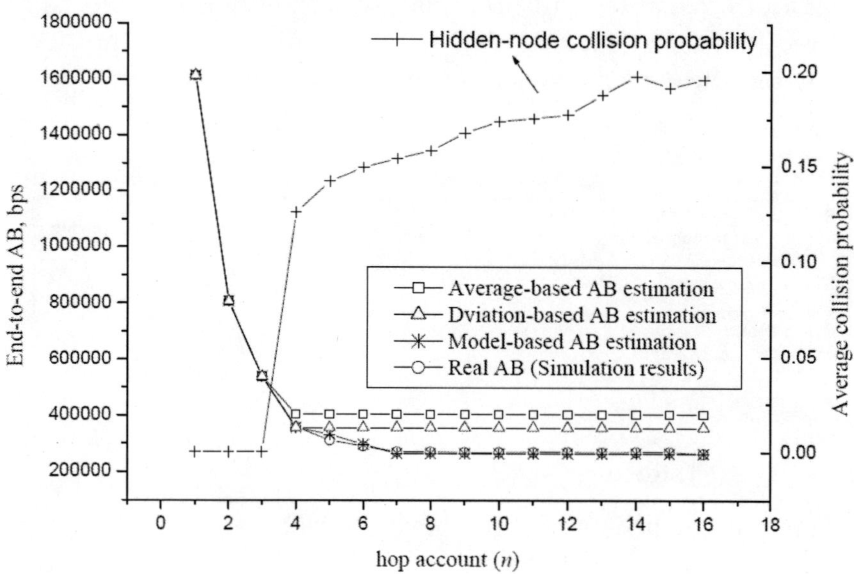

Figure. 6. End-to-end AB while varying the hop count

MODEL-BASED APPROACHES FOR AB PREDICTION

The model-based approaches are of redictive power and the current challenge is to derive more accurate and scalable analysis model. We will show our effort on this topic in this section.

Analytical Model

For a better understanding, we give an overview of our model as shown in Fig. 7. Our model takes network information (topology and existing traffic), radio-dependent parameters and incoming traffic throughput demands as input and outputs the predictive throughputs of both the incoming flow and existing flows. Such a model is a powerful tool for performing what-if analysis and facilitating network optimization and diagnosis. Although in this chapter we focus on the throughput demands, or bandwidth requirement, of the flow, there is coupling of bandwidth and delay over a wireless link as shown in (Chen, Xue et al., 2004). So the model in this chapter can potentially be extended to analyze other QoS requirements, such as delay, by relating them to the network parameters, however this is out the scope of this chapter.

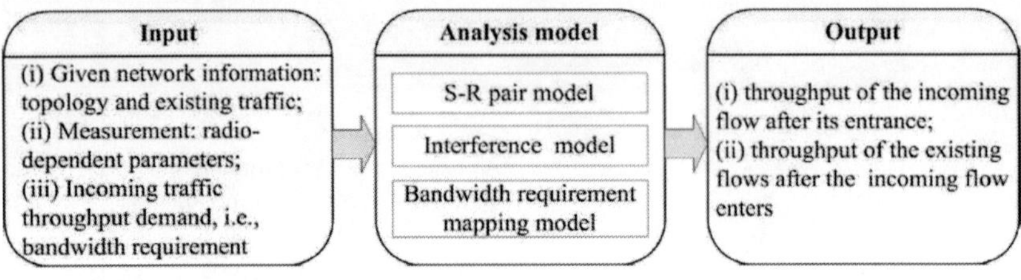

Figure. 7. Model structure

The model consists of three major components: S-R (i.e., sender-receiver) pair model, interference model and bandwidth requirement mapping model. These models will be covered in Sections 3.2, 3.3 and 3.4 respectively. The S-R pair model gives the link state from the view of an S-R pair, and considers important probabilities such as the transmission probability, the unsuccessful transmission probability, the sense busy probability and the non-empty transmission buffer probability. The interference model constructs the contention graph of the network, in order to analyze the interference of contending links. The bandwidth requirement mapping model relates the network parameters in the S-R pair model and interference model to the bandwidth requirement of the incoming flow(s). It is also important to initiate some key parameters that used in this model, which is explained in Section 3.5.

S-R Pair Model

The behavior of an S-R pair that employs an 802.11 protocol is dictated by the occupation of the 'air' around it (the channel). We denote the sender and receiver respectively as Nk-1 and Nk, and the link between them as Link k. We adopt the concept of generic slot used in (Dao & Malaney, 2008) (which is also denoted as variable length slots (VLS) in (Li, Qiu et al., 2008)), thus for the channel sensed by the Link k, 4 different states can be identified:

i. Idle—Nk-1 has seen the medium as idle and, either it has no data to send or its backoff counter has not reached 0 (i.e. backoff is in process).

ii. Successful transmission—Nk-1 has transmitted a packet, received an ACK from Nk and is about to resume backoff.

iii. Unsuccessful transmission—Nk-1 has transmitted, timed-out while waiting for an ACK from Nk and is about to resume its backoff.

iv. Sense busy—Nk-1 has detected the medium busy due to one or more other nodes transmitting, by means of either physical or virtual carrier sensing (i.e., the Network Allocation Vector, NAV), and has suspended its backoff until the NAV and DIFS/ EIFS indicate that the backoff can resume.

The average time intervals during which Link k remains in idle, successful transmission, unsuccessful transmission and sense busy are denoted by □, Tk, Ck, and Bk, respectively. □ is constant, equal to the backoff slot. The duration of the other intervals can be variable, depending on the access mechanism, the frame size, and the sending rate. From the perspective of the S-R pair, the evolution of the channel state of Link k can be abstractly represented by a temporal diagram such as the one exemplified in Fig. 8(b). So the average length of the Generic slot of link k can be expressed as:

$$E_k = \tau_k p_k C_k + \tau_k(1-p_k)T_k + (1-\tau_k)b_k B_k + (1-\tau_k)(1-b_k)\sigma \quad (10)$$

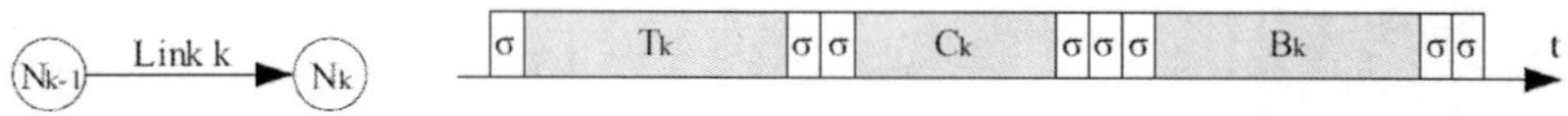

The S-R pair; (b) The state of the channel between the S-R pair

Figure. 8. S-R pair model

where τ_k represents the transmission probability on one time slot; p_k is the unsuccessful transmission probability. b_k is the channel busy probability. Then the normalized channel utilization ratio (i.e., the normalized transmitting airtime whether successfully or not, represented by x_k) and the successful transmission time ratio (represented by y_k) of Link k can be expressed as:

$$x_k = \frac{\tau_k p_k C_k + \tau_k (1 - p_k) T_k}{E_k} \quad (11)$$

$$y_k = \frac{\tau_k (1 - p_k) T_k}{E_k} \quad (12)$$

The throughput of Link k is, in pkt/s

$$S_k = \frac{\tau_k (1 - p_k) \Lambda}{E_k} \quad (13)$$

where Λ is the effective load fraction. In equation (10), the average durations of a successful transmission and of an unsuccessful one are known a priori according to the 802.11 DCF standard (see (Bianchi, 2000), here we neglect the propagation delay). They are as follows under the Basic mode and RTS/CTS mode:

$$\begin{cases} T_k^{(Basic)} = DIFS + DATA + SIFS + ACK \\ C_k^{(Basic)} = DIFS + DATA + ACK_{timeout} \end{cases} \quad (14)$$

$$\begin{cases} T_k^{(RTS/CTS)} = DIFS + RTS + CTS + DATA + ACK + 3 \cdot SIFS \\ C_k^{(RTS/CTS)} = DIFS + RTS + CTS_{timeout} \end{cases} \quad (15)$$

In single-hop 802.11 networks all nodes are synchronized

and the duration of a busy period equals the sum of the other nodes' transmitting duration. However, in the multi-hop case, transmissions of different nodes can overlap randomly due to the lack of coordination, which makes the determination of one node's busy period more complex. We take the assumption that if two links, for instance Link i and Link j, cannot sense each other, their action is independent to each other, this assumption is shown reasonable in (Gao, Chiu et al., 2006). So the overlap probability, denoted by P*overlap*(i,j), of these two links' transmitting airtime can be approximated as

$$P_{overlap}(i,j) = \frac{x_i \times x_j}{1 - \sum_{c \in v(i,j)} x_c} \tag{16}$$

where v(i) represents the set of contending links (i.e., the links that contend with each other, and we will present them in Section 3.3) of Link i and v(i,j) the set of common contending links of Link i and Link j. In Eq. (16), the numerator is the normalized probability that they transmit at the same time. When their common contending links are transmitting, neither of them can transmit, therefore the denominator represents the total time that they can use to transmit. Eq. (16) is referred to as the second-order approximation, which will be used again in our future analysis. Thus the sense busy time of Link k can be obtained via

$$B_k = \left(\sum_{i \in v(k)} x_i - \sum_{\substack{i_1, i_2 \in v(k); \\ i_1 \notin v(i_2) \cup i_2}} \frac{x_{i_1} x_{i_2}}{1 - \sum_{c \in v(i_1, i_2)} x_c} \right) E_k \tag{17}$$

A. CALCULATING THE TRANSMISSION PROBABILITY

We should keep in mind that to support an application throughput along one route, the nodes on this route may have different transmission probabilities considering they may experience different collision probabilities. But in this section we temporarily drop the subscript, k, of the symbols for brevity. A node can begin transmission when the following three conditions are satisfied: i) the node has data to transmit; ii) the link is idle; and iii) its random backoff counter reaches 0. The first one is related to the transmission queue. The last two are related to the interference by neighboring nodes. More specifically, one node's backoff counter is related to the unsuccessful transmission probability it experiences. The transmission probability □ is a function of unsuccessful transmission probability p, which is first given in (Bianchi, 2000) under saturated situations. Recently, in (Kumar, Altman et al., 2007)and (Malone, Duffy et al., 2007) similar expressions of □ as a function of p are derived respectively for a large class of backoff mechanisms and for unsaturated situations. The complete expression of τ for 802.11 that takes into account the maximum retransmission limit jointly with the maximum window size and non-saturation case is given by

$$\tau = \eta \cdot \left(\frac{q^2 W_0}{(1-q)(1-p)(1-(1-q)^{W_0})} - \frac{q^2(1-p)}{1-q} \right) \tag{18}$$

where η is the stationary probability of a node being in the state where the backoff process is complete, but the node's transmission queue is empty (Malone, Duffy et al., 2007).

$$\begin{aligned} \frac{1}{\eta} = (1-q) + \frac{q^2 W_0 (W_0+1)}{2(1-q)(1-(1-q)^{W_0})} + \frac{q(W_0+1)(p(1-q)-q(1-p)^2)}{2(1-q)} \\ + \frac{pq^2}{2(1-q)(1-p)} \left(\frac{W_0}{1-(1-q)^{W_0}} - (1-p)^2 \right) \left(\frac{2W_0(1-p-p(2p)^{m-1})}{(1-2p)} + 1 \right) \end{aligned} \tag{19}$$

And q is the probability that there is at least one packet in the queue after a transmission, which is mainly related to the traffic load and it will be discussed in Subsection D. W0 and 2mW0 are respectively the node's minimum and maximum contention window.

B. CALCULATING THE UNSUCCESSFUL TRANSMISSION PROBABILITY P

The unsuccessful transmission probability p may arise from collisions or channel failure. We identify three different categories of unsuccessful transmissions as follows: (i) due to collision between synchronized nodes, which occurs with the probability of lsc; (ii) due to hidden nodes, which occurs with the probability of lhc; (iii) due to channel errors, which occurs with the probability of le. And we assume that these three probabilities are statistically independent, then a transmission is successful if it does not suffer from any of the three types of unsuccessful transmission mentioned above (they may occur simultaneously) and thus the unsuccessful transmission probability is:

$$p = 1 - (1 - l_{sc})(1 - l_{hc})(1 - l_e) \quad (20)$$

Collisions between synchronized nodes are the traditional type of packet losses due to the MAC protocol considered in single-hop 802.11 networks (Bianchi, 2000). Indeed, when all senders are in range of each other, the DCF function is able to synchronize all nodes in such a way that all transmission attempts happen at well defined slot boundaries recognized by all nodes. As a result, in this network scenario the conditional unsuccessful transmission probability for Link k is simply given by

$$p_{sc}^{k} = 1 - \prod_{i \neq k, i \in v(k)} (1 - \tau_i) \quad (21)$$

If each node has the same transmission probability then we will obtain the same result as in (Bianchi, 2000): $1-(1-\tau)^{n-1}$, where n is the total number of nodes in the WLAN. However, in a multi-hop topology the DCF function fails to synchronize all nodes and the hidden node collision usually account for an important component of the overall packet collision probability. The hidden node collision has been modeled in (Zhao, Wang et al., 2010). If node j is node k's hidden node, the collision probability experienced at node k due to node j is as follows (using $p_{hc}^{k,j,(1)}$ and $p_{hc}^{k,j,(2)}$ to respectively denote the case when node j is the Type I and Type II hidden node2 to node k)

$$p_{hc}^{k,j,(1)} = \frac{x_j}{1 - \sum_{c \in v(j,k)} x_c + \sum_{\substack{m,n \in v(j,k);\\ m \notin v(n) \cup n}} \frac{x_m \times x_n}{1 - \sum_{c \in v(m,n)} x_c}} \tag{22}$$

$$p_{hc}^{k,j,(2)} = \frac{x_k + x_j}{1 - \sum_{c \in v(j,k)} x_c + \sum_{\substack{m,n \in v(j,k);\\ m \notin v(n) \cup n}} \frac{x_m \times x_n}{1 - \sum_{c \in v(m,n)} x_c}} \tag{23}$$

Once we know the type of hidden node to Link i, the overall hidden node collision probability is the union of, $p_{hc}^{k,j}, j \in h(k)$ ($h(k)$ represents the set of hidden node to Link k), namely:

$$p_{hc}^{k} = \sum_{j \in h(k)} p_{hc}^{k,j} - \sum_{\substack{m,n \in h(k);\\ m \notin v(n) \cup n}} \frac{p_{hc}^{k,m} \times p_{hc}^{k,n}}{1 - \sum_{c \in v(m,n)} x_c} \tag{24}$$

Here, we also use the second-order approximation to unfold the union expression. Note that the collision may not necessarily result in packet loss, considering the capture effect. The capture effect is the ability of certain radios to correctly receive a strong signal from one transmitter despite significant interference from other transmitters. It means that even when two nodes simultaneously transmit, the one with stronger power still has chance to be correctly received. We introduce a parameter $0 \leq \alpha \leq 1$ to reflect the average impact of the capture effect, which is referred to as the capture indicator in this chapter, thus

$$l_{sc} = (1-\alpha)p_{sc} \qquad (25)$$

$$l_{hc} = (1-\alpha)p_{hc} \qquad (26)$$

To obtain p, the problem is reduced to obtaining the channel error probability le and the capture indicator α. We show how to obtain them via measurement in Section 4.1.4.

C. CALCULATING THE SENSE BUSY PROBABILITY B

The sense busy probability, b, is the probability that the channel becomes busy after an idle slot due to the activity of other nodes, under the condition that link k does not start its own transmission. It is equal to the probability that at least one contending link is transmitting, whether it is successful or not

$$b_k = 1 - \prod_{i \in v(k) \bigcup k} (1-\tau_i) \qquad (27)$$

D. CALCULATING THE NON-EMPTY TRANSMISSION BUFFER PROBABILITY Q

The variable q represents the probability that there is at least one packet in the queue after a transmission. In the previous models, to analyze the performance of saturated wireless networks, each node in the network is assumed to always have a packet to transmit (i.e., q=1). But according to the work in (Zhai, Chen et al., 2006), the network does not perform best when it is saturated and extensive research has been undertaken to prevent the network from saturation. So the effect of q must be considered in the model. We introduce a parameter λ representing the rate at which packets arrive at the node buffer from the upper layers, and measured in pkt/s. The mean time between two packet arrivals is defined as the mean inter-packet time, and thus its value can be calculated as 1 /λ . A crude approximation in the unsaturated setting is to assume that packet arrivals are uniformly distributed across slots and set

$$q = \min\left\{\frac{E}{mean\ inter\text{ - }packet\ time},\ 1\right\} = \min\{\lambda \cdot E,\ 1\} \tag{28}$$

where E is the average length of the Generic slot obtained via Eq. (1) and measured in seconds. If the traffic arrives in a Poisson distribution, then probability q can be well approximated in a situation with small buffer size through the following relations as (Malone, Duffy et al., 2007) and (Daneshgaran, Laddomada et al., 2008) revealed:

$$q = 1 - e^{-\lambda E} \tag{29}$$

Here the packet arrival probability is assumed independent to the channel state. A more accurate model can be derived upon considering different values of q for each backoff state. However, it has been proved in (Malone, Duffy et al., 2007) that as state-dependent models are more computational involved, there seems little advantage in employing a statedependent model instead of the state-independent model. Thus it is a reasonable solution using a mean probability valid for the whole Markov model. Note that, in (29), placing the node in saturation by taking the limit q->1, the model is reduced to a model for saturated scenarios.

Interference Model

Given a set of wireless nodes, a network can be mapped into a contention graph (Chen, Low et al., 2005). This contention graph is used to represent interference (i.e. which link is interfering with which link) which has a consequent impact upon throughp4ut. We use contention graphs to model the interference between contending links. In the literature, contention graph models have not considered contention due to hidden nodes which is an important difference in our work. The process of mapping a network topology into a contention graph is introduced in (Chen, Low et al., 2005) and (Gao, Chiu et al., 2006). To illustrate this concept, we take the 4-hop chain network in Fig. 9(a) as a simple example, where nodes on the route are placed with the transmission distance Rtx. And RCS represents the carrier-sense range.

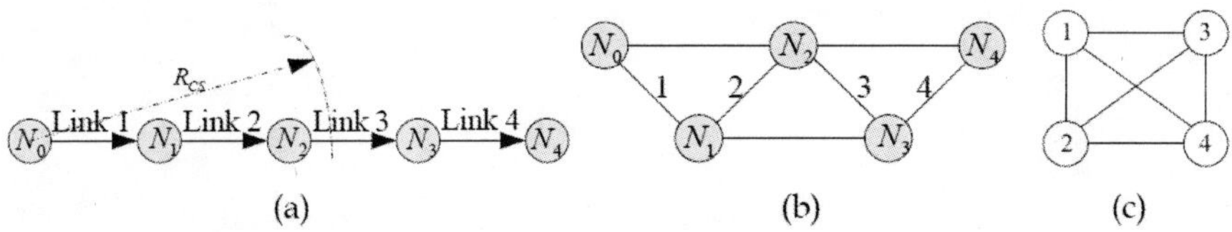

Figure. 9. Process of mapping a multi-hop route to its contention graph: (a) Example network; (b) undirected graph of the network; (c) contention graph

In Fig. 9 (b), nodes that can sense each other are connected. For instance, N0 is connected to N1 and N2 because these two nodes are within the carrier-sense range of N0 and they are considered neighbors of N0. However N3 and N4 cannot be sensed by N0 and therefore are not connected to N0. The numbers beside each edge are used to label all active links in the wireless network, i.e., Link 1, Link 2, Link 3 and Link 4. Finally, in the contention graph in Fig. 9 (c), all active links are transformed into vertices. An edge between two vertices denotes contention between two links. This can be deduced from Fig. 9(b). Two links contend with each other when either the sender or the receiver of one link is within the RCS distance of the sender or the receiver of the other, thus they are called contending link to each other. Note that previous work on contention graph only considered the interference due to neighboring nodes; while hidden node interferences were not modeled (i.e. in previous work there is no edge between Vertex 1 and Vertex 4 in Fig. 9(c)). In this research, we will consider interference due to both, neighboring and hidden nodes. Note that the aggregate successful transmission time ratio of contending links in the network should not be more than 1, thus we have the following interference constraint

$$\sum_{i \in v(k)} y_i \le 1, \ \forall k \in \mathbb{N} \quad (30)$$

where $\mathbb{N}$ is the set of all active links in the given network.

Mapping Bandwidth Requirement to the Model Parameters

In this section, we related the bandwidth requirement of a flow, to the network parameters. For instance, to satisfy the application bandwidth requirement (BW, bps), given the traffic packet size (PS, bits), the packet arrival rate is

$$\lambda = \frac{BW}{PS \cdot \Lambda} \tag{31}$$

And according to (13), we can easily obtain that the transmission probability used for this application by a link (Link k) along the path of this application is at least

$$\tau_k = \frac{BW \cdot E_k}{PS \cdot (1 - p_k) \cdot \Lambda} = \frac{\lambda \cdot E_k}{(1 - p_k)} \tag{32}$$

Recalling equations (18) and (21), the transmission probability will further affect the packet collision thus the unsuccessful transmission probability p, which will in turn affect the transmission probability, see (32). The coupling of the network parameters relates the bandwidth requirement of a flow to all the network parameters.

Parameters Initialization

We still need to obtain two radio-dependent parameters to complete the model. Those are the conditional capture indicator α and the channel failure probability le. In this section, we estimate these two parameters by conducting broadcast measurement. The key idea is that we can estimate unicast interference using broadcast packets.

First, we have one node, Node i, broadcasts packets and we keep track of the delivery rate of the packets at all other nodes in the network. Only one node is active at a time. We denote the broadcast rate as Ri and the delivery rate from Node i to Node j as Rij. Then each node broadcasts in turn. We then select a pair of nodes, Node i and Node k, and have them broadcast packets together. All remaining nodes measure the delivery rate of packets they receive from each of the two broadcasting nodes. For example, at node j, the delivery rate of packets from i is denoted by $R_{ij}^{i,k}$. Then each pair of nodes simultaneously broadcast in turn. Thus, we have carried out a total of $o(n^2)$experiments, where n is the number of nodes in the network. Using the data gathered from the above methodology, we can obtain the maximumlikelihood estimators for the channel error probability for the channel from node i and node j (denoted by $l_e^{i\rightarrow j}$) and the average capture effect experienced by the link from node i to node j (denoted by α_{ij}) as:

$$l_e^{i\rightarrow j} = \frac{R_i - R_{ij}}{R_i} \qquad (33)$$

$$\alpha_{ij} = \sum_{k\in N, k\neq i} \tau_i \tau_k \frac{R_{ij}^{i,k}}{R_{ij}} \qquad (34)$$

Model-Based Algorithms for Ab Prediction

We have built up a model considering the bandwidth requirement of a new flow and some other parameters: transmission probability, collision probability. After constructing the contention graph for a given network, we can easily perform admission control and end-toend AB estimation in order to guarantee throughputs to applications in multi-hop wireless networks.

Admission Control

Table 1. Admission control

▷ Input: bandwidth requirement, i.e., BW, of the incoming flow;
given route $\Gamma = \{N_0, N_1, ..., N_r\}$

▷ Output: whether the flow can be admitted

Initialization : *admission* = 0; $\tau_k = \tau_k^{old} + \dfrac{BW \cdot F_k^{old}}{PS \cdot (1 - l_e) \cdot \Lambda}, k = 1, 2, ..., r$

// iterative admission control (MaxIter = 20 and THD = 0.01 by default)

for *iter* = 1 **to** *MaxIter*

  update ($\{p_{i \in v(k)}, \tau_{i \in v(k)}\}$ *and* $\{p_k, \tau_k\}$) *// according to* (18) *and* (20)

  calculate ($y_{i \in N}$) *// according to* (17)

  if *any k satisfies* ($\sum_{i \in v(k)} y_i > 1$) *// interference constraint is violated*

    admission = 0; *break* *// early stop : reject*

  end if

  $\tau_k^{o} = \dfrac{BW \cdot F_k}{PS \cdot (1 - p_k) \cdot \Lambda}, k = 1, 2, ..., r$

  if ($\max_{k=1,2,...,r} \{\| \tau_k^{o} - \tau_k \|\} < THD$) *// convergence test*

    admission = 1; *break* *// early stop : admit*

  end if

end for

return *admission*, τ_k^{o}

Given the bandwidth requirement of a coming flow, the goal of admission control is to make a decision on whether the requesting flow can be admitted without impairing the QoS of existing flows. The main challenge is that we cannot make the accurate decision according to the network states before the flow entered because the entrance of the flow will change the transmission probability and collision probability. So the idea in this research is to adopt a what-if analysis, namely to check what will happen if the new flow is admitted. Since there is strong inter-dependency between the transmission probability and the loss rate of contending links: the transmission probability of Link k, τ_k, depends on its packets loss probability as well as the transmission probability of its contending links, which in turn depends on τ_k (refer to Eq. (18) and (21)). To address the inter-dependency, we use an iterative procedure to jointly estimate the transmission probabilities and loss probabilities We initialize that after a new flow entering, the collision probabilities (including collisions due to both synchronized nodes and hidden nodes) at all links for this flow are zero. We then iteratively update link transmission probabilities and packet loss probabilities based on the other links' transmission probabilities and loss probabilities derived in the previous iteration. The iterative procedure continues until the number of iterations reaches a threshold (MaxIter), or the transmission probability no longer change significantly (Less than a threshold THD), or a interference constraint (see (30)) is violated. The algorithm is outlined in Table 1. In line 1, τ_k^{old} and E_k^{old} are the corresponding parameters estimated on Link k before the entrance of the new flow. If there is no traffic on Link k before the entrance of the new flow, then $\tau_k^{old} = 0$ and E_k^{old} =Tk . This algorithm performs the admission control along a given route, and it also calculates the sending rate of the sender to guarantee the bandwidth requirement (obtained via Line 8). This algorithm can also help

End-to-End AB Prediction

Table 2. End-to-end AB prediction

```
▷ Input: given route Γ={N_0, N_1,..., N_r};
▷ Output: λ (the available bandwidth of Γ)
1: initialization : λ = λ_0 / 2    //λ_0 is the theoretic maximum capacity
   //iterative process (MaxIter = 20 and THD = 1kbps by default)
2: for i = 2 to MaxIter
3:     λ° = (1/2^i) λ_0
4:     if (λ° < THD) //convergence test
5:         break //early stop
6:     end if
7:     if (admission control(λ, Γ))
8:         λ = λ + λ°
9:     else
10:        λ = λ − λ°
11:    end if
12: end for
13: return λ
```

Let's exploit the following property in 802.11 networks (Kun, Fan et al., 2007): if the throughput of λ is feasible along a given route without violating the QoS of ongoing traffic, all throughputs smaller than λ are also feasible; while if the throughput is unfeasible, all the values larger than λ are also unfeasible. Thus, we can increase the value of λ until it is not feasible to find the end-to-end AB of path Γ without breaking the QoS demands of all existing traffic. Hence the solution can be obtained with logarithmic complexity by applying a binary search algorithm (half the search space each time). It is worth mentioning that to find the end-to-end AB is different to performing admission control, the latter is only the answer to whether a flow along a given route with a specific bandwidth requirement can be admitted, while the former need to further find out the maximum bandwidth of a flow that can be admitted. Table 2 outlines the algorithm, which takes the admission control as a sub function. In Line 1, λ 0 is the theoretic maximum capacity, which is the upper bound of our algorithm's searching space. Since the algorithm will converge very fast, the accuracy of this value will not affect the result significantly only if it is bigger than the estimated end-to-end AB. In an n-hop network, representing C as the channel physical capacity, λ 0 is set according to the following equations (i.e., the maximum capacity is limited by the number of hops due to the existence of intra-flow contention):

$$\lambda_0 = \begin{cases} C/n, & 1 \le n \le 4 \\ C/4, & n > 4 \end{cases} \tag{35}$$

CONCLUSION

With the IEEE 802.11-based ad hoc networks deployed as the vital extension to wired networks and the widespread use of multimedia applications that require QoS support, AB estimation is such an important operation that it is very necessary for research community to create an effective, general-purpose estimation method. This chapter reviews the state-of-theart of AB estimation in IEEE 802.11-based ad hoc networks, gives an analysis of the challenges on this topic. The analysis mainly focuses on fundamental problems, which rise from the nature of wireless networks and operation of DCF mode. To develop estimation tools that can work accurately in 802.11 or 802.11-alike ad hoc networks, researchers are expected to think over all these challenges. It then gives some solutions to these challenges. In particular, it presents our solutions to improve the accuracy of sensing-based AB estiamtion and modelbased AB predictation. We hope that this analysis can help to spur further work on this topic.

ACKNOWLEDGEMENTS

This work is partly supported by the National Natural Science Foundation of China (Grant No. 61002032).

REFERENCES

1. Aguayo, D.;Bicket, J., et al. (2004). Link-level measurements from an 802.11b mesh network. Proceedings of the 2004 conference on Applications, technologies, architectures, and protocols for computer communications (SIGCOMM), Portland, Oregon, USA, ACM.
2. Ahn, G.-S.;Campbell, A. T., et al. (2002). Supporting service differentiation for real-time and best-effort traffic in stateless wireless ad hoc networks (SWAN). IEEE Transactions on Mobile Computing 1(3): 192–207.
3. Bianchi, G. (2000). Performance analysis of the IEEE 802.11 distributed coordination function. IEEE Journal on Selected Areas in Communications 18(3): 535-547.
4. Chatzimisios, P.;Boucouvalas, A. C., et al. (2003). Influence of channel BER on IEEE 802.11 DCF. Electronics Letters 39(23): 1687-9.
5. Chen, K.;Xue, Y., et al. (2004). Understanding bandwidth-delay product in mobile ad hoc networks. Computer Communications 27(10): 923-934.
6. Chen, L. and Heinzelman, W. B. (2005). QoS-aware routing based on bandwidth estimation for mobile ad hoc networks. IEEE Journal on Selected Areas in Communications 23(3): 561-572.
7. Chen, L.;Low, S. H., et al. (2005). Joint congestion control and media

access control design for ad hoc wireless networks. Proceedings of IEEE INFOCOM.

8. Daneshgaran, F.;Laddomada, M., et al. (2008). Unsaturated Throughput Analysis of IEEE 802.11 in Presence of Non Ideal Transmission Channel and Capture Effects. IEEE Transactions on Wireless Communications 7(4): 1276-1286.
9. Dao, N. T. and Malaney, R. A. (2008). A New Markov Model for Non-Saturated 802.11 Networks. 5th IEEE Consumer Communications and Networking Conference (CCNC).
10. de Renesse, R.;Friderikos, V., et al. (2007). Cross-layer cooperation for accurate admission control decisions in mobile ad hoc networks. IET Communications 1(4): 577 586.
11. de Renesse, R.;Ghassemian, M., et al. (2004). QoS enabled routing in mobile ad hoc networks. Fifth IEE International Conference on 3G Mobile Communication Technologies (3G 2004)
12. Dovrolis, C.;Ramanathan, P., et al. (2004). Packet-dispersion techniques and a capacityestimation methodology. IEEE/ACM Transaction on Networking 12(6): 963-977.
13. Ergen, M. and Varaiya, P. (2005). Throughput analysis and admission control for IEEE
14. 802.11a. Mobile Network Applications 10(5): 705-716.
15. Ergen, M. and Varaiya, P. (to appear). Throughput analysis and admission control in IEEE 802.11a. ACM-Kluwer Mobile Networks and Applications, Special Issue on WLAN Optimization at the MAC and Network Levels.
16. Gao, Y.;Chiu, D.-M., et al. (2006). Determining the end-to-end throughput capacity in multihop networks: methodology and applications. Proceedings of ACM SIGMETRICS.
17. Gupta, R.;Musacchio, J., et al. (2007). Sufficient rate constraints for QoS flows in ad-hoc networks. Ad Hoc Networks 5(4): 429–443.
18.
19. Hoang, V. D.;Shao, Z., et al. (2006). A New solution to Estimate the available Bandwidth in MANETs. IEEE 63rd Vehicular Technology Conference (VTC 2006-Spring).
20. Hu, N. and Steenkiste, P. (2003). Evaluation and characterization of available bandwidth probing techniques. IEEE Journal on Selected Areas in Communications 21(6): 879-894.
21. Jae-Yong, Y. and JongWon, K. (2007). Maximum End-to-End Throughput of Chain-Topology Wireless Multi-Hop Networks. Proceedings of IEEE WCNC.

22. Jain, M. and Dovrolis, C. (2003). End-to-end available bandwidth: measurement methodology, dynamics, and relation with TCP throughput. IEEE/ACM Transactions on Networking 11(4): 537-549.
23. Johnsson, A.;Melander, B., et al. (2005). Bandwidth Measurement in Wireless Network. Sweden, Malardalen University.
24. Kapoor, R.;Chen, L.-J., et al. (2004). Capprobe: A simple and accurate capacity estimation technique. Proc. of ACM SIGCOMM.
25. Kuan, C. and Dimyati, K. (2006). Analysis of collision probabilities for saturated IEEE 802.11 MAC protocol. Electronics Letters 42(19).
26. Kumar, A.;Altman, E., et al. (2007). New insights from a fixed-point analysis of single cell IEEE 802.11 WLANs. IEEE/ACM Transaction on Networking 15(3): 588-601.
27. Kun, W.;Fan, Y., et al. (2007). Modeling path capacity in multi-hop IEEE 802.11 networks for QoS services. IEEE Transactions on Wireless Communications 6(2): 738-749.
28. Lakshminarayanan, K.;Padmanabhan, V. N., et al. (2004). Bandwidth estimation in broadband access networks. Proceedings of the 4th ACM SIGCOMM conference on Internet measurement (IMC), Taormina, Sicily, Italy, ACM.
29. Lao, L.;Dovrolis, C., et al. (2006). The probe gap model can underestimate the available bandwidth of multihop paths. SIGCOMM Computer Communication Review 36(5): 29-34.
30. Li, Y.;Qiu, L., et al. (2008). Predictable performance optimization for wireless networks. Proceedings of the ACM SIGCOMM 2008 conference on Data communication (SIGCOMM), Seattle, WA, USA, ACM.
31. Malone, D.;Duffy, K., et al. (2007). Modeling the 802.11 Distributed Coordination Function in Nonsaturated Heterogeneous Conditions. IEEE/ACM Transactions on Networking 15(1): 159-172.
32. Melander, B.;Bjorkman, M., et al. (2000). A new end-to-end probing and analysis method for estimating bandwidth bottlenecks. Proceedings of IEEE GLOBECOM.
33. Nafaa, A. (2007). Provisioning of multimedia services in 802.11-based networks: facts and challenges. IEEE Wireless Communications 14(5): 106-112.
34. Perkins, C. E.;Royer, E. M., et al. (2001). Ad hoc on-demand distance vector (AODV) routing. Qiao, D.;Choi, S., et al. (2002). Goodput analysis and link adaptation for IEEE 802.11a wireless LANs. IEEE Transactions on Mobile Computing 1(4): 278-292.

35. Qiu, L.;Zhang, Y., et al. (2007). A general model of wireless interference. Proceedings of ACM Mobicom, Montral, Qubec, Canada, ACM.
36. Ribeiro, V. J.;Riedi, R. H., et al. (2003). PathChirp: efficient available bandwidth estimation for network paths. Passive and Active Measurement Workshop.
37. Sanzgiri, K.;Chakeres, I. D., et al. (2004). Determining intra-flow contention along multihop paths in wireless networks. Proceedings of First International Conference on Broadband Networks (BroadNets)
38. Sarr, C.;Chaudet, C., et al. (2008). Bandwidth Estimation for IEEE 802.11-Based Ad Hoc Networks. IEEE Transactions on Mobile Computing 7(10): 1228-1241.
39. Strauss, J.;Katabi, D., et al. (2003). A measurement study of available bandwidth estimation tools. Proceedings of the 3rd ACM SIGCOMM conference on Internet measurement (IMC), Miami Beach, FL, USA, ACM.
40. Sun, T.;Chen, L.-J., et al. (2005). SenProbe: path capacity estimation in wireless sensor networks. the third Intl. Workshop on Measurement, Modelling, and Performance Analysis of Wireless Sensor Networks (SenMetrics).
41. Wu, H.;Wang, X., et al. (2005). SoftMAC: layer 2.5 MAC for VoIP support in multi-hop wireless networks. Second Annual IEEE Communications Society Conference on Sensor and Ad Hoc Communications and Networks (SECON).
42. Xu, K.;Tang, K., et al. (2003). Adaptive bandwidth management and QoS provisioning in large scale ad hoc networks. IEEE Military Communications Conference (MILCOM).
43. Yang, Y. and Kravets, R. (2005). Contention-aware admission control for ad hoc networks. IEEE Transactions on Mobile Computing 4(4): 363-377.
44. Zhai, H.;Chen, X., et al. (2005). How well can the IEEE 802.11 wireless LAN support quality of service? IEEE Transactions on Wireless Communications 4(6): 3084-3094.
45. Zhai, H.;Chen, X., et al. (2006). A call admission and rate control scheme for multimedia support over IEEE 802.11 wireless LANs. ACM Wireless Networks 12(4): 451-463.
46. Zhao, H.;Garcia-Palacios, E., et al. (2009). Accurate Available Bandwidth Estimation in IEEE 802.11-Based Ad Hoc Networks. Computer Communications 32(6): 1050-1057.
47. Zhao, H.;Wang, S., et al. (2009). Challenges to Estimate End-to-end Available Bandwidth in IEEE 802.11-based Ad hoc Networks Proc.

of 2009 IEEE Youth Conference on Information, Computing and elecommunication Beijing, China

48. Zhao, H.;Wang, S., et al. (2010). Modeling Intra-Flow Contention Problem in Wireless Multihop Networks. IEEE Communications Letters 14(1): 18-20.

49. Zhou, H.;Wang, Y., et al. (2006). Difficulties in Estimating Available Bandwidth. Proc. Of IEEE International Conference on Communications (ICC).

Chapter 10

TIME SYNCHRONIZATION IN WIRELESS SENSOR NETWORKS

JonggooBae and Bongkyo MoonDongguk

University-SeoulSouth Korea

INTRODUCTION

Recently small smart devices start to be embedded into the various environments in order tomonitor the events occurred in the areas such as homes, plantations, oceans, rivers, streets,and highways. These tiny and low power devices which enable sensing and communicationtasks have made sensor networks emerged. In wireless sensor networks (WSNs), especially, wireless devices get together and spontaneously form a network without any infrastructure. Due to the absence of infrastructure such as router in traditional network, nodes in a sensornetwork have to cooperate for communication by forwarding each other's packets from asource to its destination. Thus this yields a multi-hop communication environment.Meanwhile, the knowledge of time between the sensor nodes is essential that detect theevents such as target tracking, speed estimating, and ocean current monitoring. Hence, thesensed data often loses valuable context without accurate time information. With timesynchronization, voice and video data from the different sensor nodes can be fused anddisplayed in a meaningful way at the sink. Time synchronization is a critical middlewareservice required for consistent distributed sensing and control in large-scale distributedsystems such as sensor networks. That is, time synchronization in a WSN aims at providinga common time scale for local clocks of nodes in the network. Moreover, common services inWSNs, such as coordination, communication, security, power management and distributedlogging also depend on the global time scale. The most widely adapted time synchronization protocol in the internet domain is the Network Time Protocol (NTP) devised by Mills (Mills, 1991). Nodes could also be equippedwith a global positioning system (GPS) to synchronize them (Hofmann-Wellenhof et al.1997; Mannermaa et al. 1999). It is used to provide network-wide agreement among a largegroup of nodes in the Internet. NTP works well synchronizing the computers on theInternet, but is not designed with the energy and computation limitations of sensor nodes inmind. A GPS device may be too expensive to attach on cheap sensor devices, and GPS service may not be available everywhere, such as inside the buildings or under the water.Consequently, it may be useful to use NTP to discipline sensor nodes, but traditionalsynchronization schemes such as NTP or GPS are not suitable for use in sensor networksbecause of complexity and energy issues, cost and size factors. Therefore, without furtheradaptation, NTP is suitable only for WSN applications with low precision demands.Time synchronization is a key service for many applications and operating systems indistributed computing environments. WSNs are large-scale distributed systems, buttraditional distributed algorithms cannot be considered for problems due to their uniquecharacteristics, especially the severe resource constraints. In this chapter, the mechanisms tosynchronize the local clocks of the nodes in WSN have been extensively investigated.

Backgrounds and Related Works

A landmark study in computer clock synchronization is Lamport's work that elucidates theimportance of virtual clocks in systems where causality is more important than absolute time(Lamport, 1978). Though Lamport's work focused on giving events a total order rather thanquantifying the time difference between them, it has emerged as an important influence insensor networks. Many sensor applications require only relative time, for example, timingthe propagation delay of sound (Girod&Estrin, 2001), and thus absolute time may not beneeded. Mills' NTP (Mills, 1991) stands out by virtue of its scalability, self-configuration inlarge multi-hop networks, robustness to failures and sabotage, and ubiquitous deployment. NTP allows construction of a hierarchy of time servers, multiply rooted at canonical sourcesof external time.Post-facto synchronization was a pioneering work by Elson and Estrin (Elson &Estrin, 2001). In this approach, unlike in traditional synchronization schemes such as NTP, each node'sclock is normally unsynchronized with the rest of the network; a beacon node periodicallybroadcasts beacon messages to the sensor nodes in its wireless range. When an event isdetected, each node records the time of the event (timestamp with its own local clock). Afterthe event (hence the name), upon receiving the reference beacon message, nodes use it astime reference and adjust their event timestamps with respect to that reference. Thissynchronization scheme has led afterwards to their RBS (Reference BroadcastSynchronization) protocol. Elson et al. propose a scheme called Reference-Broadcast Synchronization (RBS), in which anode sends reference broadcast beacons to its neighbors using physical layer broadcasts(Elson et al., 2002). RBS gets around the non-determinism of packet send time, access time,and propagation time, while depending only on the packet receive time. Since the packetreceive time is the same for all receivers, this reference broadcast packet can be used tosynchronize a set of receivers with one another. This scheme can also be extended to a multi hopscenario. However, the impact of the translation errors and delays on the multi-hopsynchronization, which can be provided by translating the time between different broadcastdomains, still needs to be studied. In addition, they do not consider global synchronizationover the entire network.A more recently developed Time-Sync protocol for Sensor Networks (TPSN) (Ganeriwal et al.,2003) is based on similar methodology as the NTP, where the sensor nodes are organizedinto multiple levels and synchronized to the root node of the hierarchy. Unlike the Internet,the root node and nodes at different levels responsible for synchronization may fail often,which may cause synchronization problems. In addition, mobile nodes may disrupt thepredefined level-by-level synchronization procedure. On typical WSN platforms using theTPSN protocol, such as the Mica2 mote, it is possible to access directly to the MAC layer,and message time-stamping can be performed during message transmission and reception.This immediately eliminates the same three main sources of uncertainties as in RBS. With atwo-way handshake of synchronization messages, the TPSN protocol eliminates theunknown propagation time as well. Although the propagation time has been eliminated, theencoding and decoding times are not because they might not be the same on the sender andreceiver side. It is important to point out that both the RBS and TPSN protocols suffer fromthe two largest sources of uncertainty of MAC layer time-stamping: the jitter of interrupthandling and decoding time.On the other hand, the flooding time synchronization protocol (FTSP) effectively reduces allsources of time stamping errors except for the propagation time. The FTSP (Maroti et al.2004) was designed for a sniper localization application requiring very high precision(Simon et al. 2004). FTSP achieves the required accuracy by utilizing a customized MAC layertime stamping and by using calibration to eliminate unknown delays. FTSP is robustto network failures, as it uses flooding both for pair-wise and global synchronization. Linearregression from multiple timestamps is used to estimate the clock drift and offset. The maindrawback of FTSP is that it requires calibration on the hardware actually used in thedeployment (thus is not a software solution purely independent of the hardware). FTSP alsorequires intimate access to the MAC layer for multiple timestamps. However, if well calibrated, the FTSP's precision is impressive (less than 2μs).Su and Akyildiz proposed the time-diffusion synchronization protocol (TDP) for networkwidetime synchronization (Su &Akyildiz, 2005). The main idea of TDP is to start from amaster node, adjust the clocks of its neighbors, and diffuse this clock adjustment to othernodes. TDP maintains global time synchronization within an adjustable bound based on theapplication requirements. One of the benefits of TDP is that the performance of voice andvideo applications can be improved when multiple sources send data back to the sinkthrough flooding or directed diffusion (Intanagonwiwat et al. 2003). It achieves globalsynchronization by multi-hop flooding: The base station initiates the protocol by sending aspecial timing message to the entire network. Some of the nodes, upon receiving themessage, become masters by using a leader election procedure. The master nodes start thetime-diffusion procedure involving electing diffused leaders, multi-hop flooding, anditerative weighted averaging of timings from different master nodes. TDP handles nodemobility and failures by using a peer evaluation procedure.

TIME SYNCHRONIZATION

Clocks and Synchronization

Sensor Node Clock

Every sensor node maintains its own clock and this is the only notion of time that a nodehas. The clock is an ensemble of hardware and software components; it is essentially a timerthat counts the oscillations of a quartz crystal running at a particular frequency. Computingdevices are mostly equipped with a hardware oscillator assisted computer clock, whichimplements an approximation C(t) of real-time t. Let us represent the clock for node A by C(t) A . The difference in the clocks of two sensor nodes (i.e., A and B) is referred as the offseterror between them. There are three reasons for the nodes to be representing different timesin their respective clocks (Ganeriwal et al. 2008): 1) The nodes might have been started atdifferent times, 2) the quartz crystals at each of these nodes might be running at slightlydifferent frequencies, causing the clock values to gradually diverge from each other (termed as the skew error), or 3) the frequency of the clocks can change differently over time becauseof aging or ambient conditions such as temperature (termed as the drift error). These errorscan be summarized as follows:

$$\text{Offset: } \delta = C_A(t) - C_B(t) \tag{1}$$

$$\text{Skew: } \eta = \frac{\partial C_A(t)}{\partial t} - \frac{\partial C_B(t)}{\partial t} \tag{2}$$

$$\text{Drift: } \lambda = \frac{\partial^2 C_A(t)}{\partial t^2} - \frac{\partial^2 C_B(t)}{\partial t^2} \tag{3}$$

The angular frequency of the hardware oscillator determines the rate at which the clock runs. The rate of a perfect clock, which can be denoted as dCdt , would equal 1, however, all clocks are subject to a clock drift; oscillator frequency will vary unpredictably due to various physical effects. Even though the frequency of a clock changes over time, it can be approximated with good accuracy by an oscillator with fixed frequency (Sichitiu&Veerarittiphan, 2003). Then, for some node i in the network, we can approximate its local clock as:

$$C_i(t) = a_i t + b_i \tag{4}$$

Where *a* (*t*) *i* is the clock *drift*, and) (*t bi* is the *offset* of node *i*'s clock. *Drift* denotes the rate (frequency) of the clock, and *offset* is the difference in value from real time *t*. Using equation (4), we can compare the local clocks of two nodes in a network, say node i and node j as:

$$C_i(t) = a_{ij} \cdot C_j(t) + b_{ij} \tag{5}$$

We call *ija* the *relative drift*, and i_j *b* the *relative offset* between the clocks of node i and node j.If two clocks are perfectly synchronized, then their relative drift is *i* (meaning the clockshave the same rate) and their relative offset is zero (meaning they have the same value atthat instant). Some studies in the literature use "skew" instead of "drift", defining it as the *difference* (as opposed to *ratio*) between clock rates. Also, the "offset" may equivalently bementioned as "phase offset". Figure 1 shows the relationship between relative drift and offset.

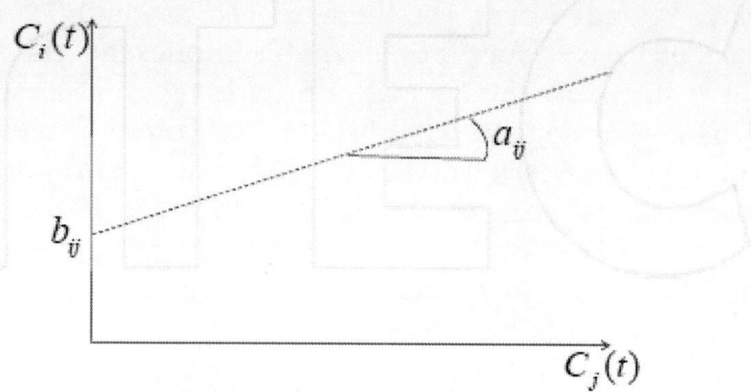

Figure 1. The relation between relative drift and offset

Although each sensor node is equipped with a hardware clock, these hardware clocks canusually not be used directly, as they suffer from severe drift. No matter how well thehardware clocks will be calibrated at deployment, the clocks will ultimately exhibit a largeskew. Since all hardware clocks are imperfect, local clocks of nodes may drift away fromeach other in time, hence observed time or durations of time intervals may differ for eachnode in the network. To allow for an accurate common time, nodes need to exchangemessages from time to time, constantly adjusting their clock values. Furthermore, nodes canconvert the current hardware clock reading into a logical clock value and vice versa(Sommer & Wattenhofer, 2009).

Hardware Clock

Each sensor node *i* is equipped with a hardware clock (×) *i H* . The clock value at time *t* isdefined as

$$H_i(t) = \int_{t_0}^{t} h_i(\tau) d\tau + \Phi_i(t_0)$$

where(t) *i h* is the hardware clock rate at time *τ* and ( ) 0 *t i* Φis the hardware clock offset at time 0 *t* . It is assumed that hardware clocks have bounded drift, i.e., there exists a constant $0 \leq \rho < 1$ such that $1 - \rho \leq h(t) \leq 1 + \rho$ for all times t. This implies that the hardware clock never stopsand always makes progress with at least a rate of $1 - \rho$. This is a reasonable assumptionsince common sensor nodes are equipped with external crystal oscillators which are used asclock source for a counter register of the microcontroller. These oscillators exhibit driftwhich is only gradually changing depending on the environmental conditions such asambient temperature or battery voltage and on oscillator aging. This allows assuming theoscillator drift to be relatively constant over short time periods. Crystal oscillators used insensor nodes normally exhibit a drift between 30 and 100 ppm (Sommer&Wattenhofer, 2009).

Logical Clock

Since other hardware components may depend on a continuously running hardware clock,its value should not be adjusted manually. Instead, a logical clock value (×) i L is computed asa function of the current hardware clock. The logical clock value L (t) i represents thesynchronized time of node i. It is calculated as follows:

$$H_i(t) = \int_{t_0}^{t} h_i(\tau)d\tau + \Phi_i(t_0)$$

where(t) i l is the *relative logical clock rate* and ( ) 0 t i θ is the clock offset between the hardwareclock and the logical clock at the reference time 0 t . The logical clock is maintained as asoftware function and is only calculated on request based on a given hardware clockreading (Sommer&Wattenhofer, 2009).

Definition of Clock Synchronization

The synchronization problem on a network of n devices corresponds to the problem ofequalizing the computer clocks of the different devices. The synchronization can be either*global;* trying to equalize C(t) i for all i = 1::n or it can be *local;* trying to equalize C(t) i for someset of the nodes that are spatially close. Equalizing just the instantaneous values of clocks bycorrecting the offsets is not enough for synchronization since the clocks will drift awayafterwards. Therefore a synchronization scheme should either equalize the clock rates aswell as offsets, or it should repeatedly correct the offsets in order to keep the clockssynchronized over a time period (Sivrikaya&Yener, 2004) .

The above definition of synchronization actually defines the strictest form ofsynchronization, where one seeks perfect matching of time on different clocks, but thisdefinition can be relaxed to different degrees according to the needs of an application. Ingeneral, the synchronization problem can be classified into three basic types (Ganeriwal et al.2003). First form of synchronization deals only with ordering of events or messages. The aimof such an algorithm is to be able to tell whether an event *E*1 has occurred before or afteranother event *E*2, i.e. just to compare the local clocks for order rather than having themsynchronized. The algorithm proposed in (Romer, 2003) is an example to this type ofsynchronization. Second type of synchronization algorithms targets maintaining relativeclocks. In this scheme, nodes run their local clocks independently, but they keep informationabout the relative drift and offset of their clock to other clocks in the network, so that at anyinstant, the local time of the node can be converted to some other node's local time and viceversa. Most of the synchronization schemes proposed for sensor networks use this model(Elson et al. 2002; Sichitiu&Veerarittiphan, 2003). The third form of synchronization is the"always on" model where all nodes maintain a clock that is synchronized to a referenceclock in the network. The goal of this type of synchronization algorithms is to preserve aglobal timescale throughout the network. The synchronization scheme of (Ganeriwal et al.2003) conforms to this model, but the use of "always on" mode is not mandatory in thescheme.

Design Factors for Time Synchronization

Some of the factors influencing time synchronization in wireless sensor networks aretemperature, phase noise, frequency noise, asymmetric delays, and clock glitches (Su &Akyildiz, 2005).

- Temperature: Since sensor nodes are deployed in various places, the temperaturevariations throughout the day may cause the clock to speed up or slow down. For atypical sensor node, the clock drifts few *parts per million (ppm)* during the day (Mills,1998). For low-end sensor nodes, the drifting may be even worse.

- Phase noise: Some of the causes of phase noise are access fluctuations at thehardware interface, response variation of the operating system to interrupts, andjitter in the network delay. The jitter in the network delay may be due to mediumaccess and queueing delays.
- Frequency noise: The frequency noise is due to the unstability of the clock crystal.A low-end crystal may experience large frequency fluctuation, because thefrequency spectrum of the crystal has large sidebands on adjacent frequencies.
- Asymmetric delay: Since sensor nodes communicate with each other through thewireless medium, the delay of the path from one node to another may be differentthan the return path. As a result, an asymmetric delay may cause an offset to theclock that cannot be detected by a variance type method (Levine, 1999). If theasymmetric delay is static, the time offset between any two nodes is also static. Thecollisions and conserve energy. However, non-determinism in transmission time caused bythe Media Access Channel (MAC) layer of the radio stack can introduce several hundreds ofmilliseconds delay at each hop. Thus, synchronization is an essential part of transmissionscheduling.

Uncertainties and Errors in Time Synchronization

Time synchronization schemes rely on some sort of message exchange between nodes inWSN. Non-determinism in the network dynamics such as propagation time or physicalchannel access time makes the synchronization task a big challenge in many systems. Notethat in short distance multi-hop broadcast, the data processing time and its variationcontribute the most to time fluctuations and differences in the path delays. Also, the timedifference between two sensor nodes may become large over time due to the wandering effect of the local clocks.

Latency estimates are actually confounded by random events thatlead to asymmetric round-trip message delivery delays; this delay prevents the receiverfrom exactly comparing the local clocks of the two nodes and accurately synchronizing tothe sender node. To better understand the source of these errors, it is useful to decomposethe source of a message's latency. Kopetz and Ochsenreiter (Kopetz&Ochsenreiter, 1987)introduced firstly four distinct components for analyzing the sources of the messagedelivery delays and later extended in (Ganeriwal et al. 2003).

- *Send Time:* The time spent at the sender to construct the message. This includeskernel protocol processing and variable delays introduced by the operating system(e.g., context switches and system call overhead occurred by the synchronizationapplication), and the time to transfer the message from the host to its networkinterface for transmission.
- *Access Time:* Each packet faces some delay at the MAC (Medium Access Control)layer before actual transmission. This delay is specific to the MAC protocol in use,but some typical reasons for delay are waiting for the channel to be idle or waitingfor the TDMA slot for transmission.
- *Propagation Time:* This is the time spent in propagation of the message betweenthe network interfaces of the sender and the receiver. When the sender and receivershare access to the same physical media (e.g., neighbors in an ad-hoc wirelessnetwork, or on a LAN), this delay is very small as it is simply the physicalpropagation time of the message through the media.
- *Receive Time*: This is the processing time required for the receiver's networkinterface to receive the message from the channel and notify the host of its arrival.This is typically the time required for the network interface to generate a messagereception signal. If the arrival time is time-stamped at a enough low level in thehost's operating system kernel, this delay does not include the overhead of systemcalls, context switches, or even the message transfer from the network interface tothe host.
- *Transmission Time:* The time it takes for the sender to transmit the message. Thistime is in the order of tens of milliseconds depending on the length of the message and the speed of the

radio Reception Time: The time it takes for the receiver to receive the message. It is thesame as the transmission time. The transmission and reception times overlap in WSN as pictured in Figure 2.

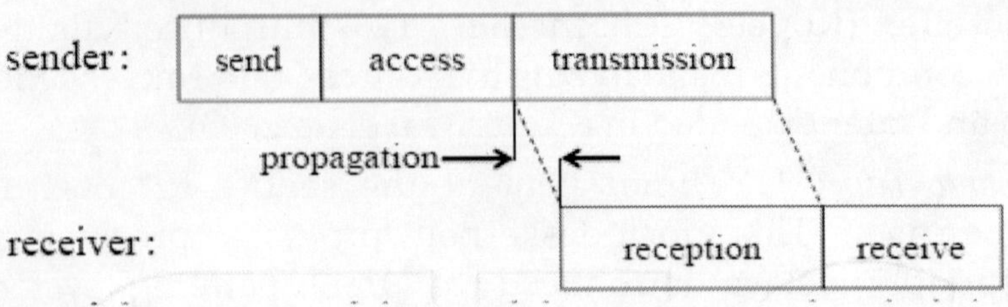

Figure 2. Decomposition of the message delivery delay over a wireless link (Maroti, et al. 2004)

Interrupt Handling Time: The delay between the radio chip raising and the microcontroller responding to an interrupt. This time is mostly less than a few microsecond (waiting for the microcontroller to finish the currently executed instruction), however, when interrupts are disabled this delay can grow large.

- Encoding Time: The time it takes for the radio chip to encode and transform a part of the message to electromagnetic waves starting from the point when it raised an interrupt indicating the reception of the idealized point from the microcontroller. This time is deterministic and is in the order of a hundred microseconds.
- Decoding Time: The time it takes for the radio chip on the receiver side to transform and decode the message from electromagnetic waves to binary data. It ends when the radio chip raises an interrupt indicating the reception of the idealizedpoint. This time is mostly deterministic and is in the order of hundred microseconds. However, signal strength fluctuations and bit synchronization errors can introduce jitter.
- Byte Alignment Time: The delay incurred because of the different byte alignment of the sender and receiver. This time is deterministic and can be computed on the receiver side from the bit offset and the speed of the radio. Fig. 3 summarizes

the decomposition of delivery delay of the idealized point of the message as it traverses over a wireless channel. Each line represents the time line of the layer as measured by an ideal clock. The dots represent the time instance when the idealized point of the message crosses the layers. The triangles on the first and last line represent the time when the CPU makes the time-stamps. Depending on the specific hardware the time stamp is usually recorded by the microcontroller when it handles the radio chip interrupts both on the sender and receiver sides. Alternatively, capture registers provided by some hardwarecan be employed to eliminate the interrupt handling time (Maroti, et al. 2004).

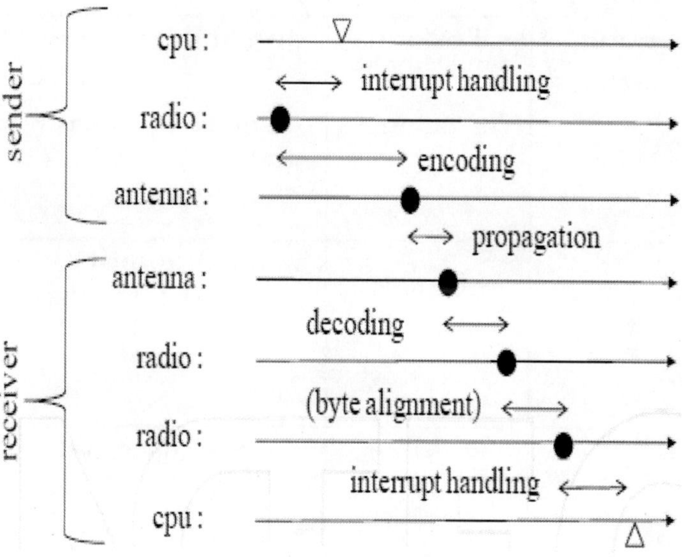

Figure 3. The timing of the transmission of an idealized point in the software (cpu), hardware (radio chip) and physical (antenna) layers of the sender and the receiver (Maroti, et al. 2004)

Table 1 summarizes the magnitudes and distribution of the various delays in message transmissions on the Mica2 platform. The block codes are used, and the idealized point of the message can also be assumed to be at a block boundary (Maroti, et al. 2004).

Table 1. The sources of delays in message transmissions (Maroti, et al. 2004)

Time	Magnitude	Distribution
Send&Receive	0-100ms	nondeterministic, depends on the processorload
Access	10-500ms	nondeterministic, depends on the channelcontention
Transmission & Reception	10-20ms	deterministic,depends on message length
Propagation	<1psfordis-tancesup to 300meters	deterministic, depends on the distance between sender and receiver
Interrupt Handling	<S11sin-mostcases, but canbeashigh as30ps	nondeterministic, depends on interruptsbeing disabled
Encoding plus Decoding	100 –200 J1S <2 J1S variance	deterministic, depends on radio chipsetand settings
ByteAlignment	O–400ps	deterministic,canbecalculated

Metrics for Evaluating Time Synchronization Schemes

The requirements for the synchronization problem can be regarded as the metrics for evaluating synchronization schemes on wireless sensor networks. Combining with the criteria that sensor nodes have to be energy efficient, low-cost, and small in a multi-hop environment, this requirement becomes a challenging problem to solve. However, a singlesynchronization scheme may not satisfy them all together since there are actually tradeoffs between the requirements of an efficient solution (Sivrikaya&Yener, 2004).

Energy Efficiency: As with all of the protocols designed for sensor networks, synchronization schemes should take into account the limited energy resources contained in sensor nodes.

- *Scalability*: Most sensor network applications need deployment of a large number of sensor nodes. A synchronization scheme should scale well with increasing number of nodes and/or high density in the network.
- *Precision*: The need for precision, or accuracy, may vary significantly depending on the specific application and the purpose of synchronization. For some applications, even a simple ordering of events and messages may suffice whereas for some others, the requirement for synchronization accuracy may be on the order of a few [1]secs.
- *Robustness*: A sensor network is typically left unattended for long times of operation in possibly hostile environments. In case of the failure of a few sensor nodes, the synchronization scheme should remain valid and functional for the rest of the network.
- *Lifetime:* The synchronized time among sensor nodes provided by a synchronization algorithm may be instantaneous, or may last as long as the operation time of the network.
- *Scope*: The synchronization scheme may provide a global time-base for all nodes in the network, or provide local synchronization only among spatially close nodes. Because of the scalability issues, global synchronization is difficult to achieve or too costly (considering energy and bandwidth usage) in large sensor networks. On the other hand, a common time-base for a large number of nodes might be needed for aggregating data collected from distant nodes, dictating a global synchronization.
- *Cost and Size*: Wireless sensor nodes are very small and inexpensive devices. Therefore, as noted earlier, attaching a relatively large or expensive hardware (such as a GPS receiver) on a small, cheap device is not a logical option for synchronizing sensor nodes. The synchronization method for sensor networks

should be developed with limited cost and size issues in mind.

- *Immediacy*: Some sensor network applications such as emergency detection (e.g. gas leak detection, intruder detection) require the occurring event to be communicated immediately to the sink node. In this kind of applications, the network cannot tolerate any kind of delay when such an emergency situation is detected. This is called the immediacy requirement, and might prevent the protocol designer from relying on excessive processing after such an event of interest occurs, which in turn requires that nodes be *pre-synchronized* at all times.

TIME SYNCHRONIZATION METHODS

Time synchronization has been a seminal topic in distributed systems (Dolev et al. 1984; Halpern et al. 1984; Lundelius et al. 1984; Lamport et al. 1985), but designing clocksynchronization algorithms in the context of a sensor network is challenging for several reasons. First, traditional distributed systems assume that all the nodes in a network can communicate directly with each other. A sensor network, however, is subject to spatialconstraints. Nodes only communicate directly with their neighbors. Communicationbetween two remote nodes is accomplished by message relay using intermediate nodes. Second, nodes in a sensor network generally rely on less information about the system than traditional distributed systems, where nodes have access to the clock values of all the other members of the system, including the faulty nodes. Third, a sensor node has only limited processing capability. The computation intensive signature algorithms, such as RSA, are not suitable for sensor networks. Instead, some light-weight algorithms (such as using a one way key chain or a key management scheme) are more suitable. The spatial constraints, the communication cost and delay, and the diminished computational capability are key reasons why localized algorithms that involve lightweight computations are preferred for sensor networks.

RBS(Reference Broadcast Synchronization)

The main advantage of RBS is that it eliminates transmitter-side non-determinism. Th disadvantage of the approach is that additional message exchange is necessary communicate the local time-stamps between the nodes. Eventually the RBS approach completely eliminates the send and access times, and with minimal OS modifications it is also possible to remove the receive time uncertainty. This leaves the mostly deterministic propagation and reception time in wireless networks as the sole source of error. The main strength of RBS is its broad applicability to commodity hardware and existing software in sensor networks as it does not need access to the low levels of the operating system (Elson et al. 2002).

The novel idea in RBS scheme is to use a third party for synchronization instead of synchronizing the sender with a receiver. This scheme synchronizes a set of receivers with one another. Although its application in sensor networks is novel, the idea of *receiver-receiversynchronization* was previously proposed for synchronization in broadcast environments. In RBS scheme, nodes send reference beacons to their neighbors. A reference beacon does not include a timestamp, but instead, its time of arrival is used by receiving nodes as a reference point for comparing clocks (Sivrikaya&Yener, 2004).

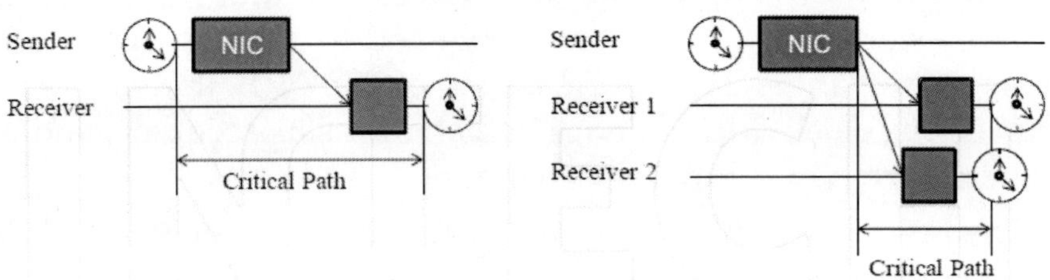

Figure 4. Critical path analysis between traditional time synchronization protocol (*left*) and RBS (*right*) (Elson et al. 2002)

By removing the sender's non-determinism from the critical path (Fig. 4), RBS scheme achieves much better precision compared to traditional synchronization methods that use two-way message exchanges between synchronizing nodes. As the sender's nondeterminismhas no effect on RBS precision, the only sources of error can be the nondeterminismin propagation time and receive time. In this scheme, a single broadcast will propagate to all receivers at essentially the same time, and hence the propagation error is negligible. This is especially true when the radio ranges are relatively small (compared to speed of light times the required synchronization precision), as is the case for sensor networks. So the only receive time errors are handled when the accuracy of RBS model is analyzed (Elson et al. 2002; Sivrikaya&Yener, 2004) In the simplest form of RBS, a node broadcasts a single pulse to two receivers. The receivers, upon receiving the pulse, exchange their receiving times of the pulse, and try to estimate their relative phase offsets. This basic RBS scheme can be extended in two ways: 1) allowing synchronization between *n* receivers by a single pulse, where *n* may be larger than two, 2) increasing the number of reference pulses to achieve higher precision.

TPSN (Timing-Sync Protocol for Sensor Network)

The TPSN algorithm first creates a spanning tree of the network and then performs pairwise synchronization along the edges. Each node gets synchronized by exchanging two synchronization messages with its reference node one level higher in the hierarchy. The TPSN achieves two times better performance than RBS by time-stamping the radio messages in the Medium Access Control (MAC) layer of the radio stack (Ganeriwal et al., 2003) and by relying on a two-way message exchange. The shortcoming of TPSN is that it does not estimate the clock drift of nodes, which limits its accuracy, and does not handle dynamic topology changes.

The first step of the algorithm is to create a hierarchical topology in the network. Every node is assigned a level in this hierarchical structure, and a node belonging to level *i* can communicate with at least one node belonging to level *i-1*. Only one node is assigned to level *0*, which is called the "root node". This stage of the algorithm is called as the "level discovery phase". Once the hierarchical structure has been established, the root node initiates the second stage of the algorithm, which is called the "synchronization phase". In this phase, a node belonging to level *i* synchronize to a node belonging to level *i-1*.

Eventually every node is synchronized to the root node and network-wide time synchronization is achieved (Ganeriwal et al., 2003).

Level Discovery Phase

This phase of the algorithm occurs at the onset, when the network is deployed. The root node is assigned a level *0* and it initiates this phase by broadcasting a *level_discovery*packet.The *level_discovery*packet contains the identity and the level of the sender. The immediateneighbors of the root node receive this packet and assign themselves a level, one greater than the level they have received i.e., level *1*. After establishing their own level, they broadcast a new *level_discovery*packet containing their own level. This process is continued and eventually every node in the network is assigned a level. On being assigned a level, a node neglects any such future packets. This makes sure that no flooding congestion takes place in this phase. Thus a hierarchical structure is created with only one node, root node, at level *0*. A node might not receive any *level_discovery*packets owing to MAC layer collisions (Ganeriwal et al., 2003).

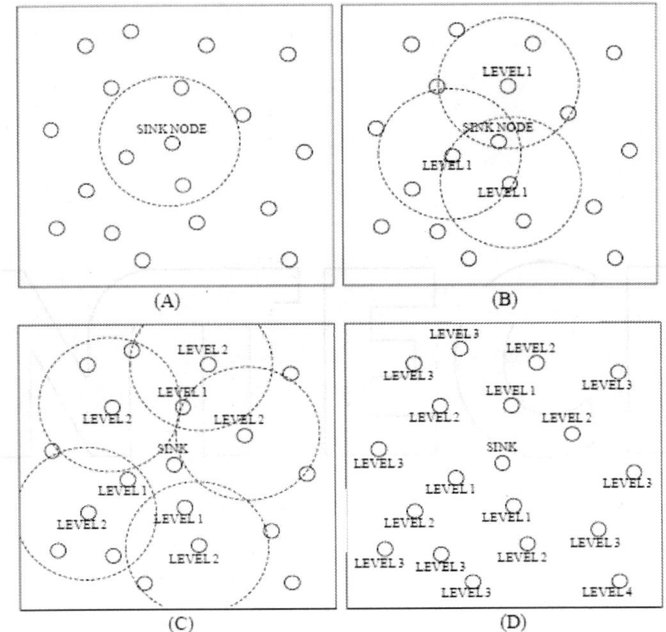

Figure 5. The Process of level discovery phase for hierarchical topology organization in TPSN

Synchronization Phase

In this phase, pair wise synchronization is performed along the edges of the hierarchical structure established in the earlier phase. The classical approach of sender-receiver synchronization (Mills, 1991) is used for doing this handshake between a pair of nodes. Fig. 6 shows this message-exchange between nodes *'A'* and *'B'*. Here, *T1*, *T4* represent the time measured by local clock of *'A'*. Similarly *T2*, *T3* represent the time measured by local clock of *'B'*. At time *T1*, *'A'* sends a *synchronization_pulse*packet to *'B'*. The *synchronization_pulsepacket* contains the level number of *'A'* and the value of *T1*. Node *B* receives this packet at *T2*, where *T2* is equal to *T1* + D + *d*. Here D and *d* represents the clock drift between the two nodes and propagation delay respectively. At time *T3*, *'B'* sends back an *acknowledgement*packet to *'A'*. The *acknowledgement* packet contains the level number of *'B'* and the values of*T1*, *T2* and *T3*. Node *A* receives the packet at *T4*. Assuming that the clock drift and the propagation delay do not change in this small span of time, *'A'* can calculate the clock drift and propagation delay as (Ganeriwal et al., 2003) :

$$\Delta = (\frac{T2 - T1) - (T4 - T3)}{2}) \; ; \; d = (\frac{T2 - T1) + (T4 - T3)}{2}) \qquad (6)$$

Knowing the drift, node *A* can correct its clock accordingly, so that it synchronizes to node *B*. This is a sender initiated approach, where the sender synchronizes its clock to that of the receiver.

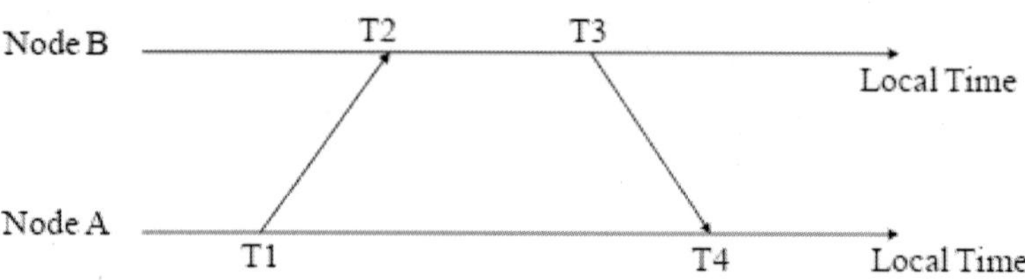

Figure 6. Two way message exchange between a pair of nodes (Ganeriwal et al., 2003)

This message exchange at the network level begins with the root node initiating the phase by broadcasting a *time_sync*packet. On receiving this packet, nodes belonging to level *1* wait for some random time before they initiate the two-way message exchange with the root node. This randomization is to avoid the contention in medium access. On receiving back an acknowledgment, these nodes adjust their clock to the root node. The nodes belonging to level 2 will overhear this message exchange. This is based on the fact that every node in level *2* has at least one node of level *1* in its neighbor set. On hearing this message, nodes in level 2 back off for some random time, after which they initiate the message exchange with nodes in level *1* (Ganeriwal et al., 2003).

This randomization is to ensure that nodes in level *2* start the synchronization phase after nodes in level *1* have been synchronized. Note that a node sends back an *acknowledgement* to a *synchronization_pulse*, provided that it has synchronized itself. This ensures that no multiple levels of synchronization are formed in the network. This process is carried out throughout the network and eventually every node is synchronized to the root node. In a sensor network, packet collisions can take place quite often. To handle such scenario a node waiting for an acknowledgement, timeouts after some random time and retransmits the *synchronization_pulse*. This process is continued until a successful two-way message exchange has been done (Ganeriwal et al., 2003).

FTSP(Flooding Time Synchronization Protocol)

The goal of the FTSP is to achieve a network wide synchronization of the local clocks of the participating nodes. In this protocol, each node has a local clock exhibiting the typical timing errors of crystals and can communicate over an unreliable but error correctedwireless link to its neighbors. The FTSP synchronizes the time of a sender to possibly multiple receivers utilizing a single radio message time-stamped at both the sender and the receiver sides. MAC layer time-stamping can eliminate many of the errors, as observed in many previous protocols (Ganeriwal et al., 2003; Woo & Culler, 2001).

However, accurate time-synchronization at discrete points in time is a partial solution only. Compensation for the clock drift of the nodes is inevitable to achieve high precision between synchronization points and to keep the communication overhead low. Linear regression is used in FTSP to compensate for clock drift as suggested in (Elson et al., 2002).

Typical WSN operate in areas larger than the broadcast range of a single node; therefore, the FTSP provides multi-hop synchronization. The root of the network, a dynamically elected single node, maintains the global time and all other nodes synchronize their clocks to that of the root. The nodes form an ad-hoc structure to transfer the global time from the root to all the nodes, as opposed to a fixed spanning-tree based approach proposed in (Ganeriwal et al.,2003). This saves the initial phase of establishing the tree and is more robust against node and link failures and dynamic topology changes.

Time-stamping

The FTSP utilizes a radio broadcast to synchronize the possibly multiple receivers to the time provided by the sender of the radio message. The broadcasted message contains the sender's time stamp which is the estimated global time at the transmission of a given byte. The receivers obtain the corresponding local time from their respective local clocks at message reception. Consequently, one broadcast message provides a *synchronization point* (a global-local time pair) to each of the receivers (Maroti et al. 2004). The difference between the global and local time of a synchronization point estimates the clock offset of the receiver. As opposed to the RBS protocol, the time stamp of the sender must be embedded in the currently transmitted message. Therefore, the time-stamping on the sender side must be performed before the bytes containing the time stamp are transmitted.

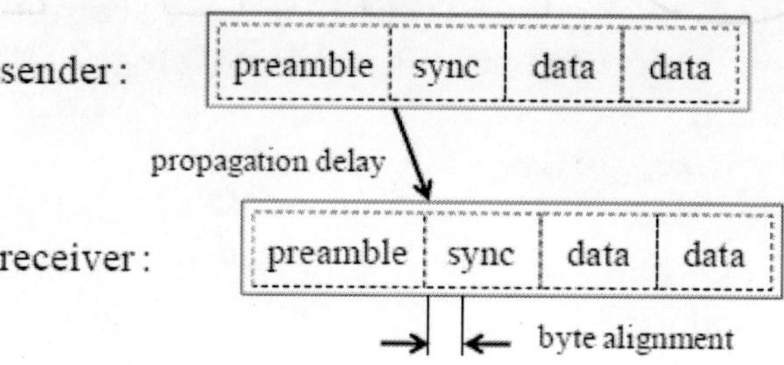

Figure 7. Data packets transmitted over the radio channel. Solid lines represent the bytes of the buffer and the dashed lines are the bytes of packets (Maroti et al. 2004)

Message broadcast starts with the transmission of preamble bytes, followed by SYNC bytes, then with a message descriptor followed by the actual message data, and ends with CRCbytes. During the transmission of the preamble bytes the receiver radio synchronizes itselfto the carrier frequency of the incoming signal. From the SYNC bytes the receiver can calculate the bit offset it needs to reassemble the message with the correct byte alignment. The message descriptor contains the target, the length of the data and other fields, such as the identifier of the application layer that needs to be notified on the receiver side. The CRC bytes are used to verify that the message was not corrupted. The message layout is summarized in Fig. 7.

The FTSP time-stamping effectively reduces the jitter of the interrupt handling and encoding/decoding times by recording multiple time stamps both on the sender and receiver sides. The time stamps are made at each byte boundary after the SYNC bytes as they are transmitted or received. First, these time stamps are normalized by subtracting an appropriate integer multiple of the nominal byte transmission time, the time it takes to transmit a byte. The jitter of interrupt handling time is mainly due to program sections disabling interrupts on the microcontroller for short amounts of time. This error is not Gaussian, but can be eliminated with high probability by taking the minimum of the normalized time stamps. The jitter of encoding and decoding time can be reduced by taking the average of these interrupt error corrected normalized time stamps. On the receiver side this final averaged time stamp must be further corrected by the byte alignment time that can be computed from the transmission speed and the bit offset (Maroti et al. 2004).

Clock drift management

If the local clocks had the exact same frequency and, hence, the offset of the local times were constant, a single synchronization point would be sufficient to synchronize two nodes. However, the frequency differences of the crystals used in Mica2 motes introduce drifts up to 40µs per second. This would mandate continuous re-synchronization with a period of less than one second to keep the error in the micro-second range, which is a significant overhead in terms of bandwidth and energy consumption (Maroti et al. 2004). Therefore, it is necessary to estimate the drift of the receiver clock with respect to the sender clock. The offset between the two clocks changes in a linear fashion provided the short term stability of the clocks is good. In this scheme, the stability of the 7.37 MHz Mica2 clock is verified by periodically sending a reference broadcast message that was received by two different motes. The two motes time-stamped the reference message using the FTSP time-stamping described in the previous section with their local time of arrival and reported the time-stamp (Maroti et al. 2004).

Tiny-Sync and Mini-Sync

Tiny-Sync and Mini-Sync are the two lightweight synchronization algorithms, proposed mainly for sensor networks, by Sichitiu and Veerarittiphan (Sichitiu&Veerarittiphan, 2003). The authors assume that each clock can be approximated by an oscillator with fixed frequency. As argued in previous section, two clocks, ( ) 1 *C t* and ( ) 2 *C t* , can be linearly related under this assumption as:

$$C_1(t) = a_{12} \cdot C_2(t) + b_{12} \qquad (7)$$

where12 *a* is the relative drift, and 12 *b* is the relative offset between the two clocks. Both algorithms use the conventional two-way messaging scheme to estimate the relative drift and offset between the clocks of two nodes; node 1 sends a probe message to node 2, time stamped with o t , the local time just before the message is sent. Node 2 generates a timestamp when it gets the message at b t , and immediately sends back a reply message. Finally, node 1 generates a timestamp r t when it gets this reply message. Using the absolute order between these timestamps and equation (7), the following inequalities can be obtained:

$$t_o < a_{12} \cdot t_b + b_{12} \quad (8)$$

$$t_r > a_{12} \cdot t_b + b_{12} \quad (9)$$

The 3-tuple of the timestamps (,,) o b r t ttis called a "data point". Tiny-sync and mini-sync works with some set of data points, each collected by a two-way message exchange as explained. As the number of data points increases, the precision of the algorithms increases (Sichitiu&Veerarittiphan, 2003). Each data point corresponds to two constraints on the relative drift and relative offset (equations 8, 9). The constraints imposed by data points are depicted in Fig. 8. Note that the line corresponding to equation (9) must lie between the vertical intervals created by each data point. One of the dashed lines in Fig. 8 represent the steepest possible such line, satisfying equation (7). This line gives the upper bound for the relative drift (slope of the line, 12 a), and the lower bound for the relative offset (y-interceptof the line, 12 b) between the two clocks. Similarly, the other dashed line gives the lower bound for relative drift (12a) and the upper bound for relative offset (12 b). Then the relative drift 12 a and the relative offset 12 b can be bounded as:

$$\underline{a_{12}} \le a_{12} \le \overline{a_{12}} \quad (10)$$

$$\underline{b_{12}} \le b_{12} \le \overline{b_{12}} \quad (11)$$

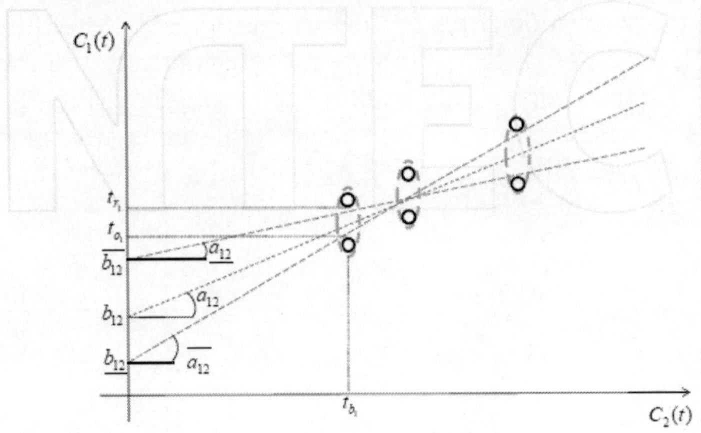

Figure 8. The constraints imposed on 12 *a* and 12 *b* by data points (Sivrikaya&Yener, 2004)

The exact drift and offset values can not be determined by this method (or any other method - as long as message delays are unknown), but they can be well estimated. The tighter the bounds get, the higher the chance that the estimates will be good, i.e. the precision of synchronization will be higher. In order to tighten the bounds, one can solve the linear programming problem consisting of the constraints dictated by all data points in order to get the optimal bounds resulting from the data points. However, this approach is quite complex for sensor networks, since it requires high computation and storage for keeping all data points in memory (Sichitiu&Veerarittiphan, 2003; Sivrikaya&Yener, 2004).

The basic intuition behind *tiny-sync* and *mini-sync* algorithms is the observation that not all data points are useful. Consider, for example, the three data points in Fig. 8 the intervals [12*a* 12 , *a*] and [12 *b* 12 , *b*] are only bounded by data points 1 and 3. Therefore data point 2 is useless in this example. Following this intuition, Tiny-sync keeps only the four constraints - the ones which yield the best bounds on the estimates- among all data points. The resulting algorithm is much simpler than solving a linear programming problem. However, the authors argue, by a counter example, that this scheme does not always give the optimal solution for the bounds: The algorithm may eliminate some data point, considering it useless, although it would actually give a better bound together with another data point that is yet to occur.

Mini-sync is an extension of Tiny-sync, such that it founds the optimal solution with an increase in complexity. The idea is to prevent the algorithm of tiny-sync for eliminating constraints that might be used by some future data points to give tighter bounds. We skipthe details here, but the authors basically define a criteria to determine if there is a chance that a constraint might be useful. A constraint is eliminated (discarded) only if it is *definitelyuseless*. The solutions found by Mini-sync are optimal (Sivrikaya&Yener, 2004).

GLOBAL TIME SYNCHRONIZATION ALGORITHMS

Li and Rus (Li &Rus, 2006) presented a high-level framework for global synchronization. The three methods are proposed for global synchronization in WSNs. The first two methods, all-node-based and cluster-based synchronization, use global information but are not suitable for large WSNs. In the third approach, diffusion method, each node sets its clock to the average clock time of its neighbors. The diffusion method thus converges to a global average value. A drawback of this approach is the potentially large number of messages exchanged between neighbor nodes, especially in dense networks.

All-Node-based Synchronization

This method is used on all the nodes in the system and it is most effective when the size of the sensor network is relatively small. In future sections of this paper, they describe ways to address scalability. They assume the clock cycle on each node is the same. They believe thisis a reasonable assumption since most sensors are programmed with the same parametersprior to deployment. They also assume the clock tick time is much longer than the packet transmission time. Finally, they assume that the message transmission time over each link and handling time on each node are roughly the same. This time can be obtained when the network traffic is small. That is, upon its initial deployment, a sensor network allows sufficient time solely for clock synchronization. The key idea is to send a message along a loop and record the initial time and the end time of the message. Then, by using the message traveling time, they can average the time to different segments of the loop and smooth over the error of the clocks. Algorithm 1 (Li &Rus, 2006) summarizes this method.

Algorithm 1 All-Node-Based Synchronization Algorithms in a Sensor Network

```
Find a ring that passes each node at least once that need to be synchronized (suppose the ring is composed of k nodes)
A message is passed along the ring starting from an initiating node
Upon receipt of the message, each node records its current local time (t_i) and its order (i) in the ring. If the node receives messages more than once, it chooses one arbitrarily
After initiating node receives the message, it sends out another message informing each node on the ring the start time (t_s) and the end time (t_e) of the previous message
for each node, to adjust its local time t do
  if ∃ m, m + 1 ≥ (t_e − t_s + 1)/k · (i − 1) ≥ t_i ≥ (t_e − t_s)/k · (i − 1) ≥ m then
    node n_i adjusts its time to t − t_i + t_s + m
  if ∃ m, m + 1 ≥ (t_e − t_s + 1)/k · (i − 1) ≥ t_i ≥ (t_e − t_s)/k · (i − 1) ≥ m − 1 then
    node n_i adjusts its time to t − t_i + t_s + m
```

Cluster-based Synchronization

The synchronization method presented in Algorithm 1 has a provable bound, but it requires all the nodes to participate in one single synchronization session. This can be mitigated using a hierarchical approach. More specifically, if the network can be organized into clusters, we propose to synchronize the whole network using Algorithm 2 (Li &Rus, 2006). In Algorithm 2, the same method as in Algorithm 1 is firstly used to synchronize all the cluster heads by designing a message path that contains all the cluster heads (they are called the initiators base). Then, in the second step, the nodes in each cluster can be synchronized with their head.

Algorithm 2 The Cluster-Based Synchronization Algorithm

1: Run any clustering algorithm to organize the network into clusters
2: Synchronize the cluster heads with a base using Alg. 1
3: **for** each cluster **do**
4: Synchronize the cluster members with the cluster head

This method can adapt to different clustering schemes. A cluster can be composed of the nodes within the transmission range of the cluster head; it can also be comprised ofnodes within some geographical area called a zone. For the first type of clustering, synchronization can be done with RBS. First, a reference broadcast is sent by the head to synchronize all the other cluster members. Then, any other node in the cluster sends out another reference broadcast to synchronize. The clock difference can be calculated with these two broadcasts and all the non head members can adjust their clocks according to the head's clock. In a zone clustering, the same method as Algorithm 1 is used to first design a cycle that includes all the nodes of the cluster and synchronize them all. The head of the cluster will be the initiator of the intra cluster synchronization (L&Rus,2006)

Diffusion-based Synchronization

The previous presented methods (cluster-based or all-node-based synchronization) use global time information sent to all the nodes and are not scalable for very large networks. The initiating node may encounter failure and, thus, the approach is not fault-tolerant. The nodes that participate in the synchronization must execute the related code approximately at the same time, which may be too hard in a large system. Now a diffusion method that is fully distributed and localized is introduced. In this method, synchronization is done locally, without a global synchronization initiator. It can also be done at arbitrary points in time as opposed to the strict timing requirements of the previous methods (Li &Rus, 2006).

The diffusion method achieves global synchronization by spreading the local synchronization information to the entire system. The algorithm can choose various global values to synchronize the network provided that each node in the network agrees to change its clock reading to the consensus value. An easy option is to choose the highest or lowest reading over the network. Synchronization to the highest or lowest value entails a simple algorithm (Li &Rus, 2006).

However, if there are faulty or malicious nodes, such a node may impose an abnormally high or low clock reading, which is likely to ruin the synchronization. To make thealgorithms more robust and reasonable, the following algorithms use the global average value as the ultimate synchronization clock reading. The main idea of the algorithms is to average all the clock time readings and set each clock to the average time. A node with high clock time reading diffuses that time value to its neighbors and levels down its clock time. A node with low time reading absorbs some of the values from its neighbors and increases its value. After a certain number of rounds of diffusion, the clock in each sensor will have the same value (Li &Rus, 2006).

There are two typical basic operations in diffusion-based synchronization scheme: 1) the neighboring nodes compare their clock readings at a certain time point and 2) the nodes change their clock accordingly. This, however, may be a problem because the clock comparison and the clock update cannot be done simultaneously (especially when clock comparison may take several steps). The clock updates based on the clock readings of the comparison time will be incorrect. The solution is to ask each node to keep a record of how much time elapses after the clock comparison on each node and use this time in the clock update (Li &Rus, 2006)

Synchronous Diffusion

Algorithm 3 (Li &Rus, 2006) shows the diffusion method. Synchronization between a sensor node and its neighbors is done by clock comparison and update operations. Because this algorithm only consider the time difference between two sensor nodes instead of the absolute clock time value, it is not required that all the sensors must do this local synchronization at the same time. In line 6, the exchanged value between sensor$i$ n and its neighbor j n is proportional to the time difference between them.

Algorithm 3 Diffusion Algorithm to synchronize the whole network

```
for each sensor n_i in the network do
  Exchange clock times with n_i's neighbors
  for each neighbor n_j do
    Let the times of n_i and n_j be c_i and c_j
    Change n_j's time to c_i + r_{i,j}(c_i − c_j)
  Change n_i's time to c_i − Σ r_{i,j}(c_i − c_j)
```

Asynchronous Diffusion

In the previous section, a synchronous diffusion-based algorithm is presented. The synchronous algorithm is localized, but it requires a set order for all the node operations. In order to remove this constraint, the extension of the diffusion synchronization algorithm is here introduced. In this algorithm, all the nodes can perform operations in any order as long as each node is involved in the operations with nonzero probability. The following asynchronous averaging algorithm (Algorithm 4) (Li &Rus, 2006) gives a very simple average operation of a node over its neighbors. Each node tries to compute the local averagevalue directly by asking all its neighbors about their values; it then sends out the computed average value to all its neighbors so they can update their values.

Algorithm 4 Asynchronous Averaging Algorithm in a Sensor Network

```
for each sensor n_i with uniform probability do
    Ask its neighbors the clock readings (read values from n_i and its neighbors)
    Average the readings (compute)
    Send back to the neighbors the new value (write values to n_i and its neighbors)
```

FAD(FAST ASYNCHRONOUS DIFFUSION) SCHEME

Several time synchronization algorithms have some problems when the algorithms escape their assumption and disconnection occurs in their network topology. For example,hierarchical topology has severe disadvantage when the network connection is broken. Thatis, all sensor nodes have to reorganize network connection and then time synchronization should be performed. Hence, asynchronous diffusion algorithm suggests new operation for global time synchronization among all the nodes in sensor networks.

$$C_{i-adjust} = \left(\frac{C_i + C_{j(neighbor)}}{2} \right) \quad (12)$$

In equation (12), *i adjust C* –presents an adjusted clock value, and *j* (*neighbor*)C is a clock value among neighbor sensor nodes. In asynchronous diffusion algorithm, a node *i n* might have several clock values adjusted by algorithm 4 since all sensor nodes are assumed to be connected. In this case, a node *i n* adjusts its local clock with the most recently received average clock value among a series of average clock values.

FAD Algorithm

Recently J. Bae and B. Moon (Bae& Moon, 2009) proposed a Fast Asynchronous Diffusion (FAD) clock synchronization algorithm in order to improve the diffusion-based asynchronous averaging algorithm (Algorithm 4). In this section, the different points about comparing asynchronous diffusion algorithm with the proposed FAD algorithm are presented. In asynchronous diffusion algorithm (Algorithm 4), each node uses the most recently received average clock value for adjusting its local clock when getting a series of average clock values. Meanwhile, the proposed scheme takes the mean of a series of average clock values received from all the neighbors under threshold for fast convergence. That is, a node adjusts its clock value with the mean of its neighbors' average clock values. Consequently the proposed algorithm (Algorithm 5) converges faster than asynchronous diffusion algorithm. The idea of FAD algorithm is expressed in equation (13).

$$C_{i-adjust} = \left(\frac{\sum_{j=1}^{N} \frac{C_i + C_{j(neighbor)}}{2}}{N} \right) \tag{13}$$

[N = number of neighbors]

FAD algorithm assumes that all the nodes in network have the same topology as asynchronous diffusion algorithm, but FAD algorithm differs from asynchronous diffusion in the process of getting average values. In other words, asynchronous diffusion scheme assumes that operating event must occurs in regular sequence, which uses average value received most recently. However, FAD algorithm doesn't consider operating sequence since it uses all the received average values (Bae& Moon, 2009).

Algorithm 5 Fast Asynchronous Diffusion(FAD) Algorithm in Sensor Network

1: **for** each node n_i with uniform probability **do**
2: Ask its neighbors the clock reading (read values from n_i and its neighbors)
3: **if** neighbor's clock < threshold
Average the reading(compute)
Send back to the neighbors the new value (write values to n_i and its neighbors)
4: **else** drop the received value
5: Each node n_i performs average operation again with all adjusted values received from its neighbors (write value to n_i)

In comparing FAD scheme with asynchronous diffusion scheme, there is actually no big difference in that more operations are required when the number of data increases in the viewpoint of algorithm complexity. But threre is an essential difference in the number of rounds needed for convergence. In next section, this difference is presented with the results of NS-2 simulation. Actually

FAD has less number of rounds than asynchronous diffusion until convergence achievement is done. That is, FAD converges faster than asynchronous diffusion scheme. Generally, FAD seems to show less performce in the aspect of energy efficiency because FAD spends more time than asynchronous diffusion in getting average value. However, the time for synchronizing all the nodes in a sensor network is reduced since FAD achieves faster time synchronization than asynchronous diffusion scheme.

Performance Evaluation

The FAD scheme (Algorithm 5) is evaluated with NS-2 simulator (version 2.30) based on IEEE 802.15.4 module. The parameters such as propagation delay, collision, packet loss, and so on are considered. The simulation also includes asynchronous diffusion scheme for comparing FAD scheme with it. The simulation for time synchronization algorithms is performed within relative error of 0.01, and all nodes are assumed to have uniform distribution. The detail simulation parameters are summarized in Table 2.

Table 2. The Parameters for Simulation

Parameter	**values**
NumberofNodes	75,90,100'125,150,200'300, 400,500
SensorField	lOOmxlOOm
TransmissionRange	15m
PhysicalLayer&MACLayer	802.15.4
RoutingProtocol	AODV
RelativeError	0.01
UniformProbability(Mean)	0.5
Threshold(PercentageofDrift)	100%,80%,60%,40%

Results and Discussions

In this simulation, the round is the number of the given algorithm performed at once. The number of operation is the sum of average operation from all nodes. In more detail, the operation ranges between zero and number of nodes participating in one round, and threshold is drift rate between received clock value and local clock value in one tick. Fig. 9 represents the comparison between asynchronous diffusion (left) and FAD (right) in the number of rounds with threshold value 40%. In this figure, the number of rounds decreases when the number of nodes increases. Each data point (*) represents the number of rounds when relative error becomes 0.01, and a line represents average value in each simulation condition.

Under this simulation, when the number of nodes is 500, FAD achieves time synchronization in average 31.7 rounds while asynchronous diffusion achieves it in average 35.8 rounds. When the number of sensor node is under 175, the time efficiency of FAD is better by 19% than asynchronous diffusion. When the number of sensor nodes is over 175, the time efficiency of FAD is better by 12% than asynchronous diffusion.

Fig. 10 shows the comparison between asynchronous diffusion (left) and FAD (right) with threshold value 40% in the number of operations. This figure represents that there is no big difference between FAD and asynchronous diffusion, and the number of total operations increases when the number of nodes increases. The reason can be explained from the results in Fig. 9. The number of rounds has exponential shape eventhought the number of wireless sensor nodes increases. It means that these algorithms have to operate even though some additional rounds are not related with increasing the number of sensor nodes. That is, when the number of nodes is especially over the specific value, the number of rounds for time synchronization are not related with the number of nodes. Moreover, the number of operations increases when the number of nodes increases since the number of rounds is similar.

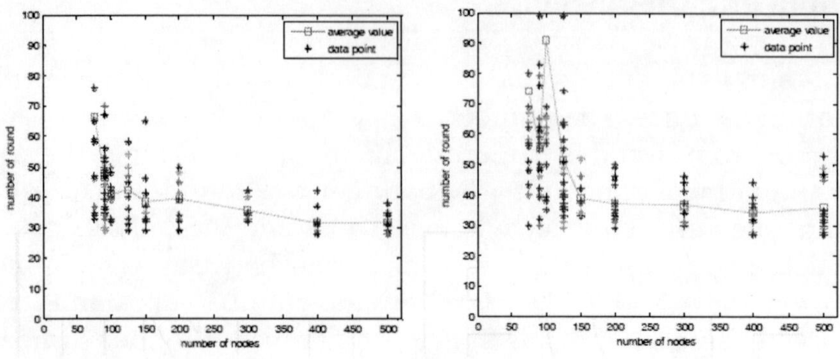

Figure 9. Comparison between asynchronous diffusion (left) and FAD (right) in the number of rounds with threshold value 40%

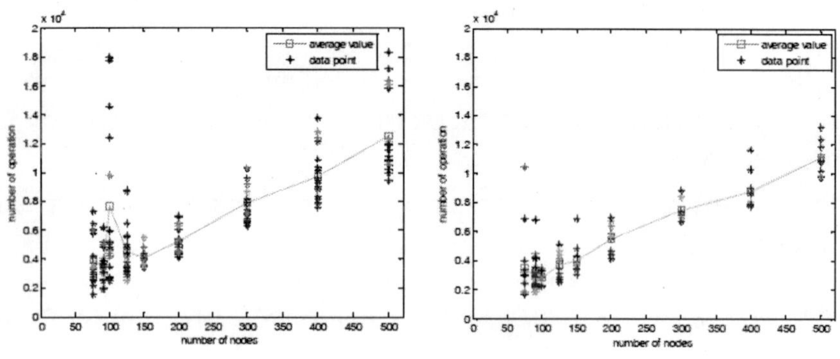

Figure 10. Comparison between asynchronous diffusion (left) and FAD (right) with threshold value 40% in the number of operations

Fig. 11 represents the comparison between asynchronous diffusion and FAD in the average number of operations (left) and the average number of rounds (right) with threshold value(log scale). Fig. 11 (left) depicts the number of average operation in this simulation. Fig. 11 (right) shows average value of rounds. When the number of nodes is over 175, FAD uses the fewer number of operations than asynchronous diffusion. When the number of nodes is over 175, it is impossible for this simulation to compare FAD with asynchronous diffusion. However, when the number of nodes is under 175, FAD has better performance than asynchronous diffusion.

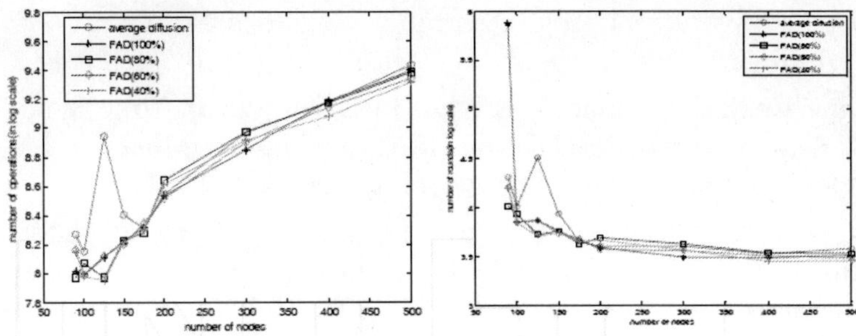

Figure 11. Comparison between asynchronous diffusion and FAD in the average number of operations (left) and the average number of rounds (right) with threshold value(log scale)

CONCLUSION

Time synchronization is very useful function for improving device performance in WSN. In this chapter, we investigated time synchronization algorithms in WSN. Even though many algorithms are proposed until now, the best solution doesn't seem to exist since diversity devices are used in WSN. For the future research, meanwhile, time synchronization among heterogeneous devices will be new challenges.

REFERENCES

1. Bae, J., & Moon, B. (2009). Time Synchronization with Fast Asynchronous Diffussion in Wireless Sensor Network, *International Conference on Cyber-enabled DistributedComputing and Knowledge Discovery (CyberC 2009)*, China, Zhangjiajie, October
2. Dolev, D.; Halpern, J., & Strong, H. R. (1984).On the Possibility and Impossibility of Achieving Clock Synchronization, *Proc. ACM Symp. Theory of Computing (STOC)*, May
3. Elson, J. &Estrin, D. (2001). Time Synchronization for Wireless Sensor Networks, *Proceedings of the 2001 International Parallel and Distributed Processing Symposium (IPDPS),Workshop on Parallel and Distributed*

Computing Issues in Wireless and Mobile Computing, San Francisco, California, USA, April

4. Elson, J.; Girod, L. &Estrin, D. (2002).Fine-Grained Network Time Synchronization Using Reference Broadcasts, *Proc. Fifth Symp. Operating System Design andImplementation(OSDI 2002),* Dec.
5. Ganeriwal, S.; Kumar, R. &Srivastava, M. (2003). Time Sync Protocol for Sensor Network, *The First ACM Conference on Embedded Networked Sensor System (SenSys),* Los Angeles, Nov., pp. 138–149.
6. Ganeriwal, S.; Pöpper, C., Čapkun, S. &Srivastava, M. (2008), Secure Time Synchronization in Sensor Networks, *ACM Transactions on Information and System Security (TISSEC),* Vol.11, no.4, July, ISSN:1094-9224
7. Girod, L. &Estrin, D. (2001). Robust range estimation using acoustic and multimodal sensing, *Proceedings of the IEEE/RSJ International Conference on Intelligent Robots andSystems (IROS2001),* March
8. Halpern, J.; Simons, B. & Strong, R. (1984). Fault-Tolerant Clock Synchronization, *Proc. ACM Symp. Principles of Distributed Computing (PODC),* Aug.
9. Hofmann-Wellenhof, B.; Lichtenegger, H., & Collins, J. (1997). Global Positioning System: Theory and Practice, *4th ed. Springer Verlag.*
10. Intanagonwiwat, C.; Govindan, R., Estrin, D., Heidemann, J. & Silva, F. (2003). Directed Diffusion for Wireless Sensor Networking, *IEEE Trans. Networking,* vol.11, no.1, pp.2–16, Feburuary
11. Kopetz, H., &Ochsenreiter, W. (1987).*Clock* Synchronization in Distributed Real-Time Systems, *IEEE Transactions on Computers,* C-36(8), p.933–939, August
12. Lamport, L. (1978). Time, clocks, and the ordering of events in a distributed system, *Communications of the ACM,* vol.21, no.7, pp.558–565
13. Lamport L. &Melliar-Smith, P. M. (1985).Synchronizing Clocks in the Presence of Faults, *J. ACM,* vol.32, no.1, pp.52-78, Jan.
14. Levine, J. (1999). Time synchronization over the internet using an adaptive frequency-lockedloop, *IEEE Trans. Ultrason., Ferroelectr., Freq. Contr.,* vol.46, no.4, pp.888–896, Jul.
15. Li, Q., &Rus, D. (2006). Global Clock Synchronization in Sensor Network, *IEEE Trans. Computer Society,* vol.55, pp.214-216, Feb.
16. Lundelius, J. & Lynch, N. (1984).A New Fault-Tolerant Algorithm for Clock Synchronization, *Proc. ACM Symp.Principles of Distributed Computing (PODC),* pp. 75-88, Aug.
17. Mannermaa, J; Kalliomaki, K., Mansten, T. &Turunen, S. (1999).

Timing performance of various GPS receivers, *Proceedings of the 1999 Joint Meeting of the European Frequencyand Time Forum and the IEEE International Frequency Control Symposium*, pp.287–290, April

18. Maroti, M.; Kusy, B., Simon, G. &Ledeczi, A. (2004). The flooding time synchronization protocol, *Proceedings of the ACM Conference on Networked Sensor Systems (SenSys'04)*,ACM Press, New York, pp.39–49
19. Mills, D. L. (1991). Internet Time Synchronization: The Network Time Protocol, *IEEE Transactions on Communications*, COM 39, no.10, pp.1482-1493, October
20. Mills, D. L. (1998).Adaptive hybrid clock discipline algorithm for the network time protocol, *IEEE/ACM Transactions on Networking*, vol.6, no.5, pp.505–514, Oct.
21. Romer, K. (2003). Temporal Message Ordering in Wireless Sensor Networks, *IFIP MedHocNet*, Mahdia, Tunisia, June
22. Sichitiu, M. L., &Veerarittiphan, C. (2003). Simple, Accurate Time Synchronization forWireless Sensor Networks, *IEEE Wireless Communications and Networking Conference (WCNC) 2003*, New Orleans, LA, USA, March, vol.2, pp.1266 - 1273
23. Simon, G.; Maroti, M., Ledeczi, A., Balogh, G., Kusy, B., Nadas, A., Pap, G., Sallai, J. &Frampton, K. (2004). Sensor network-based counter sniper system, *Proceedings of the2nd International Conference on Embedded Networked Sensor Systems (Sen Sys)*, ACM Press, New York
24. Sivrikaya, F. &Yener, B. (2004). Time Synchronization in Sensor Networks: A Survey, *IEEE Network*, vol.18, no.4, pp.45 – 50, July-Aug
25. Sommer, P. &Wattenhofer, R. (2009). Gradient clock synchronization in wireless sensor networks, *Proceedings of the 2009 International Conference on Information Processing inSensor Networks*, pp. 37-48,
26. Su, W. &Akyildiz, I. F. (2005). Time-Diffusion Synchronization Protocol for Wireless Sensor Networks, *IEEE/ACM Transactions on Networking*, vol.13, no.2, pp.384–397, April
27. Woo, A., & Culler, D. (2001). A Transmission Control Scheme for Media Access in Sensor Networks, *International Conference on Mobile Computing and Networking, (Mobicom)*, pp. 221–235, July
28. Yoon, S.; Veerarittiphan, C. &Sichitiu, M. L. (2007). Tiny-sync: Tight time synchronization for wireless sensor networks, *ACM Transactions on Sensor Networks (TOSN)*, vol., no.2, June

Citations

CHAPTER 1

Meir A, Rubinsky B (2009) Distributed Network, Wireless and Cloud Computing Enabled 3-D Ultrasound; a New Medical Technology Paradigm. PLoS ONE 4(11): e7974. doi:10.1371/journal.pone.0007974

CHAPTER 2

Wang XY, Wong A (2013) Multi-Parametric Clustering for Sensor Node Coordination in Cognitive Wireless Sensor Networks.PLoS ONE 8(2): e53434. doi:10.1371/journal.pone.0053434

CHAPTER 3

Zussman, G.; Segall, A. "Energy efficient routing in ad hoc disaster recovery networks", INFOCOM 2003. Twenty-Second Annual Joint Conference of the IEEE Computer and Communications. IEEE Societies, On page(s): 682 - 691 vol.1 Volume: 1, 30 March-3 April 2003

CHAPTER 4

Daniele De Caneva, Pier Luca Montessoro and Davide Pierattoni (2010). Communication Strategies for Strip-Like Topologies in Ad-Hoc Wireless Networks, Mobile and Wireless Communications Network Layer and Circuit Level Design, Salma Ait Fares and Fumiyuki Adachi (Ed.), ISBN: 978-953-307-042-1, InTech, DOI: 10.5772/7713.

CHAPTER 5

Cattuto C, Van den Broeck W, Barrat A, Colizza V, Pinton J-F, et al. (2010) Dynamics of Person-to-Person Interactions from Distributed RFID Sensor Networks. PLoS ONE 5(7): e11596. doi:10.1371/journal.pone.0011596

CHAPTER 6

Georgios I. Tsiropoulos, Dimitrios G. Stratogiannis and Eirini Eleni Tsiropoulou (2010). Call Admission Control in Mobile and Wireless Networks, Mobile and Wireless Communications Network Layer and Circuit Level Design, Salma Ait Fares and Fumiyuki Adachi (Ed.), ISBN: 978-953-307-042-1, InTech, DOI: 10.5772/7715.

CHAPTER 7

Nan Hua and Yi Guo (2010). Mechanism and Instance: a Research on QoS Based on Negotiation and Intervention of Wireless Sensor Networks, Smart Wireless Sensor Networks, Yen Kheng Tan (Ed.), ISBN: 978-953-307-261-6, InTech, DOI: 10.5772/13380.

CHAPTER 8

Meir A, Rubinsky B (2009) Distributed Network, Wireless and Cloud Computing Enabled 3-D Ultrasound; a New Medical Technology Paradigm. PLoS ONE 4(11): e7974. doi:10.1371/journal.pone.0007974

CHAPTER 9

Haitao Zhao, Jibo Wei, Shan Wang and Yong Xi (2011). Available Bandwidth Estimation and Prediction in Ad hoc Networks, Mobile Ad-Hoc Networks: Protocol Design, Prof. Xin Wang (Ed.), ISBN: 978-953-307-402-3, InTech, DOI: 10.5772/13110.

CHAPTER 10

Jonggoo Bae and Bongkyo Moon (2010). Time Synchronization in Wireless Sensor Networks, Smart Wireless Sensor Networks, Yen Kheng Tan (Ed.), ISBN: 978-953-307-261-6, InTech, DOI: 10.5772/13869.6

INDEX

D

E

F

G

H

I

L

M

U

V

W